ST. FRANCIS OF ASSISI

St. Francis of Assisi
A Biography

Omer Englebert

franciscan
media
Cincinnati, Ohio

IMPRIMI POTEST: Dominic Limacher, O.F.M., Minister Provincial
NIHIL OBSTAT: Mark Hegener, O.F.M.,
IMPRIMATUR: Most Rev. Cletus F. O'Donnell, D.D.
Vicar General, Archdiocese of Chicago
April 16, 1965

The *Nihil Obstat* and the *Imprimatur* are official declarations that a book or pamphlet is free of doctrinal or moral error. No implication is contained therein that those who have granted the *Nihil Obstat* and Imprimatur agree with the contents, opinions, or statements expressed.

Cover and book design by Mark Sullivan
Cover image: St. Francis by Cimabue (Cenni di Pepo)
www.bridgemanart.com

LIBRARY OF CONGRESS CATALOGING-IN-PUBLICATION DATA
Englebert, Omer, 1893-1991.
[Vie de saint François d'Assise. English]
St. Francis of Assisi : a biography / Omer Englebert. — Second English Edition / revised and augmented by Ignatius Brady, O.F.M., and Raphael Brown.
pages cm
Originally published: Chicago : Franciscan Herald Press, 1966.
Includes index.
ISBN 978-1-61636-608-7 (alk. paper)
1. Francis, of Assisi, Saint, 1182-1226. I. Title.
BX4700.F6E613 2013
271'.302—dc23
[B]
2012044862
ISBN 978-1-61636-608-7

Published by Franciscan Media
28 W. Liberty St.
Cincinnati, OH 45202
www.FranciscanMedia.org

Printed in the United States of America. Printed on acid-free paper.
17 18 19 20 21 5 4 3 2

CONTENTS

INTRODUCTION

FRANCIS OF ASSISI has been the most beloved and popular of saints, a man who has inspired Christians of all traditions. His ideal of evangelical poverty has challenged Christians for eight centuries. His spirit of uncompromising commitment to the Gospel has endured as a force for renewal in the Church. His teaching about intimacy with God and wholehearted love of Jesus Christ molds our vision of the spiritual life. Above all, Francis's personal magnetism continues to attract men and women today, as it evidently attracted those in his own unhappy age. Generations of writers and artists have studied his words and told and retold his story in all media—from the frescos of the twelfth century to the movies of the twentieth. Fr. Omer Englebert, the author of this biography, put it well when he wrote that "Francis is one of those men of whom humanity will always be proud."

Francis is universally admired, but he has not always been universally understood. As with Jesus Christ, another universal figure, Francis's admirers often try to remake the saint in their own image. Modern romantics are beguiled by Francis the nature lover, the man who talked to the birds. We have Francis the social worker, the humanist, the lyric poet, the dropout. At the other extreme, Francis is viewed through the prism of religious sentimentality. The Poverello—the "little poor man"—charms us with a sweet gentleness. Or he chills us with his fasts, his stigmata, his heroic and unfathomable asceticism.

Yet, as Fr. Englebert shows, there was nothing esoteric, effeminate, or intimidating about Francis's spirituality. In this widely admired biography, he portrays Francis as a whole man. Francis was a gentle man, but also a fierce one when opposing those who opposed his Lord. He loved God's creation as intensely as any man ever has, but he renounced material comforts and showed his followers how to live for the things of the spirit. He was no lovable eccentric, but a man who heard God's call and followed it with utmost consistency.

In *St. Francis of Assisi: A Biography,* Omer Englebert tells the Poverello's story with spiritual insight and careful historical judgment. His work is unique among contemporary biographies of Francis in that it is a much-admired classic that also represents the best of contemporary scholarship. First published in French in 1947, the book was revised in French in 1956, translated into English, and then revised and retranslated in a new English edition in 1964. This edition is based on the 1964 revision and retranslation. The revision was done by Fr. Ignatius Brady, O.F.M., and Raphael Brown, two leading Franciscan scholars. The translation is by Eve Marie Cooper.

Englebert continually refers to his primary sources in the text of his biography. Thus they will be briefly discussed here.

The primary sources for Francis's life consist of a small body of his own writings and a larger collection of writings about him by his early associates and by St. Bonaventure.

Francis's own writings consist of two rules for the order he founded, a testament dictated before his death, some letters, and a few exhortations and prayers.

The most important of the writings by Francis's associates were written by Thomas of Celano and three early Franciscans who wrote under the direction or in the spirit of Brother Leo, the saint's confessor and best friend. These writings present reliable historical information, but they were not written as history in the sense that modern readers understand the term. They were all of the genre of medieval writing called *legenda* or "legends." These were stories compiled to inspire readers and to call them to greater faith and zeal for the kingdom of God. The spiritual purpose of the legends should not disturb modern readers who have a greater interest in precise fact than the medieval chronicler did. Indeed, men and women continue to read lives of saints in order to grow in faith and zeal. In this, the life of Francis is unsurpassed. His life inspired readers of the early legends; it continues to do so today through Englebert's biography and others.

Nevertheless, assessing the early sources for Francis's life challenges the historian's judgment and skill. He must balance the somewhat different pictures of the saint they present, using each source to correct the others. Critics have admired Englebert's ability to determine the accurate historical data while preserving the spiritual truth the legends also contain.

Thomas of Celano was Francis's first biographer. A talented writer and careful historian who had been received into the Franciscan order by the saint himself, Thomas was chosen by Pope Gregory IX to write the saint's life immediately after Francis's death in 1226. This work was Thomas's *vita prima*. Twenty years later, Thomas undertook a *vita secunda* at the request of the Franciscan minister general. He drew on the recollections of many of Francis's earliest followers and completed the work in 1247. Finally, Thomas wrote the *Treatise on the Miracles of St. Francis* between 1250 and 1253.

The same minister general who asked Thomas to write the *vita secunda* also asked three of Francis's closest associates to record their memories of him. The three were Brothers Leo, Rufino, and Angelo; the book attributed to them is called the *Legend of the Three Companions*. This source preserves many anecdotes and personal details about the saint.

St. Bonaventure's life of Francis was written between 1260 and 1263—a generation after the saint's death, at a time of growing tension within the Franciscan order over steps to modify the founder's original rule. Bonaventure, who was minister general of the order at the time, wanted to present an accurate life of Francis as part of his effort to mediate between factions and set firm direction for the order. Another early source for Francis's life is also the most widely known. This is the collection of tales known as the *Fioretti* or, in English, the *Little Flowers*. The *Fioretti* were not written until a hundred years after Francis's death, but scholars agree that they accurately reflect an oral tradition that extends back to Francis's earliest followers.

The *Fioretti* and the other early sources for Francis's life contain many miracle stories, some of them straining credulity. The modern temper is decidedly skeptical about miracles of any kind, and it is important to mention Englebert's approach, as a Christian and as a historian, to the miracle stories that make up so much of the early source material for the saint's life. Englebert believed that the miracle stories contained truth. While conceding the possibility—even the likelihood—that the miracle stories were sometimes embellished, he resolutely rejected the rationalist skepticism that marked many early biographies of Francis. He wrote: "We are not sufficiently convinced that the first Franciscan biographers were less intelligent and honest than we are to dare dispute with them on so delicate a matter." He records many of the miracle stories while carefully attributing them to their sources in the *legenda*.

As a historian, Englebert's intention was to follow the rules of good criticism and to rely on the weight of the historical record. As he put it, "We have—insofar as possible—let those speak who knew him, believing that once in possession of authentic evidence, the reader will be able to draw his own conclusions."

With such a scrupulous and faith-filled guide, the reader can confidently study the most human and esteemed of saints.

CHAPTER ONE

Francis's World

IN ST. FRANCIS'S day, the world known to the west was limited to Europe, North Africa, and the Near East, where the Crusaders had fought and traded for a century.

The political and social configuration of the European states was by no means that of today. France was only half as big; Spain was partly in the hands of the Moors; and England continued to exercise her suzerainty over Normandy, Brittany, and the Aquitaine. The Holy Roman Empire embraced not only Germany, Austria, Switzerland, and Bohemia, but also spilled over into the Walloons, Lorraine, Burgundy, and Provence. To this, Italy—except for the Pontifical States—also belonged.

In the Italian peninsula, however, frequent revolts flared, which Frederick Barbarossa (1152–1190), Henry VI (1190–1197), Otto IV (1197–1214), and Frederick II (1214–1250), had the utmost difficulty in quelling. To maintain his domination, the emperor relied on the nobility, whose members held their fiefs from him and exercised the functions of podestas, judges, and consuls in his name.

Born of the necessity of keeping in check the anarchy following upon the barbarian invasions, the feudal regime comprised, as we know, two classes of men—the *majores* or *boni homines* (the great, or the nobility) and the *minores* (the common people).

The *majores* were the nobles, the knights, the lords, who constituted in those times of general brigandage a permanent police force. Everyone was born into his hereditary rank (duke, marquis, count), with his local position and landed property, with the certainty of never being abandoned by his liege lord, and also with the obligation, should need arise, of dying for him. Thanks to these warriors, the *minores* were protected. They could work in peace and eat their fill—no longer in fear of being liquidated or led away at the point of the lance as captives with their families. But they paid dearly for this protection, sometimes in quitrents and service, and sometimes even with the loss of freedom.

The *minores* were of two sorts: villeins and serfs. The latter, attached to the lord's land, belonged to their master like so much livestock and enjoyed no independence whatever. The others, farm laborers in the country, craftsmen, or merchants in the towns, were free men, with the right to own property and move about freely. The serf, then, was really a slave; the villein was free in body, but subject to taxation and forced labor. The noble, who shared with the churches and monasteries nearly all the wealth of the period, was not taxed, owing only a vassal's homage to his lord.

The Crusades, which were in part commercial expeditions, transformed the feudal system. Up to then, craftsmen and laborers worked for the local market, with no other outlets than the castle or monastery. After the discovery and pillage of the treasures of the Byzantine Empire, hitherto unsuspected routes opened up to trade and industry. Innumerable ships dotted the Mediterranean; the Roman highways, destroyed by the barbarian invasions, were rebuilt; and from one end to the other of Europe raw materials and manufactured products were exchanged. Many artisans became rich, and some merchants reaped immense fortunes.

These newly rich remained nonetheless villeins or *minores*, crushed beneath the burden of quitrents and services, deprived of any voice in the government of the towns. Their fortunes, however, soon permitted their voices to be heard. They compelled the temporal and spiritual lords to grant them economic privileges and to admit them to their councils, thus becoming themselves *majores*.

From concession to concession, the lord, who up to then had made all appointments to public employment, was also constrained to grant to other citizens consuls of their own choosing, charged with lawmaking, administrating, and handing down justice. From then on, the commune was born, a sort of new suzerainty, bound like any vassal domain to its lord, and like it, obliged by the feudal oath to place troops at his service.

The serfs did not benefit from the social transformation. For to become a freeman and lay claim to the title of "citizen," one must own a house and enjoy a certain revenue. Consequently, only a small number of privileged villeins could belong to the commune. The serfs on the glebe and of the crafts thus remained just as poor and enslaved as before. Indeed, their plight was often worse than before, so greedy and cruel did their new masters prove to be. Having no protection, the greater part among them began to form a wretched proletariat in the outskirts of the city, whose freemen were concerned only with sending them off to fight.

Now the Italian citizens of the time declared war, and fierce war, at will. These associated merchants constituting the commune were insatiable—forever having some quarrel to pick with their neighbors. When these neighbors blocked off the roads with taxes and tolls, they attacked them, if they felt themselves strong enough. If they were too weak, they allied themselves with other merchants, with some powerful lord, even with the emperor, so as to snatch the coveted river, bridge, forest, or strip of land from the rival commune.

And woe to the vanquished! Their city was razed, entire villages were destroyed, and crops burned. Prisoners—those who escaped from the massacre—were mutilated or tortured with a refinement of cruelty. At Forli, for instance, men were shod like mules. And, lest any should forget, annual festivals were celebrated in which pigs, rams, asses, and other grotesque animals appeared on the scene, charged with making the hereditary enemy seem despicable.

Thus to the old seignorial rivalries were now joined undying hatreds and feuds between the communes, while within their walls they were often torn apart by partisan or family struggles, to the loss of their inner peace. "We learn," wrote Innocent III, "that you continue to lay waste cities, destroy castles, burn villages, oppress the poor, persecute churches, and reduce men to serfdom. Murder, violence, and rapine are rife, with quarreling and wars."

At the time of St. Francis's youth, at any rate, these reproaches of the pope were deserved as much by Assisi as by the communes of the marches to which they were addressed. "Not only had war, with its orgies and disorders, become a necessity and a habit, but it had become the preferred occupation, the ruling passion, and the whole life of this city, in which the word 'peace,' no longer had any meaning."

It is a mistake, then, to see in the end of the twelfth century and in the beginnings of the thirteenth a sort of golden age wherein peace and the practice of the Gospel flourished. It is true that in this period men built hospitals for the sick and abbeys whose walls resounded to the chanting of the divine praises, the land was adorned with a white flowering of churches, prayers and pilgrimages multiplied, Crusades were preached, knights professed to defend the widow and the orphan, and troubadours went all over Europe singing their courtly refrains. But if we stop to think that these hospitals, these cathedrals, and monasteries were often the "remorse in stone" by means of which great sinners attempted to atone for their crimes and violence, and if we observe in addition that heresy and immorality corrupted Christian people, and that never before had the "little man" been the victim of so much social injustice, we may well conclude that the times of St. Francis yielded to none in calamities and scandals.

Umbria, where St. Francis's life was spent, is situated in central Italy, between the march of Ancona and Tuscany. This region, full of contrasts and beauty, affords to man's spirit a variety of scenery which is truly captivating: solitary peaks and charming valleys, streams lazily meandering along the plain, torrents cascading down ravines, fields of wheat and unproductive volcanic soils, forests of ilex and fir, silver-leaved olive trees, engarlanded vines running along the mulberry trees, and clumps of black cypress mounting guard at wayside chapels. The winter is rugged, the summer scorching, autumn and springtime marvelously mild. The people are handsome, kindly, and thoughtful.

The artistic riches of the country are scarcely inferior to its natural beauties. Rarely does one see so many masterpieces accumulated in so small a space. For without mentioning the churches and palaces, who does not know Perugia with its Signorellis, its Lorenzos, and its Peruginos; Assisi with its Giottos and its Cimabues; Spoleto and its Filippo Lippis; Spello and its Pinturicchios; Montefalco with its Benozzo Gozzolis; and finally, Trevi, Cortona, and Foligno? "Florence and Pisa seem almost Boeotian to me, after seeing Perugia and Assisi," wrote Renan.

Perched almost all of them on hilltops, these little towns appear ethereal in the diaphanous light that bathes them. The crenelated battlements of their ancient walls speak eloquently of the struggles which blood-reddened them for centuries—but these are memories that the gentle Franciscan legend has now obliterated. For Umbria, "the Galilee of Italy," has long been the country of the Poverello, the kingdom of peace in which poets and mystics alike have been spiritually naturalized.

Assisi, where Francis was born toward the close of 1181 or the beginning of 1182, then belonged to the Empire.

The city's founders, so it is said, were those Umbrians who, overcome by the Etruscans, joined with their conquerors and were subsequently beaten with them by the Roman legions in the third century before Christ. It became a Roman municipality, and later gave birth to the poet Propertius, if we are to believe the inscription on the temple of Minerva still standing in the piazza. The sight of that edifice threw Goethe into an extraordinary state of exaltation. "It was," he exclaims, "the first monument of antiquity that it was given me to see; and I could not see enough of it."

It is claimed that the city was evangelized about the year AD 50 by St. Crispoldo, a disciple of St. Peter; but it is St. Rufino who is reputed by the Assisians to have really converted them two centuries later. Condemned to death and drowned in the Chiascio, he was first buried in a temple to Diana, near this river; then in 412 his body was solemnly brought into the city.

The latter had, in the thirteenth century, the same boundary lines as in the time of St. Rufino. It has changed little since, with its sloping streets and its old houses of rose-colored stone; and its population is still below ten thousand. Terraced on a spur of Mount Subasio, whose summit soars some four thousand feet, Assisi beholds at its feet the vast plain extending from Perugia to Spello, Foligno, and Spoleto. Here silence, solitude, and peace reign supreme. In the evening one may hear—so still is it—the murmur of the water in the fountains. We must climb to the ruins of the Rocca, the ancient feudal castle, to have a sweeping view of the entrancing landscape.

On our right, our gaze extends over the immense Valley of Spoleto; on our left, there is the wild desolation of the mountains; behind, an arid ravine; ahead, the city with its somber towers, its crenelated gates, its houses that seem to stand on tiptoe to see better; and finally, its Franciscan monuments which form its immortal glory: the grandiose basilica, with its two superimposed churches, guarding the tomb of St. Francis; the Chiesa Nuova, over the site of the family residence; the Cathedral of San Rufino where he was baptized; the Basilica of St. Clare, replacing the Church of San Giorgio, where he learned to read; the bishop's palace where he stripped off his garments to give them to his father; the home of Bernard of Quintavalle, his first disciple; the Church of San Nicolo, where the two consulted the Gospels to learn their vocation; the Church of San Damiano which the Poverello restored with his own hands; and finally, down in the plain, St. Mary of the Angels, the Portiuncula, where he died.

Some traces still remain of the house where Francis passed the first twenty-five years of his life. If it resembled its neighbors that are still standing, the house had five or six rooms.

Peter Bernardone, father of the future saint, was one of the richest cloth merchants in the city. Pica, his mother, gave birth to at least two children; of whom one, Angelo, had two sons, Piccardo and Giovanni.

In the sixteenth and seventeenth centuries, when men too readily "discovered" noble lineages for the saints, writers boasted of Bernardone's noble origin and gave him the Moriconi of Lucca for ancestors. But such a genealogy was a pure fabrication. Besides, Francis often affirmed that he was born a commoner. All that can actually be said is that at this time when the cloth trade led so often to wealth, and wealth to nobility, Bernardone could hope to see his son become a knight, and therefore a gentleman.

If he himself was not born to the purple, did Francis's father at least marry a noblewoman? To prove that he did, French historians have had her born in Provence, alleging the authority of the seventeenth-century French author Claude Frassen. "Pica," he writes, "comes from the illustrious house of Bourlemont, as appears in an ancient manuscript preserved in the archives of that house." But it is difficult to attach any importance to this unverifiable testimony.

Peter Bernardone was on one of his frequent trips to France when his son was born.

Thanks to the peace maintained by Barbarossa in the empire, central Italy enjoyed great prosperity, and the cloth trade especially flourished. As Italian wools, however, were good only for the manufacture of coarse stuffs, to find better materials, merchants of the peninsula were obliged to frequent the fairs of Provence and Champagne, where Europe, Asia, and Africa exchanged their products.

Without waiting for the father's return, Dame Pica had the newborn baby carried to the baptismal font of San Rufino Church, where he was christened John. Was this name afterward changed into another, not found in the martyrology? Celano, who mentions the fact, gives no reason. He observes, though, that the Poverello always celebrated the feast of his heavenly patron, St. John the Baptist, with special devotion. "It was the father," says the *Three Companions,* "who,

in his joy, had him named Francis on his return from his far journey."
Was it a compliment on his part to the country where he traveled so
much and did so much business?

But those who did not take everything in the *Legend of the Three
Companions* for Gospel truth rather surmise that John was dubbed
"Francesco" when later on people saw that he enjoyed speaking
French so much and singing the songs and plays of the French troubadours. His father knew French, and no doubt, taught it to his son,
for French at that time served as a business medium everywhere in
the West.

Francis's biographers have noted that he was "a man without
learning." That is, he studied neither theology nor canon law, and
was unversed in any of the ecclesiastical or profane sciences of the
time. Is this one of the reasons why everything about him arouses
so warm a response in men of every clime and culture? Men taught
him the catechism and the alphabet. God and his own native genius
taught him the rest.

A few steps away from the family home stood a school that was
an annex of San Giorgio Church. There it was that Francis learned
to read and write. This elementary schooling included Latin, often
used still in sermons and public deliberations. As for writing, it
would seem that Francis never became very proficient in it, as in the
rare autographs we have of him the handwriting is quite ordinary.
Besides, he wrote little. Ordinarily, he dictated to Brother Leo, and
for signature drew a T-shaped cross.

The school from which the young man derived the most benefit
was that of the songs of chivalry and of the *gai savoir* which was then
all the rage.

For years, the most famous troubadours of France wandered
through Italy, visiting the castles, enlivening gatherings and

tournaments, bringing the Courts of Love into style, endlessly rhyming the legendary history of Charlemagne, of the knights of the Round Table, and of the doughty warriors who emulated them. They also sang of woman; for as Don Quixote says, "There can no more be a knight without a lady than a tree without leaves or a sky without stars." But the love they celebrated was the love that is purified by sacrifice and loyalty, and the heroes whose exploits they extolled were always "knights without fear and without reproach."

The troubadours had for pupils and interpreters the *jongleurs*, with whom the land teemed. They expressed themselves in a "Franco-Italian" jargon, spoken nowhere and yet understood by all. They were to be met on pilgrim routes and in cities, parroting over and over in their peculiar style the consecrated themes, before their enthusiastic—or resigned—hearers. The use of rhyme became so trite that professionals complained: "We shall have to give up singing, for there isn't a drunkard now who doesn't set his hand to writing a song."

At every step in the life of St. Francis, we shall be reminded of the songs of chivalry, of the troubadours, and even of the *jongleurs*. Like Ronald of Montauban, the cousin of the brave Roland, we shall see him building churches to atone for past sins. Like King Arthur, he will assemble his knights of the Round Table at the Chapter of Pentecost. He will compose music and verse, and will praise the Lord in song while pretending to accompany himself on the viol. We shall hear him make use of phrases from the poetry of chivalry to express his inmost being and to draw men after him.

If we are to believe Thomas of Celano, the upbringing of the little Bernardone boy was dreadful. "In our day, and even from the cradle," he writes, "Christian parents are wont to bring up their boys in softness and luxury. These innocents are barely able to lisp when they are taught shameful and abominable things. They are scarce weaned before they are forced to utter obscene words and commit indecent acts. Should they attempt to resist, the fear of ill-treatment would get the upper hand over their resistance. The more perverted they become, the more pleased are their parents; and when they grow up, they rush of their own accord into more and more criminal practices." And the diatribe continues with a profusion of redundant and balanced phrases.

But we should remind ourselves here that Friar Thomas is one of those authors who sometimes let themselves be carried away with words—stopping only when they run out of them. Writing more calmly, St. Bonaventure states that in his youth Francis "was nurtured in vanity among the vain sons of men"; which adds up to saying that he was not sanctified from the cradle and that his character training may have been sketchy.

His father, however, does not seem to have been a bad man. A domineering and vain burgher, he was fond of his gold, liked to be in the public eye, and was desirous of rising in the social scale. He was an ordinary Christian, in no rush to get to heaven and putting off all active concern for his salvation. Meanwhile, happy and prosperous in this life, he was intent on seeing that his son did not run through his property and that he should be an honor to him.

Noblewoman or commoner, Pica was in any case his superior. Ordinarily she was a meek creature, submissive and retiring, but one who, on occasion, dared brave her husband's wrath. "A friend of everything good," wrote Thomas of Celano, correcting in his second *Legend* the exaggerations of the first, "she practiced every virtue in a rare degree, and reminds one of St. Elizabeth by the name she had prophetically given to her child. 'You shall see,' said she to those scandalized by his youthful errors, 'that he will become a son of God.'"

Peter Bernadone lost no time in introducing his son into his business.

It was the custom then to advertise one's wealth by one's clothing, and luxury was, for the most part, confined to dress. Men vied with one another in wearing the richest and most showy textures. Even some priests sought to distinguish themselves in this respect, since a decree of 1213 had to forbid them to ape the sartorial luxury of the ladies.

So Francis waited on customers in a well-patronized shop. He went on horseback to the fairs of Spoleto, Foligno, and other places. He may have accompanied his father to Champagne and to Provence. Later on, he declared that he loved France in a special manner and desired to end his days there, because (he said) there, more than anywhere else, men showed reverence for holy things and particularly for the Blessed Sacrament. Was this an observation that he had already made in the course of his youthful journeys?

At any rate, never did anyone see a more affable and charming merchant. In addition he was, says Thomas of Celano, "most prudent in business." But it soon became evident that if Francis excelled in making money, he was still better at spending it.

Naturally liberal, he gave abundant alms. "Love for the poor was born in him," writes St. Bonaventure; and he had made a special resolution never to refuse anyone who solicited alms in God's name. Only once, detained by a customer, did he brusquely turn away a beggar, but he regretted it at once. "What!" he said to himself, "if this man had come to borrow money for one of your noble friends, you would have been proud to give it to him; and you dare to show him the door when it is the King of kings who sends him to you?" And dashing out after the beggar, he made amends.

It was not just in charity, however, that Francis spent his money.

By his way of looking at things, observes one of his biographers, he was the exact opposite of his father. "Much more whimsical and less thrifty, he lived above his station, rushing pell-mell into pleasure and throwing away everything he earned on feasts and sumptuous clothing." He even rigged himself up like a *jongleur* "by sewing pieces of sacking onto his best clothes. Prompt to leave the dinner table or his father's counter at the first signal from his friends, he was always ready, day or night, to run singing with them through the town."

At that time there were youth groups in Assisi, in which boys from middle-class homes, mingled with a few nobles, had good times together. And the year round, there were well-wined banquets, noisy gatherings, farandoles danced through the streets of the little city, and nocturnal serenades beneath the balconies of local beauties. There was feasting and laughter, poetry and music, eccentricities and follies, and also (alas!) real disorders. For debauchery was rife in Assisi, and the excesses of these night prowlers often compelled the authorities of the commune to intervene.

"Certain it is that from time to time Francis's parents reproached him for his conduct; 'You are no prince's son,' they would say to him, 'to throw money away like water, and feed so many parasites at your expense.' But rich and indulgent, they overlooked his vagaries and avoided crossing him."

After all, this prodigal youth was a charming and affectionate son, who would eventually "straighten out"; and meanwhile, Peter Bernardone must have been flattered to see him getting in with the nobility.

One naturally wonders just how far the young man's wayward-ness actually went during this period of his life, of which, later on, he was so bitterly to reproach himself with having "lived in sin." In what sense are we to take this rather vague expression? In order not to say—on this delicate subject—more than we know, let us limit ourselves to citing the evidence.

First of all, we have Thomas of Celano putting the final brushstrokes to the somber picture whose first lines we have quoted:

> What do you think becomes of them [these children whose fearsome training he has depicted], once they pass through the portals of youth? Free at last to pursue their inclinations and swept up in the maelstrom of pleasure, these voluntary slaves of sin, whose members serve only iniquity, eagerly rush into every vice. There is no longer anything Christian about them but the name, and they become boastful sinners who would deem it a disgrace to preserve a semblance of decency. Such was the miserable apprenticeship which made up the youthful existence of the man whom we now venerate as a saint. He wasted his life up to his twenty-fifth year, surpassing his comrades in foolishness, and drawing them with him into vanity and evil. He was fond of jests and songs and jokes, liked to dress in fine and flowing garments, and was lavish with his money, thereby attracting to his retinue many youths who made a career of wickedness and crime.
>
> Thus he went on, the proud and magnificent leader of this perverse army, through the streets of Babylon. And so it went, until that day when—to keep him from utter loss of his soul—the hand of the Lord fell upon him and transformed him. Then was Francis converted; so that sinners, following his example, might henceforth trust in God's mercy.

This language is clear. True, quite a bit of rhetoric is mixed in; but not enough, it would seem, to take all the meaning out of the words. And it must be agreed that Friar Thomas, had he so willed, might have employed his rhetoric to say something else. For instance, it would have been easy for him to show the flighty youth remaining pure in spite of his bad company; and certainly, nothing prevented him from retracting on this point in his second *Legenda*, as he did for several others. Yet he changed nothing.

All the accounts written in the next thirty years give us the same theme. Seven or eight years later, Julian of Speyer, using Thomas of Celano's very words, cited St. Francis's example to sinners, to inspire them likewise to trust in God's readiness to forgive.

In 1238, Pope Gregory IX, the intimate friend of the Poverello, praised St. Francis for "having embraced chastity, after having given himself over to the seductions of the world."

Finally, preaching to a General Chapter of the Order, Cardinal Eudes of Chateauroux did not hesitate to declare that "in the beginning, Francis was a great sinner; but, sated with carnal pleasures, he took the road leading to holiness, so that no sinner need thenceforth despair of his salvation."

His Franciscan audience could not have been offended at this portrait of the culpable youth of their founder since they themselves when chanting Matins alluded to it in the following antiphon:

Hic vir in vanitatibus
Nutritus indecenter
PLUS SUIS NUTRITORIBUS
SE GESSIT INSOLENTER.

"As a child, he received a very bad upbringing, and later he did not scruple to go beyond his masters in immorality."

The first Friars Minor believed then that their father had been a sinner. But those of the following generation found this to be an inadmissible stain in so sublime a life. It pained them to admit that the flesh marked by the sacred stigmata had ever been defiled, and that the purity of the seraphic Francis had been less than that of St. Dominic, of which the Friars Preachers were so proud.

Then it was that the Chapter of 1260 recast the last two verses of the compromising strophe, making it read that, fortunately, divine grace had preserved the seraphic father from every error:

Hic vir in vanitatibus
Nutritus indecenter
DIVINIS CHARISMATIBUS
PREVENTUS EST CLEMENTER.

At almost the same time, St. Bonaventure definitely settled the question by writing that "despite the young debauchés he had associated with, Francis had never yielded to the seductions of the flesh"; and as henceforth his *Legend* had the sole right to exist, this became the prevailing opinion.

But sinner or not, it would be an error to think of the youthful Francis as a rake. One cannot imagine him as either corrupt or corrupting; and if there were some weaknesses in his life, assuredly baseness was not among them. No one (thank God) has revealed to us the name of the little lady who may have momentarily captivated his heart. But if Francis loved, it was nobly and in the manner of the knights of chivalry whose ideals he shared. He was prey to temptations of the flesh (since we shall see him later rolling in the brambles and in the snow to get rid of them); but his deportment and his speech were always perfectly proper. "Never did an offensive or coarse word come from his mouth; and if anyone spoke improperly to him, he resolved not to reply."

His nobility of soul extended to everything. He was, we are told, dignity and graciousness itself. "Avoiding wounding anyone, and being most courteous to all, he made himself universally loved. To see the refinement of his manners, one would have taken him for the son of some great nobleman." In short, he was born a prince, and everyone gladly forgave him "for wanting to be in the forefront of things. Thus he soon came to be known beyond his immediate circle, and many began to predict for him a glorious destiny."

Among them was "that simple man, somewhat of a prophet," writes St. Bonaventure, "who never met him without taking off his cloak and spreading it under his feet, replying to the mockers that, in honoring Peter Bernardone's son in this way, he was but anticipating the universal homage of posterity."

It may well be imagined that Francis's ambitions were not confined to measuring out cloth in his father's house and to feasting in company with the fops whom he fed at his expense. He had faith in his star, and he dreamed of becoming famous.

At that time, fame was to be acquired in war, and those who liked fighting found opportunities galore.

Francis himself had grown up in an atmosphere of civil war. For almost thirty years, his native city had been demanding its freedom. In 1174, the merchants of Assisi had tried to shake off the imperial yoke; but they had run up against something stronger than themselves; and in 1177, Frederick Barbarossa, going up to La Rocca, had installed his lieutenant, Duke Conrad of Urslingen, charged to hold them in check. From that time onward, the great feudatory lords regained the upper hand; and the middle class, stripped of all political rights and burdened with taxes, meditated projects of vengeance.

Peter Bernardone's son was about fifteen, when in 1197 the succession of Henry VI, owing to the rivalries to which it gave rise, had momentarily placed the affairs of Germany in an evil pass. This was the signal in Italy for a general uprising against German supremacy. The communes seized the goods of the empire, drove out its representatives, and occupied its fortresses. Innocent III profited by the interregnum to support the revolted cities and to attempt to bring several of them under his authority. Specifically, he ordered Duke Conrad to turn Assisi over to him. Betraying the cause of the empire, the duke left La Rocca and hastened to Narni to do homage for his fief to the papal legates. No sooner had he set off than the Assisians rushed to attack the German garrison defending the fortress. It was in vain that the papal legates called on the besiegers to surrender the keep. With no great desire to give themselves a new master, the latter braved the papal excommunication, took the citadel by storm, and totally demolished it. They thereupon formed a communal government, whose first concern was to provide the city with a stout enclosure, so as to forestall any renewed offensive by the enemy. These ramparts—parts of which still stand—were finished with incredible speed, and stones from the dismantled fortress were used in their construction. Can we doubt that Francis took part in this work, learning as he did so the building trade in which we shall see him excel?

One would prefer to believe, however, that he took no part in the massacres which followed.

Not content with having driven out the Germans, the next thought of Assisi's burghers was to rid themselves of the feudal aristocracy, which, by its toll charges and vexations of every sort, hampered the city's trade. Then began dreadful reprisals. The castles dominating the heights were burned and many of their owners executed. The lords found in the city were put to death and their palaces demolished. The goods of all those nobles in whom the German hegemony found its support were confiscated.

Delivered from its oppressors, was Assisi at last to enjoy its newly won liberty in peace? Not so, for Perugia, the eternal rival, aroused by the nobles of Assisi who took refuge in it and who burned to recover their lost status, now entered upon the scene. In 1201 Perugia declared war on her neighbor, and a fierce duel between the two communes ensued which lasted for at least a decade.

It was during this murderous period that in November 1202, the battle of Ponte San Giovanni was waged by the Tiber below Perugia. Francis fought in it bravely, was taken prisoner, and carried away as a hostage to Perugia. His captivity probably lasted until the month of November 1203, though the war continued—interrupted by truces and new massacres—up to 1210, when Francis perhaps contributed to restoring peace to his fellow townsmen.

Meanwhile, the long months he passed in the Perugian prison dampened neither his military ambitions, his knightly courage, nor his gaiety.

> As he lived in the manner of the nobles, it was with the knights that he was imprisoned. Now, while the latter were bewailing their fate, he laughed at his chains, and always appeared cheerful.
>
> "Are you crazy?" asked one of his companions, "to crack jokes in the fix we're in?"

"How can you expect me to be sad," he replied, "when I think of the future that awaits me, and of how I shall one day be the idol of the whole world?"

Among the captives, there was an unbearable young noble, shunned by all. Francis alone did not turn his back on him. In fact, he did so well that he ended up taming him and reconciling him with his companions. For already, no one could resist his charm and goodness.

CHAPTER TWO

Conversion

SEVERAL PAINTERS OF the thirteenth century have preserved for us the features of the Little Poor Man. We admire, "as if he were living in our time, this slight Italian figure, slender and pale, with his beautiful large eyes, his fine and regular features, his smiling, almost merry, countenance, and extreme expressiveness."

Of all these paintings, that of Cimabue in the Lower Church of the saint's Basilica in Assisi is perhaps the most faithful. It dates from around 1265 and corresponds quite well with Thomas of Celano's description:

> Francis was a man of almost medium height, rather slight of build, joyous and kindly of countenance. He had a round head, a low forehead, kind, black eyes, straight brows, a straight well-shaped nose; small, and as it were, uptilted, ears. His speech was penetrating and ardent; his voice, strong and musical. His teeth were well-spaced, even, and white; his mouth small, and his beard scanty. He had a slender neck, short arms, tapering fingers and nails. He was lean, with slender legs, and small feet.
>
> He had a good intellect and an excellent memory. His great eloquence melted men's hearts. Ever courteous and

mild, he was open-handed, seldom angry, quick to forgive, knew how to keep a secret, and adapted himself to the most diverse temperaments. Though one of the greatest of the saints...

But let us not anticipate. We are only in 1203; and that year, the aspirant to knighthood who leaves the Perugian prison has not yet dreamed of sainthood.

On the contrary, he resumed his life of business and pleasure, and then fell gravely ill. "In fact, Francis never had any health," affirm those who knew him. "From his youth, he could live only surrounded by constant care."

Had his long imprisonment weakened him? Or, once liberated, anxious to make up for lost time, had he overtaxed his strength? At any rate, he now spent long weeks in bed; during which time his thoughts began to take a different tack.

"When he was out of danger," writes Thomas of Celano, "he arose, and, leaning on a cane, began to take a few steps in his room. Shortly after, he was able to venture outdoors for the first time; and wanted to go and enjoy the country, which had always been enough to make him happy. But this time, neither the beauty of the fields and the smiling vineyards, nor anything pleasant to the sight was able to charm him. Astonished at the change, he reflected that it is foolish to become attached to those things that lose their appeal from one day to the next; and, profoundly disillusioned, he sadly returned home.

"These, however," Thomas adds, "were but surface impressions. Vice is second nature; and those bad habits which have taken root in the soul are not eradicated all at once. So, as soon as he felt really well again, Francis began to prepare for new exploits."

He continued to dream of military glory and of chivalry. Chivalry was the nobility of the times. It was not, moreover, reserved to the sons of aristocrats. Those of the upper middle class could also aspire to it, if they were able to furnish their equipment and were deemed worthy to be dubbed a knight. Being knighted involved the double ritual of the conferring of knighthood and the accolade.

The first consisted in the conferring of the armor. The accolade was the symbolic blow with the fist the new knight received from his sponsor. The candidate passed the night before the altar on which his armor reposed. In the morning, he heard Mass, and on his knees, took the oath to use his sword in the service of God and the oppressed. His sponsor then gave him the accolade on the back of his neck and embraced him, saying: "In the name of God, of St. Michael, and of St. George, I dub you knight. Be brave, courageous, and loyal."

Francis had just learned that a count of Assisi, perhaps named Gentile, was preparing to leave for Apulia, where the eternal struggle between church and state had flared up anew.

By his marriage with Constance, heiress of the Norman princes, the Emperor Henry VI had added to his crown the title of "King of the Two Sicilies." After his death, his widow had decided to confide the tutelage of their son, the young Frederick II, to Pope Innocent III. But the German princes were too fearful lest the patrimony of St. Peter should aggrandize itself at their expense, to brook that so able a pope should be the protector of their future emperor. So they arrayed themselves on the side of Markwald, the former lieutenant of Henry VI, who, on the strength of an alleged will made by the dead king, claimed the precious guardianship for himself. Now the interests of both sides were too involved to permit them to come to an understanding, so it was necessary to have recourse to arms.

Thus had the struggle continued since 1198. At first, the pontifical armies had been defeated. But the situation changed when in 1202 Gautier de Brienne entered the service of Innocent III. The Norman captain scored victory over victory; and those interpreters of the populace who did not like the Germans—the Provençal and Italian troubadours—sang his exploits far and wide. From the entire peninsula, soldiers rushed to range themselves under the banner of the glorious knight.

Francis likewise decided to join the papal armies. "He was certainly less opulent and less wellborn than the lord of Assisi, his companion," we are told; "but he set off moved by noble sentiments. The other thought especially of the spoils, while Francis thought only of glory" and of being knighted on the field of battle.

Feverishly, he made ready.

The equipment of a knight cost a small fortune; and that is why so many young lords, unable to defray the cost, were finally eliminated from the ranks of the nobility. It consisted of the hauberk or coat of mail, and the cuisse covering the thighs to the knees, the greaves or jambeaux and sollerets, protecting the shins and feet, the helmet covering the head, the sword whose hilt was a reliquary, the lance with its pennant, the buckler with its coat of arms, and the surcoat or flowing robe which covered the whole person. In addition, there was the horse and its armor, consisting of chain mail protecting the flanks and the chamfron protecting the head; and finally, the squire, likewise armed and mounted, by whom the knight was attended as he set out for war.

One may well imagine that Francis, who had no intention of being outdone by anyone, did things in the grand manner.

Meanwhile, "he met a knight so ill-clad that he was almost naked."

Did the seedy warrior implore his charity? Or was Francis spontaneously touched by his dilapidated appearance? Be that as it may, the fact is that "he gave to him generously, for the love of Christ, the sumptuously embroidered garments he was wearing."

He had acted like St. Martin, Thomas of Celano writes, and like St. Martin, he received his reward from God in a symbolic vision that he had the following night:

> He saw in a dream his father's house changed into a marvelous palace filled with arms. The bales of cloth had disappeared, and were replaced by magnificent saddles, shields, lances, and all kinds of knightly harness. Moreover, in one room of the palace a beautiful and charming bride was waiting for her bridegroom. Francis, thunderstruck, was wondering what all this could mean when a voice revealed to him that the soldiers and this beautiful lady were reserved for him. He awoke with happiness, since this vision, as he thought, could only be symbolic of the success he was to achieve.

> Such was not, however, the true interpretation of this strange dream, and doubtless, the ambitious youth became aware of this, when his joy was followed by a deep gloom and he found he had to make a real effort to get started on his way.

> But off he went. One morning, his kinsfolk saw him galloping off on horseback, followed by his squire, on the road which winds along the flanks of Mount Subasio. From Foligno, he headed toward Spoleto, whence he could reach Rome, then southern Italy. But it was written that he should nevermore serve under an earthly standard, and should thenceforth have no other master but God.

At Spoleto, where he stopped for the night, the mysterious voice spoke to him again in his sleep. "Francis," it said to him, "where are you going like this?"

"I am going to fight in Apulia," he replied.

"Tell me," the voice continued. "From whom can you expect most, the master or the servant?"

"From the master, of course!"

"Then why follow the servant, instead of the master on whom he depends?"

"Lord, what would You have me do?"

"Return to your own country. There it shall be revealed to you what you are to do, and you will come to understand the meaning of this vision."

Francis awoke, and unable to go back to sleep, spent the rest of the night in reflection. Abandoning his project, he took the road back to Assisi the next day. He was then about twenty-five years old.

All were amazed that he appeared in no way humiliated at his setback, and that, on the contrary, he appeared gayer than ever, saying: "You will see that some day I am going to be a great prince just the same!"

"But he was a changed man," observes Friar Thomas, "as his friends soon found out."

The chronicler gives us a most realistic account of his last party:

His friends had come to propose him as "king of youth", and had given him the scepter of his new dignity, which (if truth be told) merely signified their desire to fill their bellies at the expense of the so-called "king." Too polite to refuse, Francis offered them once more one of those banquets which permitted them to surfeit themselves with food. Then these gluttons spilled out over the sleeping city, singing their drunken refrains. Francis came behind them, his fool's scepter in his hand. But far from joining in with their songs, which disgusted him, he began to pray.

Then it was that divine grace came upon him, enlightening him as to the nothingness of earth's vanities and revealing to him the invisible realities. Suddenly, he was inundated with such a torrent of love, submerged in such sweetness, that he stood there motionless, neither seeing nor hearing anything. They might have cut him to pieces, he said later, and he would not have moved.

His companions, however, missing him, turned back to look for him. But they scarce recognized him, so changed was his countenance. "What's wrong with you," they asked, "that you're not following us anymore? Are you planning to get married? And has your sweetheart turned your head?"

"You're right!" replied Francis. "I *am* thinking of marrying! And the girl to whom I intend to plight my troth is so noble, so rich, and so good, that none of you ever saw her like!"

Who was the lady of his thoughts? Francis himself did not know yet. It was only later that he was to find her. While waiting, he sought her, created her little by little (if I may dare so to speak), up to the day when the Gospel disclosed the features and name of his future bride.

Certain it is that this feast was Francis's last, and that he thereafter remained faithful to the mysterious bride his heart had chosen. "He tried hard," says Thomas of Celano, "to conceal from everyone the change that had been wrought in him; but he nonetheless lost all taste for business, and gradually he was seen to withdraw from the world."

Here, as elsewhere, we shall make no attempt to explain the workings of grace in the soul of St. Francis. Who would presume to indicate the why and wherefores of similar phenomena? Neither St. Luke, writing of Mary Magdalene, nor St. Paul and St. Augustine, writing of themselves, ever attempted to show how faith succeeds doubt, nor the way whereby the soul suddenly passes from indifference or hate to fervor and mystical love. Has the Almighty, who can do more than we can ever comprehend, ever revealed those laws on which his miracles depend?

All that anyone can say is that Francis is now a man who has found love and who claims to be enlightened from on high. And he will act as such, consenting to pass for a religious visionary in the eyes of the blind who walk in darkness, and accomplishing acts described as "madness" by those who have never loved.

One might add that all that was best of his youthful ideals and ambitions was to survive in him. Like an artist who, changing his inspiration, does not thereby change his technique, he will shed nothing of his nobleness or his originality. A knight was what he had dreamed of becoming; a knight he will remain till his death.

His biographers often call him *miles Christi*. But the expression should not be taken as St. Paul understood it when speaking of Christians, or St. Augustine, Jerome, and Benedict when speaking of monks. To them, *miles* evoked the Roman legionary, the brave foot soldier who endured war's fatigues and won the victory.

The word took on a nobler meaning in the Middle Ages. It no longer designated the soldier who goes on foot, but the mounted warrior, the lord, the knight. *Miles Christi,* as pictured by historians of the Crusades, is the brother in arms, the champion, the "vassal of Christ." And so it is that Francis is to look on his service of the suzerain chosen by him in the night of Spoleto.

He is to proclaim himself the "herald of the Great King," and the "standard bearer of Christ," and he will call his followers his "companions of the Round Table." He is to wear a sack in the form of a cross, to recall together his Master's death and the colors of his Lady Poverty. We shall see him a knight in his joyous enthusiasm, his courtesy, his liberality, his uprightness, his horror of minutiae. He is to be chivalrous in thought, deed, and troth. For these things were, as we know, fundamental points in the code of chivalry.

The liege man (*homo legalis*) was obliged to respond to the call of his suzerain, to fight, and if need be, to die for him. To withdraw from this engagement out of cowardice or through some legal loophole would be a breach of faith, a dishonor, and for the felon it meant the death penalty on earth, while waiting "to go and burn in hell-fire with the devils."

Honor and undying fidelity were to characterize the holiness of the Poverello. Once he has paid homage to the Master, who said: "Whoever does not follow me is not worthy of me," Francis, filled with valor, will think only of imitating him in his life of poverty and suffering; constantly conceiving new exploits, endeavoring to vie with him in love and goodness, burning to become a martyr, and finally dying marked with the stigmata of his passion.

At this point in our story, however, young Francis, who has just broken with his past, and who seeks another goal for his life, is still ignorant of the road to follow to the happiness promised him. But he relies on God to show him the way; and that he may hear the Lord's voice again, he meditates and prays.

He also seeks to unburden himself to a friend. He makes a confidant of a young man of his own age who shared his tastes and consented to accompany him on his walks. Both went by preference to a grotto near town; and as they walked, they talked of the precious treasure for which they aspired.

Arriving at the grotto, Francis would go in alone, and remain alone with God. And there, in a long and anguished prayer—for his soul, torn by a thousand conflicting thoughts, could not find peace—he would implore God to show him the way. He would bewail his past sins, which he now held in horror, trembling lest he fall into them again. And all this made him suffer so intensely that his face would be drawn when he rejoined his companion.

One day, however, he came forth in peace, for God had delivered him from uncertainty and had enlightened him. He was so brimming over with joy that no one could help noticing it. As he could neither explain his joy nor contain it, he would put people off by saying that if he had come back from Apulia before he got there, it was that he might accomplish his exploits in his own country. Or else he would start talking again about the peerless princess whom he hoped to wed.

This princess was Lady Poverty.

Loving poverty does not mean limiting yourself to loving the poor, while taking care that you yourself lack nothing. It means becoming poor with them. It means refusing to enjoy yourself while they are suffering; and it means to embrace, as our Lord did, their state and their neediness. Such is the form of heroism that the sanctity of St. Francis was to take. People remarked that his love for the outcasts had increased. He gave them, we are told, more and more alms. If he had no money, he would give them his cap, his belt, some portion of his clothing—sometimes even his shirt. He also bought sacred vessels for needy priests. And when his father was absent, he would place much more food than was necessary on the family table, thinking of the beggars who would come after the meal for the leavings. This little stratagem, of course, did not escape his mother; but she said nothing against it, for she loved and admired him more than her other children. In short, Francis reached the point where he was concerned solely with the poor and was happy only in their company.

"The truth was," writes Thomas of Celano, "that he had become one of them, thinking only of sharing their life of privations." He loved Poverty itself.

In the course of a pilgrimage made to Rome, an opportunity was afforded him to wear the colors and livery of his austere princess. It may have been his confessor who imposed the journey on him as a penance; or perhaps the idea came to him of its own accord, since he had—like all Christians of his time—a great devotion to the apostles.

Arriving at St. Peter's tomb, he was scandalized to see the pilgrims so niggardly with their money and making such mean offerings. "Really!" he thought. "This is no way to honor the prince of the Apostles!" And taking his purse filled with gold, he flung it toward the altar. The gold pieces rolling on the pavement caught the attention of the crowd, who marveled at such munificence. The gesture was chivalrous and right in St. Francis's style, for he was never one to stop and look at the sordid side of things; and so it was a matter of indifference to him, should his gold go to prelates, already, perhaps too rich.

When Francis had finished his devotions, he went out, encountering in front of St. Peter's the beggars with whom this place teems at all times. There it was that he proposed to one of them that they exchange clothes—an offer which, as one may well imagine, was not turned down. Putting on the wretched fellow's rags, and mingling with the troop of beggars, he begged along with them, shared their sordid meal, and found so much happiness in his taste of this kind of life that he would have asked nothing better than to keep on with it. Indeed he would have become a beggar there and then, had it not been for his desire to spare his family the shame of seeing him in this state.

After his return to Assisi, he became more solitary than ever and gave himself over more and more to prayer. Sometimes he was tempted to quit, and for some time he was troubled by a strange obsession.

There was a woman in the city, some devout old crone, perhaps, who had so ugly a hump on her back, that the poor old creature appeared a monster. For a long time, Francis was obsessed with the fear that this same hump would grow on his back if he kept on in this way of life. It was the Devil, (a fallen angel, and therefore grotesque) who suggested this ridiculous thought to discourage him. But God came to his assistance. "Francis," said the well-known voice, "if you would find Me, despise earthly things; deny yourself, and prefer bitterness to sweetness. For this is the price you must pay to understand all these things."

The young man "promised to obey," and God soon sent him a final trial.

The saint himself has related in his Testament how he became "converted."

"During my life of sin," he writes, "nothing disgusted me like seeing victims of leprosy. It was the Lord Himself who urged me to go to them. I did so, and ever since, everything was so changed for me that what had seemed at first painful and impossible to overcome became easy and pleasant. Shortly after, I definitely forsook the world."

If we are to believe the chronicler, Matthew of Paris, there were no fewer than twenty thousand lazarets in Europe at that time. Everywhere, one would run across these unfortunates, whose putrefying flesh, oozing ulcers, and pestilential odor brought disgust. The young dandy had such a horror of them that if he saw one two miles away, he would turn his horse's head and gallop off, holding his nose. And he sent someone else to take alms to him.

But one day, at a bend in the road, he suddenly found himself facing a man afflicted with leprosy. His first reaction was to turn back. But he immediately changed his mind; and dismounting, he embraced the wretch, gently putting some coins in his hand. He thereupon felt a great happiness pervade his whole being. It was God keeping his promise and changing bitterness to sweetness for him who had preferred bitterness to sweetness.

But the young man was not content with his first victory. He sprang to the saddle and rode to a neighboring lazaret, apparently, San Lazaro d'Arce, about two miles from Assisi. Francis entered this "last refuge of all human misery." He assembled its unfortunate inmates and begged their pardon for having so often despised them; he lingered some time in their company; and while waiting to come and live near them, "he distributed money to them and left only after kissing them all on the mouth."

CHAPTER THREE

The Restorer of Churches

ABOUT THREE-QUARTERS of a mile below Assisi stands the little convent of San Damiano. Built on a hillside, on an elevation from which the whole plain may be viewed through a curtain of cypresses, it has become the residence of the Friars Minor after having been that of the Poor Ladies.

But in the spring of 1206, all that was there among the wheat fields sparsely set with olive trees was a ruinous chapel. Within, suspended over the altar, hung a mild and serene Byzantine crucifix. Although the church was no longer frequented, an indigent priest was still attached to it, living, no doubt, on alms and the suffrages of the faithful.

"Now one day as Francis was passing, he entered the chapel. Kneeling before the wooden crucifix, he began to pray, when suddenly the figure of Christ, parting its painted lips, called him by name and said, 'Francis, go repair My house, which is falling in ruins.'

"It would be impossible," the biographer continues, "to describe the miraculous effect that these words produced on the hearer, since the latter declared himself incapable of expressing it. But one may reverently conjecture that Christ then impressed on his heart the sacred wounds with which he was later to mark his stigmatized body.

For how many times in the future was not the blessed man to be met along the road, shedding compassionate tears over the Savior's Passion?"

It was not a rare thing for knights to become builders of churches, in expiation of the faults committed in their adventure-filled lives. Had not one of the four sons of Aymon, men said, abandoned his military career to help build the Cathedral of Cologne?

Francis may have believed himself called on to imitate him; for, taking literally an order evidently applying to the Church of Christ itself, he at first thought that he was to restore the chapel of San Damiano. He at once offered the priest money for oil and a lamp, so that a suitable light might burn before the image of Christ crucified. But where was he to find the necessary resources for rebuilding the chapel?

That need not be an obstacle! Francis thought of his horse and the bales of cloth at home. He returned home, made up a bundle of the most precious stuffs, then fortifying himself with the sign of the cross, leaped to the saddle and set off at a gallop for Foligno. There (as he usually did) he met customers who bought his merchandise. He also sold them his horse, so that he had to make the ten miles back to Assisi on foot.

When he returned, the priest of San Damiano was in the chapel. Francis kissed his hands, detailed his plans to him, and attempted to give him the receipts for his sale. But the priest took this at first for a practical joke. Was not this risky money, which might embroil him with Francis's family? And then, how was a man to believe in the sudden conversion of this young fop, who even yesterday was scandalizing the whole town by his follies? So Francis did not succeed in having his gift accepted. But he did win the priest's confidence and got his permission to stay with him. As for the purse that was burning his fingers, he tossed it like a dead weight into the corner of a window and thought no more about it.

Meanwhile, Peter Bernardone was in a towering rage and deeply distressed at learning what his son had done. Assembling his friends and neighbors, he rushed to San Damiano "to seize the fugitive and bring him home."

Fortunately, the new hermit had taken care to secure a place of refuge—a sort of dugout under a house that no one, except a friend, knew about. As the conspirators drew near, he ran and hid in it, and let them shout it out. He hid for a whole month, eating in his cave the little food that was brought him, and beseeching God to help him carry out his plans. And in this dark retreat, the Lord sent him such consolation and delight as he had never known.

The time came, however, when, blushing at his fears, he left the hiding place; and resolved to face the music, he headed for town. He was exhausted by his austerities. People seeing him gaunt and wan— he who a short time before had been so full of life—thought that he had lost his mind, and began to yell, "Lunatic! Madman!" Urchins slung stones and mud at him; but he went on, without appearing to notice their taunts.

Hearing the hullabaloo, Peter Bernardone came out of the house and saw that it was his son they were harrying. He became furious. Hurling himself on Francis like a fierce wolf on an innocent lamb, he dragged him into the house, where he chained him and shoved him into a dungeon. He spared neither arguments nor blows to wear down the rebel, but the latter refused to be shaken.

Personal business, however, obliged the father to leave; and Francis's mother profited by this to try her hand at swaying her son.

Seeing that he remained inflexible, one day when she was alone in the house, she broke his chains and set him free. The father's fury knew no bounds, when, on his return, he learned of the prisoner's escape. He launched into reproaches against his wife; then attempted a final move at San Damiano, where Francis had again settled.

But trial had steeled his courage. He went forth now with assurance, with peaceful heart and joyous mien. He calmly walked up to his father, declaring that he no longer feared either irons or blows and that he was ready to endure all things for the love of Christ. Feeling that all hope was lost for the time being, Peter Bernardone concerned himself only with recovering the Foligno sales money and sending the young rebel into exile. This respectable citizen hoped in this way to get the son who shamed him out of the way, and perhaps by cutting off his living, to bring him back home someday.

Shouting angrily on the way, he rushed to the palace of the commune, and swore out a warrant before the consuls. The magistrates charged a town crier to summon Francis to appear before them. But the young man, who was bothered neither about exile nor about giving back the money, refused to obey; and claiming that having gone into God's service, he was no longer under civil jurisdiction, he declined to appear. The consuls declared themselves incompetent and rejected the plaintiff's claim, leaving him with no recourse but to appeal to the jurisdiction of the Church.

The Bishop of Assisi at that time was Lord Guido, who occupied his diocese until after the saint's death. He formally bade the accused to appear before his tribunal. "I will go before the bishop," replied Francis, "for he is the father and master of souls."

The judgment was most probably rendered in public, in the piazza of Santa Maria Maggiore, in front of the bishop's palace.

"Put your trust in God," said the bishop to the accused, "and show yourself courageous. However, if you would serve the Church, you have no right, under color of good works, to keep money obtained in this way. So give back such wrongly acquired goods to your father, to appease him."

"Gladly, my Lord," replied Francis, "and I will do still more."

He went within the palace and disrobed; then, with his clothing in his hands, he reappeared, almost entirely nude, before the crowd. "Listen to me, everybody!" he cried. "Up to now, I have called Peter Bernardone my father! But now that I purpose to serve God, I give him back not only this money that he wants so much, but all the clothes I have from him!" With this, Francis threw everything on the ground. "From now on," he added, "I can advance naked before the Lord, saying in truth no longer: my father, Peter Bernardone, but: our Father who art in Heaven!"

At this dramatic climax the bishop drew Francis within his arms, enveloping him in the folds of his mantle. The spectators, catching sight of the hair shirt that the young man wore on his skin, were dumbfounded, and many of them wept. As for Peter Bernardone, unhappy and angry, he hurriedly withdrew, taking with him the clothing and purse.

And that was the way Francis took leave of his family.

One would like to think that he saw his mother again, and from time to time showed some mark of tenderness toward this woman who admired him and had had an intuition of his sublime destiny. But the biographers make no further mention of her.

For some time after that, Francis did no more about San Damiano. The funds on which he had counted had vanished, and he had not yet learned that poverty sufficeth for all things. He had first to go in search of suitable clothing, since all that he had to cover him was a little coat full of holes that the bishop's gardener had given him after the scene of the day before. He drew a cross on it with chalk by way of a coat of arms; then he set out through the woods singing the Lord's praises in French at the top of his lungs.

His heart was overflowing with joy. There was to be no more now of circumspection and feeling his way. A pathway of light opened straight before him. He was consecrated to the Master's service; he had just been made Christ's knight and had solemnly espoused Lady Poverty. God was rewarding him by making him happy.

He was making the woods ring with his songs when some robbers, scenting a prey, rushed up. This man with his threadbare cloak was a disappointment to them. "Who are you?" they asked.

"I am the herald of the Great King!" replied Francis with assurance.

As he did not yet have the gift of taming wild beasts, the robbers beat him up and threw him into the snow at the foot of a ravine. "There you are, oaf!" they shouted as they made off. "Stay there, God's herald!"

Francis climbed out of the slush-filled hole only with great effort, and when the ruffians were out of sight and hearing, he went on his way, singing louder than ever. He then directed his footsteps to a monastery, where he thought the monks would consent to clothe him in exchange for work.

The monks took him on as a kitchen helper but gave him nary a stitch to cover him. For food, they let him skim off a little of the greasy water they fed the pigs. It is true that afterward, when Francis's reputation for sanctity began to be established, the prior was ashamed at the way he had treated him and came to beg his forgiveness. And he obtained it easily, for the saint said that he had very pleasant memories of the few days spent in his kitchen.

It was at Gubbio that an old friend gave him something to wear. So afterward men saw him wearing a hermit's garb—a tunic secured at the waist by a leather belt, sandals on his feet, and a staff in his hand. He next stayed a while with the lepers, living in their midst, bathing their sores, sponging off the pus from their ulcers, and giving them loving care for the love of God.

Then he went back to San Damiano.

There, the chaplain still recalled recent events, and Francis had to reassure him by telling him of the bishop's encouragement and approval. After this, the restoration of the chapel could begin.

As Francis had no money with which to buy materials, he was obliged to beg for them. He went through the city crying, "Whoever gives me a stone will receive a reward from the Lord! Whoever gives me two will have two rewards! Whoever gives me three will receive three rewards!" Sometimes, like a *jongleur* who sings in order to earn his salary and repay his benefactors, the collector would interrupt his rounds to sing to the glory of the Most High.

And whether he addressed himself to God or to men, whether he begged for hewn stone or celebrated the divine attributes, the Little Poor Man (his biographers observe) "always spoke in a familiar style, without having recourse to the learned and bombastic words of human wisdom." Is this an allusion to the jargon and to the false science that flourished in the schools? One thing certain is that here you have defined the man and the style, which go together in St. Francis.

Simple he was in his person, having but one aim and one object, honestly and openly sought. Simple he was in speech, knowing what he said, and saying only what he knew; avoiding lengthy, pompous, and obscure discourse, speaking—like Jesus in the Gospels—to make himself understood and to be useful to others. Picturesque and sublime, his talks, coming from the heart, reached men's hearts, delivering them from their sadness and their sins, and revealing to them the happiness that comes from belonging to God.

Moreover, if many still held the new hermit to be a madman and persisted in insulting him, many already were beginning to understand him; and, moved to the depths of their being, they wept as they listened to his words. They saw him carrying stones on his back and striving to interest everyone in his project. Standing on his scaffolding, he would joyously hail the passersby. "Come here a while, too," he would shout, "and help me rebuild San Damiano!"

It may be that crews of masons responded to his appeals, and working under his direction, helped him in his tasks. It was then, accounts tell us, that he predicted that virgins consecrated to God would soon come and take shelter in the shadow of the rebuilt chapel.

One can imagine how he drove himself—he who had always been petted and pampered by his parents. Taking pity on him, his priest-companion began—poor as he was—to prepare better food for him than that with which he himself was satisfied.

Francis, at first, raised no objections; but seeing that he was being mollycoddled, he said to himself: "Francis, are you expecting to find a priest everywhere who will baby you? This is not the life of poverty that you have embraced! No! You are going to do as the beggars do! Out of love for Him who willed to be born poor and to live in poverty, who was bound naked to the cross, and who did not even own the tomb men laid Him in, you are going to take a bowl and go begging your bread from door to door!"

So Francis went begging through the town, a large bowl in his hands, putting everything that people gave him into it. When it came to eating this mess, he felt nauseated. He managed, however, to get it down, and found it better than the fine food he used to eat at home. He thereupon thanked God for being able—frail and exhausted as he was—to adjust himself to such a diet; and from then on, he would not let the priest prepare anything special for him.

Let no one imagine, however, that he was not sometimes subject to false shame. For instance, one day when oil was needed for the chapel lamp, he went up to a house where a party was in progress, with merrymakers overflowing into the street. Recognizing some old friends and blushing to appear before them as a beggar, he started back. But he soon retraced his steps and accused himself of his cowardice before them all. Then, making his request in French, he set off again with his oil.

Thomas of Celano observes here that "it was always in French that St. Francis expressed himself when he was filled with the Holy Ghost; as if he had foreseen the special cult with which France was to honor him one day," and wanted to show himself grateful in advance.

No one, though, ever loved his homeland more than he did, or was more beloved by its people. But the veneration of his fellow citizens did not come in a day. A considerable number of them began by mocking him at will, including his brother, Angelo, eager to show himself for once witty at Francis's expense.

This happened very likely in a church, where Francis was praying one wintry morning, shivering with cold beneath his flimsy rags. Passing near him with a friend, the brother remarked to his companion, "Look! There's Francis! Ask him if he won't sell you a penny's worth of his sweat!"

Francis could not help smiling. "It's not for sale," he replied gently. "I prefer to keep it for God, who will give me a much better price for it than you."

The barbed shafts no longer struck home. Only one thing continued to distress him, and that was his father's attitude toward him. For every time that Peter Bernardone met his son, he became infuriated and cursed him.

A son like Francis could not remain under the spell of a father's curses. So to an old beggar named Albert, he made the following offer: "Adopt me as your son, and I will share the alms I receive with you. Only whenever we meet my father and he curses me, you make the sign of the cross over me and give me your blessing."

The arrangement was to Albert's advantage, and we may be sure that he had no scruples about giving so many blessings as there were curses to ward off. So, addressing the wrathful merchant, Francis would say to him, "You see that God has found a way to offset your curses, for he has sent me a new father to bless me."

Evidently Peter Bernardone was sensitive to ridicule and ended by taking things more calmly, for we hear no more of him in the biographies. No doubt, he lived long enough to behold the rising star of the Little Poor Man. And who knows if, on seeing his son honored by important personages, he did not put as much zeal into acknowledging him as he had into denying him?

CHAPTER FOUR

First Recruits

WE DO NOT know how many churches Francis repaired during the two or three years he gave himself up to this occupation, while continuing to care for lepers. Biographers mention three, all of them in the neighborhood of Assisi: San Damiano, which we know already; probably San Pietro della Spina on the plains west of San Damiano; and finally, the Portiuncula, lost at that time in deep woods, and today enclosed within the walls of the basilica of St. Mary of the Angels.

The Portiuncula belonged to the Benedictine Abbey of Mount Subasio; but the monks had long since abandoned it and cared less and less about it. "The chapel was, then, completely deserted, and no one ever set foot in it," writes Thomas of Celano, "when, pained at this state of things, Francis, the devoted client of the Virgin Mary, resolved to settle there and restore it."

The Portiuncula, which was to become the cradle of the Franciscan epic, "was the place that Francis loved most in the whole world," wrote St. Bonaventure. Everything conspired to endear it to him: its name, linking the concept of poverty to the name of the Mother of God; its isolation in the midst of the great silent forest; without counting the proximity of the Santa Maddalena and San Salvatore leprosaria situated about three miles from there, and both of them near Assisi.

It was while hearing Mass in the restored chapel that Francis received the revelation of his true vocation. This event probably took place on the twenty-fourth of February 1208, the feast of St. Matthias, while the priest was reading the Gospel passage in which Jesus maps out a rule of conduct for his apostles. "Go," said the Savior, "and preach the message, 'the Kingdom of Heaven is at hand!'…. Freely you have received, freely give…. Do not keep gold, or silver, or money in your girdles, no wallet for your journey, nor two tunics, nor sandals, nor staff, for the laborer deserves his living.

"And whatever town or village you enter, inquire who in it is worthy; and stay there until you leave. As you enter the house, salute it, saying, 'Peace to this house.'"

Francis had made great spiritual progress and received much light since beginning his life of penance and charity; but this time, he felt that God had taken away the last veil and finally illumined his path.

The better to understand these sacred lines, he asked the priest to explain them and comment on them. The priest, perhaps a Benedictine from Mount Subasio, explained the Gospel passage— that Christ's disciples had been commanded to preach repentance everywhere, to take nothing with them, and to trust in God alone to supply all their needs.

Francis thrilled with happiness at this revelation and exclaimed enthusiastically: "That is what I want! That is what I seek! I long to do that with all my heart!" On the instant, he threw away his staff, took off his shoes, and laid aside his cloak, keeping only a tunic; replaced his leather belt with a cord, and made himself a rough garment, so poor and so badly cut that it could inspire envy in no man.

That, as Francis recalled in his Testament, was a day of decision, a day to be remembered, in which "the Most High personally revealed to me that I ought to live according to the Holy Gospel"; and in which he himself, in his childlike candor and knightly loyalty, adopted forever this literal way of interpreting the Savior's words. For (Thomas of Celano observes here), "it was not as a deaf man that he heard the Lord's words"—as a deaf man who opens and closes his ears according to circumstances and his own convenience. As for him, "not only did he learn by heart all our Lord said, but he never lost sight of it, and constantly endeavored to observe it to the letter."

Francis knew now that it was not to build chapels that God was calling him, but to cooperate in the restoration of the Church. So he lost no time in setting joyfully to work to preach penitence.

To everyone he met he now gave the Gospel greeting: "The Lord give you peace!" Coming from a man whose voluntary poverty permitted him to enjoy this supreme benefit, these words were not without effect, for many to whom they were addressed made peace with their enemies and with their own conscience.

It was at this time that Francis gave his first sermon in the church of San Giorgio, where he had gone to school and in which he would at first be buried. "He began," continues Thomas of Celano, "by wishing peace to the congregation, speaking without affectation, but with such enthusiasm that all were carried away by his words."

From now on the mockers held their peace. The influence of the Poor Man of Jesus Christ and God's Troubadour was spreading. People began to listen to this sunny prophet who preached redemption to sinners and to sad hearts the secret of regaining joy and gladness.

Unlike the lay reformers who swarmed through Europe in those days, he hurled no anathemas at the times and inveighed against no one. He limited himself to relating the Gospel with such humility,

charm, and assurance that he gave it back its effectiveness and fresh-
ness. After all, this time the disciple reminded men of the Master,
and the virtue of the preacher lent credence to his message. Had they
not seen him for over two years living like the least of the poor and
devoting himself to the relief of the lepers?

All this burst upon men in those days as a kind of revelation.
Certainly it was an awakening and a new beginning. And as the habit
St. Francis wore designated him as a guide, some thought that a new
form of religious life had been born; and disciples eager to follow it
soon presented themselves.

In a few months, they were eleven.

"The first was a man from Assisi, simple and good," of whom nothing
else is told us and who disappears at once, like a wraith. The second
was Bernard of Quintavalle; the third, Peter Catanii; the fourth,
Giles. Then, in uncertain order, come Morico, the Crosier from
the leprosy hospital of San Salvatore; Barbaro, Sabbatino, Bernardo
Vigilante, John of San Costanzo; Angelo Tancredi, the knight; Philip,
who "preached admirably, and interpreted the Scriptures perfectly
without having studied in the schools"; and, finally, the Judas of the
new apostolic college, that Giovanni della Cappella, later known as
"John of the Hat," who, according to the *Fioretti*, "apostasized, and
hanged himself by the throat." He was, it appears, very disobedient;
he flatly refused to go without a hat, whereas the other brothers were
content with their hoods.

Bernard was a rich and important citizen of Assisi, thoughtful and
of exemplary conduct. Greatly impressed by young Bernardone's
conversion, he began to consider following his example and leaving
the world. Meanwhile, to test him, he often received him as a guest
in his home.

One night when both were sharing the same room, Francis promptly pretended to be sound asleep. Bernard, likewise feigning sleep, began to snore loudly—though he kept one eye open. He soon saw his companion rise cautiously, kneel down, and begin to pray. And all night, he could hear Francis, on his knees, with loving sighs, conversing with God. Bernard was now completely won over. In the morning, he asked his guest, "What would you say a man should do who wanted to get rid of his money?"

"It would seem to me that he ought to give it back to the Master he received it from."

"Well, then, I've decided to follow your advice!" replied Bernard.

"In that case," said Francis, "we shall go and consult the Gospels to find out what Christ's will is for you."

At daybreak they set out for the Church of San Nicolo to hear Mass, taking with them Peter of Catanii, who had likewise resolved to leave the world. They opened the missal three times at random. The first time, their eyes fell on these words: "If you will be perfect, go, sell what you have, and give to the poor." The second time, they read: "Take nothing for your journey"; and the third time: "If anyone wishes to come after Me, let him deny himself, and take up his cross, and follow Me."

"Here," said Francis, "is what we are going to do, and all those who shall afterwards join us."

We do not know if Peter of Catanii, who was a jurist, had means; and if so, how he got rid of them.

As for the wealthy Bernard, of whom Thomas of Celano declares that he "made haste to sell his property down to the last penny" the *Fioretti* depict him stationed in front of his door, distributing his possessions to the poor who rushed up for the handout. Even so, he seemed in more of a hurry to get rid of his money than the poor to receive it. Like a farm woman in the midst of the hen yard, he tirelessly reached into the folds of his cloak and gave fistfuls of money to every comer. Standing beside him, Francis helped to hurry things along.

While this was going on, a priest named Sylvester squeezed through the crowd, and going up to Francis, reminded him of an old overdue bill. "By the way," he said, "there are still some stones you bought from me to repair your churches that have never been paid for."

"That's quite possible!" replied Francis, "but never mind!" And plunging both hands into Bernard's cloak, he gave him a handful of silver. "Here you are!" he said. "If you want more, you have only to say the word!"

But it must have been the right amount, for the avaricious priest asked no more and left—greatly embarrassed.

Shortly after, renouncing his stones and other goods, Sylvester the priest also embraced the life of poverty.

Peter and Bernard were persons of too much prominence for their vocation not to be heralded abroad. Seven days later, Giles heard of it from his kinsfolk, who, it seems, were farmers in the outskirts of Assisi. As for a long time he had been greatly concerned with his soul's salvation, he was delighted to learn that Francis was receiving companions. The next morning—April 23, 1208—he said farewell to his family and went to hear Mass in the Church of St. George on its titular feast day. Then he proceeded to the Portiuncula. A little way past the San Salvatore lazaret, he met Francis coming out of the woods. Running up to him and throwing himself at his feet, he begged him to receive him.

"Dear Brother," said Francis, raising him up, "it is a great favor that you have received today! If the Emperor, coming to Assisi to choose a knight or a chamberlain, had let his choice fall on you, you would feel proud, and rightly so! Well, it is God himself who invites you to His court, by calling you to serve Him in our little band."

Taking Giles by the hand, Francis led him to the hut where Bernard and Peter were. "Here," he said, presenting him, "is a good brother God has sent us! Let us sit down to table to celebrate his coming."

After the meal, he took him to Assisi to find something with which to make him a habit. On the way, a beggar woman asked for charity. Francis said to his companion, "Give her your fine cloak." Brother Giles obeyed, and afterward related that "his alms had appeared to fly up to Heaven," and himself with it, so happy he felt. But his happiness "grew still greater" when, shortly afterward, he saw himself "wearing the coarse tunic" in which Francis had clothed him.

The four new apostles lost no time in trying out their strength, and went forth in two groups for their first mission. Accompanied by Giles, Francis reached the march of Ancona and the others went in a direction not disclosed to us.

The crowds had not yet started to run after the Little Poor Man. So he limited himself to singing songs —like the minstrels—in the public squares; and to recommending to the few listeners gathered to hear him to love God above everything else and to repent of their sins. Never being much gifted in public speaking, Brother Giles kept still, and intervened only to applaud his master's speech. "Do everything that my spiritual father tells you to do," he would say. "For you can believe me, he is quite right, and no one could tell you anything better."

According to the *Three Companions*, our missionaries did not enjoy great success at this time. Their strange garb did not add to their prestige. What did these ragamuffins want with their ragged clothes, their sermons, and their songs? People generally took them either for fanatics or fools. Young women fled at sight of them, as if they had the evil eye. "They are either madmen or saints," thought the wise-acres, not venturing to express an opinion.

As for Francis, he radiated hope, and already saw himself at the head of a great army, made up of the flower of chivalry. He confided to Brother Giles: "Like the fisherman who, hauling up all kinds of fish into his nets, throws out the little fish and keeps only the big ones, so we should choose and keep only the best."

Back at the Portiuncula once more, Francis received four new brothers, equally natives of Assisi: Philip; the Crosier, Morico, whose Order ministered to the San Salvatore leprosarium; Sabbatino; and probably Giovanni della Cappella.

The people of Assisi did not take kindly to this increase in the brotherhood. They forgave Francis, so long as he was one of a kind; but when they saw that he was gathering recruits, they anxiously asked themselves where it would all end, and also how many of these healthy men—who so often came begging to their doors—they would have to feed. "If they had held onto their own property," people grumbled, "they wouldn't be reduced to eating other men's bread."

Thus the penitents of the Portiuncula now received more insults than alms.

Things had come to such a pass that Bishop Guido thought it his duty to intervene. He too, when he had encouraged Francis, never dreamed that the latter would gain adherents. "Your way of life appears too hard and impractical to me," said he, wishing to induce Francis to give up so radical a poverty.

But Francis replied: "My Lord, if we owned property, we should need arms to defend it. Besides, property engenders many disputes and lawsuits harmful to love of God and neighbor. That is why we do not want to have anything of our own here below."

Unless he was prepared to say the Gospel was wrong, there was nothing to reply; and Bishop Guido, who sometimes lost his lawsuits, declared himself convinced. Doubtless, to completely satisfy the bishop, Francis explained to him that, far from being idle, his followers would busy themselves in earning their living and have recourse to public charity only when absolutely necessary.

Our penitents strove, then, not to be a burden to anyone. Some of them hired themselves out as laborers in monasteries and private homes. Others helped farmers in the field, and still others took care of victims of leprosy in the neighboring lazar houses. But the demands made by the common life and the apostolate, the needs of the sick, and the fact that Francis, in conformity to the Gospel, was "opposed to receiving money and thinking about the morrow"—all these things made mendicancy inevitable.

Now unless he is born a slave, what man does not have a horror of a state wherein one receives without giving and must accept insult and injury without repaying in kind?

The brothers would gladly have dispensed themselves from begging, and at first Francis tried to spare them. Every day, notes *The Three Companions*, it was he who, despite his frail constitution and impaired health, took the bowl and went out begging.

But he finally succumbed to the task, and as no one stepped forward to take his place, he said to the brothers: "My little children, you must make up your minds to go out begging, since, following the example of our Lord and of His most blessed Mother, you have chosen the way of perfect poverty. And do not believe that it is so difficult and humiliating. You have only to say, 'Charity, for the love of God.' And since, in exchange for what they give you, your bene-factors will receive the incomparable blessing of God's love, you will therefore be in the position of someone who offers a hundredfold for one. So be not ashamed, but go forth with joy."

The brothers were not yet numerous enough to go out two by two (which would have made them bolder). So each went alone. But everything went along famously; and when the brothers returned at night, there was not one of them who did not declare himself satis-fied with his daily "stint." They also amused themselves by comparing results—those having the fullest sacks were, naturally, the proudest. Their father congratulated them; and from that time onward, the brothers vied at being the ones to receive permission to go out begging.

Francis spent the summer and fall of 1208 at St. Mary of the Angels, devoting himself to his spiritual family.

By making the brothers poor and destitute, he had constrained them to trust in God and to seek him alone. But he still had to form them in the spiritual life and show them the special way whereby he wished to lead them. So he instructed them, encouraged and corrected them, teaching them to pray, exercising them in humility and penance, training them in perfection; and—like those artists to whom one gives a good model so that they may paint a good picture— he continually placed before them the person of our Lord. "When the Lord gave me brethren," he declares in his Testament, "no one save the Most High taught me what I must do." By this, we see that the founder of the Franciscans did not feel that he owed anything to the doctors and founders of Orders who had preceded him.

When winter came, he decided to undertake a new crusade with his sons. Calling them together, he said to them: "Since it is God's will for us to work, not only for our own salvation, but also for the salvation of others, we will go all over the world to preach—by example, even more than in words—penitence and peace. Among those whom you will meet, some will give you a good reception and will listen to you; but the greater part will reject you and revile you. Reply humbly to those who question you; and as for those who shall persecute you, show them your gratitude."

At these words, which reminded them of their unpleasant experiences and predicted more to come, the brothers began to tremble so much that their father had to reassure them. "Do not feel sad at my ignorance and your own," he said to them. "God will keep His promise and speak by your mouth. Besides, the time is at hand when wiser men will come and help us. And do not be discouraged any more about your small number. There is something of which I should not speak to you, if charity did not oblige me. But I can tell you confidentially that the Lord has revealed to me in a vision that our Order is to spread over all the earth. And even yet there rings in my ears the sound of the footsteps of men hastening from France, from Spain, from England, and from Germany, to join up with us." This talk restored their courage.

Francis divided them, then, into four groups of two. It was agreed that Bernard and Giles should go in the direction of St. James of Compostella. He himself with a companion would go as far as the Valley of Rieti. As for the others, other regions were assigned to them.

All dropped to their knees. Francis blessed them and tenderly embraced them, saying to each: "Dear brother, put your trust in the Lord, who will take care of you." He then dismissed them.

The brothers kept the recommendations made to them as best they could.

When they passed near a crucifix, they would keel down and say a *Pater*. When they entered a church, they would say the following prayer: "We adore You, O Lord Jesus, here and in all the churches of the entire world; and we bless You, because by Your holy Cross You have redeemed the world." They greeted all whom they met with their usual, "God give you peace!" letting it be understood, no doubt, that they themselves possessed this peace and found it good.

But some surly folk, displeased at this salutation, replied, "What are these new manners? Why can't you greet people the way other religious do?"

They were so gruff that a timid brother asked St. Francis not to have to greet people in this way. But the saint said to him, "Let them be, as these men do not discern yet what comes from God. For the Lord Himself revealed this greeting to me. And it is the Lord, too, who has raised up our little brotherhood, which is bound to distinguish itself from others in this—that all its wealth must consist in possessing Him alone."

If well-disposed listeners consented to hear more, the brothers would address this short sermon to them, known as the "exhortation to repentance":

"Fear and honor, praise and bless, thank and adore the Lord God Almighty, in Trinity and Unity, Father, Son, and Holy Spirit, Creator of all things. Do not put off any longer confessing all your sins, for death will soon come. Give and it will be given you; forgive and you will be forgiven.... Blessed are they who die repentant, for they shall go to the Kingdom of Heaven! But woe to those who are not converted, for these children of the Devil will go with their father into everlasting fire. Be watchful, therefore. Shun evil, and persevere in well-doing unto the end."

An enemy of verbosity, and knowing what danger and uselessness for his brethren lay in long sermons on apologetics and dogma, Francis had prudently enjoined his friars to stick to this little speech.

Here again, they had more opportunity for practicing patience than eloquence.

People had never seen men dressed that way before. So sometimes they were taken for savages, and sometimes for sneak thieves in disguise who ought to be driven off with clubs. Many wondered where they came from, and if they were not dangerous heretics. People kept asking them who they were. "We are Penitents, from the city of Assisi," they would reply. This was their first name, a fact which reassured no one. And they made them repeat it so often, writes the biographer, that this was not the least of their fatigues. Some threw mud at them. Others, grabbing them by their hoods, dragged them behind them like so many sacks. In some places they were disrobed in public. But they did not resist, refusing—so as to keep the Gospel—to resist evil, and waiting for people to have the charity to give back their clothes. Brother Giles once gave his cowl to a pauper and traveled without it for twenty days.

Brother Giles, as we have said, set out toward St. James of Compostella with Brother Bernard. In the course of this journey, they passed through Florence, where they met with the worst possible reception.

It was in the dead of winter, and night had fallen before they could find shelter. They finally prevailed on a pious lady to let them sleep in the bake-house under the porch. But when her husband came home, he was very annoyed. "Why," he demanded, "did you let those low fellows spend the night under the porch?"

The woman replied that at any rate she had not been so imprudent as to let them in the house; and as for whatever wood was left in the bake-house, it would be no great loss if they walked off with it.

"In any case," replied the husband, "I forbid you to give them any blankets."

Now it was very cold, "so that the slumbers of Brother Bernard and Brother Giles were quite light that night, they having only the garments of Lady Poverty to cover themselves and the zeal of their devotion to warm them."

The next morning, as the pious lady entered a church, she found the two brothers deep in prayer. "If they were thieves as I thought," she said to herself, "they would not pray so well." Continuing to observe them, she saw a man named Guido go up to them to give them alms. They refused. "Why don't you take money like other beggars?" he inquired.

"Because we have embraced poverty voluntarily," replied Bernard.

"You had means before?"

"Oh yes! A great deal!" responded Bernard, speaking mostly for himself. "And if we have no money left now, it is because we gave it away for the love of God."

The lady, who had heard the entire conversation, now approached, this time to offer them decent hospitality in her home. But as they had just accepted the same invitation from the charitable Guido, they thanked her humbly and followed their new friend. They spent several days with him, and so thoroughly edified him that after their departure, people noticed that he gave still more alms than before.

But, according to The Three Companions, the adventures of the brothers rarely turned out so well; and one should say rather that they failed all along the line.

As for Francis, he had better success in the Valley of Rieti, where entire populations who had become almost pagan were converted by his words. There, in the person of the knight Angelo, he made one of his best recruits. "You have worn," said he to him, "the belt, the sword, and the spurs of the world, long enough. Come with me and I will arm you as Christ's knight."

The ex-warrior obeyed. Within the Order, where he was called Brother Angelo, his refined courtesy remained proverbial; and after the death of his master, he formed—together with Brother Leo and Brother Rufino—the group known as the "Three Companions."

It was at that time that Francis had the consolation of knowing that his sins were forgiven.

For long hours he prayed near Poggio Bustone, in a grotto far above the valley—trembling with anguish at the thought of the sinful years of his youth. "Lord, I beseech you," he would repeat weeping, "have mercy on me, a sinner!"

Suddenly an immense sweetness filled his soul and he swooned with happiness. When he came to, his darkness and anxieties had vanished. He had become a new man; and from that time onward, he possessed the certainty of having been restored to God's grace.

But this sentiment of his justification never prevented him from considering himself a great sinner. Just as a true artist sees better than all others the distance separating him from absolute beauty, so did he measure only too well the depth of the abyss separating the divine perfection from our human misery to cherish any thoughts of vain glory. And such was his eagerness to excuse others that he adjudged all to be better than himself. Men could not humiliate him—he humiliated himself.

After having preached for some time in the Valley of Rieti, Francis felt a great longing to see his brothers again and prayed the Lord to bring them back to him. His prayer was answered; for with no signal having been given, all soon regained the Portiuncula.

Great was their joy at seeing their father again. They related to him the blessings with which God had favored them, made accusation of their faults, and humbly accepted needed admonitions.

Four new recruits, "virtuous men full of merit," now brought the number of the growing brotherhood up to twelve. The saint then disclosed to them his plan to write a Rule and to seek its approval by Pope Innocent III.

CHAPTER FIVE

Before Pope Innocent III

To those who consider the thirteenth century the "great Christian century," and the age in which St. Francis lived "one of the finest types of human civilization," it is natural that the pontificate of Innocent III should appear as "one of the most glorious in history."

No pope was ever closer to making the "theory of the two swords" a triumphant reality. This doctrine maintained that the Church having received power in heaven and on earth, God had given it at the same time jurisdiction over all earthly sovereigns and authority to depose them if they so deserved. There was, so to speak, no country in which Innocent III had not succeeded in imposing his will. In Italy he ousted the emperor and drove his officials from the pontifical states. In Sicily he received the homage of the regent, who entrusted to him the tutelage of her son, the future emperor. In Germany he dethroned Philip of Swabia and gave the crown to his rival, Otto of Brunswick, next excommunicating the latter to enthrone Frederick II in his place. In England, John Lackland became his vassal, as were already the kings of Hungary, Aragon, and Castile. France alone attempted to resist him in the person of Philip Augustus.

This glorious picture of pontifical policy had its counterpart, however, in the scandals then desolating Christianity. For without speaking of the princes who, contesting the theory of the two swords, braved excommunication, warred against the pope, and taught the people to despise the spiritual prerogatives of the Bishop of Rome, truth compels one to confess that many clergy at this period afforded a most afflicting spectacle.

Living under the regime of landed property, the clergy were absorbed in the management of temporal affairs, to the neglect of their priestly ministry. Priests preached little, studied not at all, practiced simony, and lived loosely and lazily—having, it would seem, no other concern than the exercise of power and the possession of honors, pleasure, and money. Many prelates made a display of unheard-of luxury, and had recourse to traffic in church benefices to maintain it. They would even sell these benefices at public auction; as for example Ralph, Bishop of Liege, who had them sold by a city butcher along with his meat. As for the people, their moral and religious status was on a par with that of their pastors.

In brief, the evil was so serious and so widespread that Innocent III himself said that it "would take fire and sword to cure it," and everywhere men talked of reform. Never had one seen so many self-styled "prophets" and "reformers" as at this period.

Prophets and prophetesses foretold purifying chastisements and the coming of a better age.

"Woe to all nations!" cried St. Elizabeth of Schonau (1126–1164), "for the world has become darkness! The Lord's vineyard has perished; the Head of the Church is sick and his members are dead! Do you sleep, shepherds of the flock? But I know how to awaken you!"

"God's justice is about to strike!" prophesied St. Hildegard (1098–1179). "His judgments shall be accomplished; the empire and the papacy have fallen and shall go down together. But from their ruin, to rise. All men shall be converted, and the angels shall return in confidence to dwell among the children of men."

The most extraordinary of these prophets was Joachim of Fiore (1145–1202), who had an enormous influence, notably on the Spiritual Franciscans. His exegesis and calculations led him to announce that the existence of the human race on earth was divided into three periods, over which presided respectively the Father, Son, and Holy Spirit. The first period is that of the Mosaic law, of servile obedience and fear. The second period is that of grace, of filial obedience and faith. As this period has been far from perfect, and even ends badly, a third period would succeed it in 1260, inaugurating the reign of the Spirit, of liberty and of love, and would last until the end of the world.

But all was not raving on the part of the Calabrian Cistercian. This pure and gentle man had a burning love for Christ. He had a deep love for and feeling of kinship with nature; he tenderly rested the faces of the dying against his breast to warm them and so make dying easier; he lived in destitution, professing that nothing brings man close to God like voluntary poverty; and he showed much distaste for useless learning. "Dialectics," he wrote, "closes what is open, darkens what is clear, and engenders idle speech, rivalries, and blasphemy; as is proven by those arrogant scribes, who by dint of their reasoning, founder in heresy."

The reformers, for their part, wanted to go back to the Gospel. Unfortunately, many among them who aspired to instruct the Church fell into heresy or schism. However, the Vaudois, or "Poor Men of Lyons," had started out well.

Their founder, Peter Valdes, a rich merchant of Lyons who had given up his property to practice and preach the Gospel, had gained a number of adherents, attracted by his ideals and virtue. These lived in poverty, penance, and perfect equality, and from time to time met in chapters.

When they began to lash out against the laxity of the clergy, the Archbishop of Lyons excommunicated them. They appealed to the pope and were received at the Vatican. Alexander III embraced Peter Valdes, congratulated him on his vow of poverty, and authorized him and his followers to address moral exhortations to the people, wherever the bishops permitted, on condition that they should not attempt to interpret the Scriptures or teach theology. The fault of the "Poor Men of Lyons" lay in their overstepping these orders.

As all roads lead to Rome, and these penitents always declared that they were on their way to the tomb of the apostles, they soon spread all over Europe, reading the Gospel to the people in the vernacular and seasoning it with commentaries displeasing to the clergy. The prelates wished to impose silence on them; but they continued to preach more than ever, and Pope Lucius III finally condemned them in 1184, including them in the same anathema as the Cathari. It is not certain that Peter Valdes was still their head at this time.

What we do know is that the greater part of his disciples, out of hatred for the teaching Church, became heretics (known as Waldenses), placing the authority of the Bible above that of the pope, affecting to confess to virtuous laymen rather than to priests of evil life, and rejecting purgatory, indulgences, and the veneration of the saints, on the pretext that these things were profitable to the clergy.

Many, however, submitted in an exemplary manner, some acting under the influence of the German, Bernhard Prim, and others under that of the Spaniard, Durando of Huesca. Durando's disciples took the name of "Poor Catholics," and one might almost look on them as pre-Franciscans.

In 1208, they went to Innocent III, promising him to obey their bishops and to preach only with their permission. They likewise agreed to receive the sacraments from any priest with faculties to administer them and to stop discouraging the faithful from paying the tithes required by the Church. The pope then permitted them to keep on with their way of life. They proposed to follow the Gospel counsels as if they were precepts, to despise gold and silver, and take no thought for the morrow. The clerks gave themselves over to study and engaged in polemics with the heretics, and the laymen did manual labor. All wore the religious habit with sandals, kept two Lents a year, and said a certain number of Paters and Aves seven times daily at the canonical hours.

As the bishops, however, continued their opposition, the "Poor Catholics" were finally obliged a few years later to become absorbed in the Augustinian Order.

Let us likewise mention the "Humiliati," who took their rise in Lombardy, and in 1216 had up to a hundred and fifty communities in the Milan diocese alone. Their name came from the ash-grey habit they wore. Because they resembled the Waldenses and Cathari they were looked on at first with suspicion until Innocent III approved them in 1201.

The Humiliati were made up of three orders, one of brothers, one of sisters, and a "third order" composed of seculars. The members of the third order remained in their state of life and with their families; but professed to avoid immodesty in dress and all disputes, to assist the poor and the sick, to listen to a pious exhortation on Sunday, to fast twice a week, and to say seven Our Fathers during the day.

As for the religious, they lived in convents, dividing their time between manual labor and the chanting of the Divine Office. If the product of their labor was insufficient for their needs, they went out begging. If it was more than sufficient, they gave the surplus to the poor. As their rule did not forbid them to own property in common, they wound up in most comfortable circumstances, and even with a monopoly on the woolen industry in Lombardy.

Among the malcontents of the period, there assuredly were very holy souls who thought only to follow the example of Christ and the apostles. There were likewise a goodly number of utopians and stiff-necked persons, who were still more insufferable than the ones over whom they set themselves as censors. Some there were who, under the cloak of reform, were literally leading the world into chaos. Such were the Cathari, called in Italy the Patarini, in France the Albigensians, in Eastern Europe Bogomiles, and in the northern countries Bulgars or Bulgarians.

Born or resurrected no one knows where, but probably imported from the Balkans, their doctrine was allied to that of the ancient gnostics. Like them, the Cathari believed in the existence of two creative principles.

One of these principles is good, and is God, Author of all good, and in particular of spiritual souls which exist since time immemorial. The other is evil, and is Satan or Jehovah, author of evil, suffering, and all material objects. Man is their common work, since he owes his soul to God and his body to Satan. And as the flesh comes from the latter, it is clear, for example, that Christ's body was only an appearance. Jesus assumed human form merely to incite us to revolt against Satan and against the Church of Rome, his representative here below, and to invite us to belong to the church of the Cathari. This church, moreover possessed everything needful to lead man to heaven. It had its priests or "perfect," its faithful or "believers," its liturgy, its grace, its parishes, its schools, and even a number of convents.

The "perfect" were those who had received the *consolamentum* or laying on of hands, and who, in order to keep themselves thereafter from all stain, had renounced marriage and all property, enfeebled themselves with fasting and mortification, refusing in addition to use meat, milk, butter, or cheese, claiming that the souls of sinners accomplished their time of expiation in the bodies of animals before ascending to heaven.

It devolved on the "perfect" to administer the *consolamentum* to the "believers," and to restore to them the Comforter, the Holy Spirit, who had left them at their birth and was to take them back to heaven after death. For greater safety, the majority of "believers" did not receive this sort of baptism until the hour of death. Meanwhile, the priests urged them frequently to formulate a desire to receive it, and to come every month to pray with them, promising them that thanks to these desires and prayers, the grace of the *consolamentum* would not be refused them.

The Cathari apostles displayed an extraordinary zeal, becoming merchants in order to frequent the fairs and preach to the people, schoolmasters for the formation of youth and, above all, doctors in order to assist the sick and dying. People admired their austerity and enjoyed their diatribes against the laxity of the clergy. The nobility in particular flattered themselves that they would inherit the riches of which they proposed to despoil the Church. Many people were overjoyed to hear them say that receiving the *consolamentum in extremis* was sufficient to save their soul; and when they denounced marriage as an invention of Satan to perpetuate suffering and the world, all those who preferred license to the duties of domesticity could not be otherwise than grateful.

Along the way, the Cathari absorbed the disciples of Arnold of Brescia, who denied the validity of sacraments administered by bad priests. Together they spread all over Italy.

From Lombardy they entered the Papal States and made their way as far as Calabria. In Rome itself, in 1209, when Otto IV came to receive the imperial crown, he discovered a school where Catharism was publicly taught. Neither repressions nor excommunications succeeded in reducing these stubborn men. They triumphed at Ferrara, Verona, Rimini, and Treviso. At Piacenza they drove out the Catholic clergy and prevented their return for three years. At Viterbo, where they had many consuls, Innocent III had to tear down their houses to obtain their submission. In 1203, the city of Assisi itself had a Patarin for podesta.

As for the heretics of Languedoc, it is well known only the massacres of the Albigensian War of 1209 subdued them.

Such was the assortment of reformers and rebels with which the Roman Curia was at grips when Francis presented himself to obtain the approval of his Rule. The time was probably April or May 1209.

The twelve "Penitents of Assisi" set out from the Portiuncula. "Let us choose a leader whom we will obey as to the Lord," said Francis as they were leaving. "We shall take the roads he points out and lodge in the places he designates." They elected Brother Bernard, and the journey went off well.

Every night they found charitable people to give them lodging. Every day they went happily on, assured of success, for Francis had divulged a recent vision to them. He had dreamed that, coming across a great tree with an immense number of branches on his way, he had stopped to admire it. Suddenly a supernatural force had made him grow as tall as the treetop. Effortlessly, he put out his hand and bent the tree to the ground. To him, this was a presage of the ease with which—by God's grace—the mighty Innocent III would let himself be swayed. And then, was not the Gospel Rule he was going to show him the charter of his alliance with the Lady Poverty? And since she was Christ's spouse, Christ's Vicar could not fail to recognize and receive her.

The reception was, at first, very chilly, if we are to believe Matthew of Paris. This contemporary chronicler relates that going into the Lateran Palace, Francis walked in unceremoniously and went up to where the pope was. But he looked so shabby with "his poor tunic, his tangled locks, and his great black eyebrows," that Innocent III pretended to take him for a swineherd.

"Leave me alone with your rule!" said he. "Go find your pigs instead. You can preach all the sermons you want to them!"

Francis did not wait to be told twice. He dashed to a pigsty, smeared himself with dung, and reappeared before the pope.

"My lord," he said, "now that I have done what you commanded, please be good enough to grant me my request." The pontiff had to admit that this petitioner did not appear to be a rebel. So, "thinking it over," writes Matthew, "he regretted having given him so ill a reception: and after sending him away to wash up, promised him another audience."

Is the anecdote true? At any rate, it offers nothing improbable, either on the part of Francis, who sought out humiliation, or on the part of Innocent III, who sometimes used strong words when he was angry. Did he not write in 1205 to Tignosi, the administrator of Viterbo: "You fear neither God nor man. Wallowing in your sins like an ass in its dung, you stink so that everything around you smells, and God himself is nauseated."

We shall soon see what the pope decided to grant to the Little Poor Man, but it is fitting at first to know what this Rule was that he was asked to approve.

Very short it was, we are told, and made up of a series of Gospel texts and of some regulations needed to guide the life of the friars. It is true that we no longer have it in its original form, but the scholarly reconstructions which have been made of it, permit us to summarize it as follows:

Preamble. Francis and his successors promise obedience to Innocent III and to succeeding popes, and the Brethren were to obey Brother Francis and his successors.

What the Rule is. It obliges the friars to conform to the kind of life imposed by Christ on his apostles, that is, the integral practice of the Gospel. In this lay its great and complete novelty, for never before had a monastic rule made the Gospel taken literally the foundation of the religious state. Certain of these rules, by imposing the vow of stability on the monk and diverting him from preaching, even prevented him from leading the apostolic life.

How new Brethren are to be received. All those whom God shall induce to enter the brotherhood are to be affectionately received; but they are to be admitted only after they have abandoned all their goods, and, if possible, distributed them to the poor.

The habit. They are to wear a tunic with hood, a cord, and trousers. The place for men in rich clothing being, according to the Gospel, in kings' palaces, the Brethren are to wear mean clothing, which they can mend by sewing on coarse pieces, with God's blessing.

Of precedence. Our Lord having declared that it is for heads of state to act as masters and for the great to give orders, the Brethren, for their part, are not to have any authority over one another; and he among them who would be first, shall place himself in the lowest place, making himself servant of all.

Of charity and humility. Let no brother cause pain to another. Let all avoid anger, calumny, detraction, and murmuring. Rather than dispute with any man, they will keep silent or else humbly reply, "We are useless servants." Instead of judging or condemning anyone, let them rather consider their own faults. Let them show great condescension and meekness toward all men, and let even thieves and robbers be kindly received by them. If a brother fall ill, the others shall take care of him; and all shall show the same love and care toward one another as a mother has for her child.

Of work and poverty. If possible, the Brethren shall follow their former trade. If they are in the service of others, they shall not fill the position of treasurer or of other employment of a nature to harm their soul or scandalize their neighbor. In exchange for their labor, they shall be content with food and clothing. If necessary, they will beg alms, but they are never to receive money. It is forbidden for them to have animals for hire or anything else whatever save their tools. They shall not even appropriate their hermitages for themselves, or defend them against anyone to keep them.

How they are to behave in the world. The Brethren are to carry nothing with them for the road, neither sack nor provisions. Their greatest joy shall be to mingle with victims of leprosy, beggars, and other wretches. When they enter a house, they shall say: "Peace be to this house!" and shall eat whatever is set before them.

Of preaching. The Rule inserts here the little penitential exhortation that we quoted above, and which Francis bids the Brethren to address on occasion to the people.

Orthodoxy. Let the Brethren, under pain of being expelled from the fraternity, always conduct themselves as good Catholics. Let them follow the customs and usages of the Church of Rome, and defer to the teachings of the secular and regular clergy in everything that is not contrary to their Rule; and if they go to confession, let it be to whatever priest is approved by the Church.

The reader, like the Roman Curia of the time, will not fail to note the analogies offered by this Rule with the program of the Reformers of the period. Are these chance resemblances, the result of inevitable influences, or genuine borrowings? We should like to discuss this question if only the necessary documents were not entirely lacking. All that we could do, then, would be to build up vain hypotheses. So, as things stand now, the problem cannot be solved.

Certainly, it is unlikely that Francis would not have heard of Joachim of Fiore and of Peter Valdes, since everybody was talking about them; or that he never came across any Cathari, since these were everywhere, even in Assisi and Spoleto. But the fact is that he never mentioned the names of these people, and that unlike the "Poor Catholics," the Cistercians, and St. Dominic, he never disputed with heretics.

He evidently knew of the way of life and evangelical tendencies of the former, and he was not ignorant of the ranting and ravings of the others, but was he influenced by them?

All that we are able to say is that Francis declared that the Lord alone had shown him what he must do, that his Rule resolved in an orthodox manner those difficulties to which his contemporaries often presented heretical solutions, and that he himself seemed to take from the reformers of the time whatever they had that was good, conducting himself as if he wished to render them all useless and harmless.

Meanwhile, as we have said, he was obliged to enter into contact with the Roman Curia and obtain the approval of Innocent III.

Again, it was the Bishop of Assisi who came to his assistance. It so happened that the bishop was in Rome. Surprised at meeting some of his flock there, he anxiously asked himself if the brothers had left his diocese for good. They reassured him and informed him of the purpose of their journey. Guido presented them to his friend, Cardinal John of St. Paul, who offered them hospitality.

This prelate was a man of God whose piety was outstanding even among the most virtuous members of the Sacred College. It was he who had been charged the previous year with preparing the case against the Waldensians. The bishop vouched for the Penitents of Assisi as having only deference for the clergy, and the cardinal himself was able to appreciate the fervor and humility of his guests. He nonetheless sought to dissuade Francis from founding anything new and counseled him instead to enter one of the old Orders with his followers.

Such a solution was prudent and shrewd, but Francis remained unconvinced. He defended his Rule so persuasively that he brought the cardinal over to his way of thinking. John of St. Paul spoke about the matter to the pope, and the young founder had an audience at which he could put forward his plans.

Now the prodigious sagacity of Innocent III has never been called in question; but his detractors have claimed that, absorbed in his great temporal plans, he was somewhat lacking in a Christian outlook. Thus St. Ludgard (1182–1246) is said to have seen him condemned to purgatory until the Last Judgment. But the holiest of women are not infallible. The fact is that the conduct of Innocent III was always exemplary; the reform of the Church was the thing he had most at heart; and on this occasion he conducted himself with wholly supernatural wisdom.

The cardinals cried out in protest when they heard Francis explain his program. No doubt they wondered if he were not some new "poor man" from Lyons or elsewhere, come to have some supposedly evangelical rule approved, so he could go out and stir up the people against the prelates. Besides, it seemed impossible to them for a religious institute to subsist without property or revenues.

Thus all were of the opinion that so literal an interpretation of the Gospel went beyond human strength, and the pope himself declared, "Although your zeal, my dear sons, reassures Us, We must nevertheless think of your successors, who may find the path you wish to follow too austere."

But the Cardinal of St. Paul replied, "If we reject this poor man's request on such a pretext, would not this be to declare that the Gospel cannot be practiced, and so to blaspheme Christ, its Author?"

These words made so strong an impression that Innocent said to Francis, "My son, pray God to manifest His will to Us. When We know it, We shall be able to give you an answer with perfect surety."

This second interview with the pope already was a great step forward over the first one—if there was a first one.

The third was a complete success. For this Francis prepared himself by beseeching God to touch the heart of the pope. Thereupon, Christ (so say the biographers) sent a dream to his earthly vicar and inspired the saint with a parable. It was this parable that Francis recounted to the Holy Father when, a few days later, he reappeared in his presence.

> "Your Holiness," he began, "once upon a time in the wilderness, there was a very poor, but very beautiful woman, whom the king had loved, and who had had many sons by him. When these sons had grown up, their mother said this to them: 'My sons, do not be ashamed to be poor, for you are

74

the king's sons.' And addressing the eldest sons, she said, 'Go to your father, who will not fail to recognize you and take care of you.'

"As soon as they arrived at the court, the king, struck by their handsome appearance, discovered that they resembled him. 'Who is your mother?' he asked. They replied that she was a poor woman living in the wilderness. Filled with joy, the king pressed them to his heart.

"'Do not be afraid,' he said, 'for I am your father. And if I receive so many strangers at my table, how much more reason have I not to admit my sons!' And he asked the mother to send him his other sons also, so that he could lodge them all in his palace."

"Your Holiness," continued Francis, "the wilderness is this world, barren of virtue. This poor woman whom the king made fruitful is I, to whom Christ has given sons who strive to reproduce the features of their father by imitating his poverty. Finally, the sons who sit at the king's table are my brothers, whom the Lord will never leave in need, He who so bounteously feeds all His creatures, even sinners."

If he had any of the poet about him, Innocent must have been won over by this troubadour in tatters who sang with such gusto the joy of being poor. At any rate, he realized that this reformer was not dangerous. He was no Cathar cursing a wicked god for having inflicted life on him, nor some other zealot drawing from his gloomy virtues the right to demand perfection of all men and to hurl invectives at the whole world. This was a humble child of God who condemned neither clerics nor laymen, and whose sole ambition was to share his inner joy with those who wished to possess it.

The great statesman likewise realized the assistance that Francis could bring to the Church. He was reminded of a dream he had had a few nights previously. He had seen, writes Thomas of Celano, the Lateran basilica—head and mother of all churches—leaning to one side, ready to topple over. Suddenly, a little religious ran up, who with a simple push of his shoulders raised it and straightened it once more. The pope now recognized the providential man of his dream in this humble suitor who simply sought, without wishing to disturb anyone, permission to live according to the Gospel.

He verbally approved the Rule, and, after numerous commendations, charged Francis with the direction of the brotherhood. The brethren made a vow of obedience to Francis, who, in turn, promised to obey the pope. Those among them who were still laymen received the small tonsure; and all were given the right to "preach penitence," that is, to address moral exhortations to the people. It is thought that it was then that Francis was ordained a deacon.

So the Franciscan Order was attached to the Church of Rome. She did not give it a definite approval, but she did give it a chance to win its spurs. "Go, brethren," said the pope, dismissing the twelve Penitents, "and may the Lord be with you! If it please Him to increase you, come and tell me about it. And I shall see then about granting you more numerous favors and entrusting you with a more important mission."

The mission that the pope had in mind was probably that of preaching the crusade against the Saracens or the heretics, as others already were doing. As for the "favors" he held out, they would consist of a Bull giving the Rule its official consecration.

Being no stickler for formalities, Francis felt no regret at leaving without anything in writing. The pope's word was enough for him.

His dearest wish having been fulfilled, he thanked God, prayed before the tomb of the apostles, then left the city with his companions.

Along a dusty and monotonous road, the little group went up the Tiber to Orte. There they entered the wooded ravine along which coursed the turbulent waters of the Nera.

The brothers interrupted their journey, writes Thomas of Celano, to stop not far from Orte in a complete wilderness. There they spent two weeks with Holy Poverty, tasting such delights that they resolved never more to leave her chaste embrace. Their destitution was total, and no man came to interrupt their prayer. While part of them went into town to beg from door to door, the rest prayed and waited for them. Then all ate together the collected food, thanking God for treating them so well. If there was anything left over and no one was found to give it to, it was put away in an old Lombard tomb for the next day. The friars came to prize this solitude so much that they feared lest they become too attached to it, and so miss their vocation.

For some of them were strongly attracted to the solitary life and did not want to go back among men. But Francis reminded them that in imitation of Christ, they were to win souls for God. And he set off with them on the road to Assisi.

CHAPTER SIX

Rivo Torto

ON THEIR RETURN, the brothers settled in a place called Rivo Torto. The "crooked stream" from which this spot derived its name has disappeared; and topographers argue as to whether Rivo Torto was located near the old Santa Maria Maddalena leprosarium about fifteen hundred yards from the Portiuncula, or if it occupied the site of the present church of Rigobello, a mile farther on, in the direction of Foligno.

It would seem that the brothers passed the autumn and winter there. They made good use of an abandoned hut that could serve as a shelter when it rained. It was hardly big enough to hold them all; but Francis used to say that a man gets to heaven more quickly from a hovel than from a palace. He wrote their names with chalk on the beams so that when they wished to pray or rest, each might find his place without letting their being cramped disturb their quiet peace of mind.

Rivo Torto is the brief and wonderful springtime in which the fairest Franciscan virtues flourished—those virtues which God's troubadour praised in the following salutation:

Hail, O Wisdom, Queen! May the Lord keep you, and your sister, pure and holy Simplicity!

Hail, O holy lady Poverty! May the Lord keep you, and your sister, holy Humility!

Hail, O holy lady Charity! May the Lord keep you, and your sister, holy Obedience!

For it is from the Lord, most holy virtues, that you proceed. And there is not one among you that one may practice without being dead to self; and whoever possesses one of you, possesses all; and who offends one of you offends all.

Francis shows next how holy patience foils the wiles of the devil, how holy and pure simplicity confounds the wisdom of the world and of the flesh, and, how finally, holy obedience disposes the body to obey the spirit and men to obey their neighbor.

"And it is not just men," he adds, "that the true Christian obeys, but also animals, so that even fierce beasts may do with him whatever God wills."

Of all these virtues, poverty is the one that was to impart its originality to the Franciscan Order and constitute its "true foundation."

Voluntarily poor one may be from philosophy or asceticism, for reasons of zeal, of charity, and others still. But Francis was poor from love. He made himself poor because his beloved Christ had been poor. He espoused Poverty because she had been "the inseparable companion of the Most High Son of God," and because for twelve centuries she has wandered about forsaken.

In truth, it was a wonderful union. Never was a loved woman the object of a more chivalrous and loyal cult, of more impassioned and more charming homage.

It is to the *Sacrum Commercium* rather than to the biographers that we shall go for the story of the espousals of the Little Poor Man. No document so well expresses his sentiment or better reproduces the way in which he spoke of the chosen lady of his heart.

This little song of chivalry opens with the questing of God's servant: "I pray you, point out to me," he said to two old men encountered in the country, "the dwelling place of Lady Poverty, for I faint with love for her."

The old men disclose to him the place of her abode, but they add, "A man must be naked and free of every burden if he would attain the mountain top where she has taken refuge. Take also with you companions who will help you in your painful ascent. But woe to him who is alone, for if he chances to fall, he has none to aid him."

Francis then chooses a few faithful friends, and with them, presents himself to the forlorn princess:

> We come to you, O Lady, because we know that you are the Queen of the virtues; and prostrate at your feet, we beseech you to join with us and become our way leading to the King of Glory, as you were the way for Him when He came to help those sitting in the shadow of death.
>
> For, leaving His royal abode, the Son of the Most High sought you whom all men flee. Enamored of your beauty, it was you alone whom He desired to wed on earth. You had prepared for Him a fitting throne within a most poor Virgin; from which throne He came forth to manifest Himself to the world. It was you again who provided Him an abode in that miserable stable when at His birth there was no place for Him in the inn. There, you became, His whole life long, His inseparable companion. For the foxes have holes and the birds of the air their nests, but He had no place to lay His head. Again, when He who had once opened the lips of the prophets opened His own mouth, it was to praise

you; saying: "Blessed are the poor in spirit for theirs is the Kingdom of Heaven." And it was for love of you that instead of rich merchants He chose poor fishermen as ministers and witnesses of His preaching.

And you, most faithful spouse and sweet lover, never left Him for an instant, and were never closer than when you saw Him despised by all men. Had you not been with Him, He would never indeed have been so contemned by all. You were at His side when He was outraged by the Jews, insulted by the Pharisees, derided by the princes of the priests. You were with Him at the buffeting, the spitting, and the scourging; and when He came to die—naked, arms outstretched, feet and hands pierced—you were His only companion and went up with Him on the Cross. At last, before He returned to Heaven, He left you the sign of the Kingdom of God with which to mark the elect; so that whoever seeks after the kingdom everlasting must needs come to you.

O Queen, have pity on us! Mark us with the sign of your favor! For love of Him who loved you so much, despise not our prayers, but deliver us from every danger, O Virgin filled with glory and with blessing.

At these words, the Lady Poverty thrilled with happiness, and in a voice filled with sweetness, bade her visitors to listen to her long tale.

How many vicissitudes in her life, from the Garden of Eden where she kept Adam company as long as he stayed naked, and whom she left when she saw him prefer the pursuit of earthly goods to the service of God! "As Abraham, Isaac, and other patriarchs likewise loved riches, I wandered on earth for centuries, sad and solitary, until that day when the Son of God came to fulfill those things which you have brought to mind."

Here Poverty quotes the "covenant" and "immutable decree" which Christ left his disciples before he ascended again into heaven: "Take nothing with you, neither gold nor silver.... Do not resist those who would take away your goods.... Do not be anxious about tomorrow." She celebrates the heroism of the first faithful, "who sold their goods, had all things in common and lived in perfect equality." Then she adds something of her later history:

> So long as the blood of the Crucified Poor Man was fresh in their memory, and the chalice of His Passion inebriated their heart, Christians practiced poverty. But then came peace, which for me was worse than war and renewed my sufferings. Once more all forsook me, including those so-called religious who had promised me to be faithful. How many there are among them who, in the world, lived poor, hungry, and lean, lacking even lowly bread, and lodging 'neath the sweet-briar, and who, once united to me, have grown fat in their cloisters, have sought to appear great in man's eyes, and have come and spat in my face.

These complaints bring tears to the eyes of Francis and his followers, who swear eternal fidelity to the forlorn and lovely lady. She consents to follow them to their hermitage.

"Let me first visit," she says upon arrival, "your cloister, your refectory, your kitchen, your dormitory, your stables, your fine furniture and magnificent establishment; for thus far I have seen only your radiant and friendly faces."

"Dear Lady and Queen," they replied, "your servants are weary from our journey, and you too must be tired. So with your kind permission, we shall begin to dine. When we shall have recovered somewhat, we shall carry out your wishes."

"Gladly, but I must first wash my hands."

They went and fetched—for want of better—a chipped earthen pot, filled with water. She asked for a towel, but when they did not find any, one of the friars offered his tunic instead.

They then led the princess to the table, that is, before a few pieces of barley bread spread out on the grass. Everyone sat down on the ground; and after giving thanks to God, the Lady Poverty pretended to wait for cooked food to be served up on plates. But only a bowl of fresh water was brought in, in which everyone dipped his crust.

"Don't you have some fresh vegetables to top off our menu?" she inquired. The brothers excused themselves for having neither a gardener nor a garden and they went off to gather some wild fruits and herbs in the forest.

"Don't you have at least a little salt to season these bitter herbs?"

"Lady," they replied, "we should have to go to the city to get some."

"Then salt is not necessary. Please pass me a knife to cut this bread with, for it is really quite dry."

"Alas, dear Lady, we have no maker of knives on hand. Meanwhile, we pray you to use your teeth."

"Will you not let me taste of your wine?" she asked.

"O Queen! We never use it, and it seems to us that Christ's spouse as well ought to shun wine like poison."

After they were thus satisfied, all rose, and joyously intoned their thanks anew. As the Lady Poverty expressed the desire to rest a few moments, they showed her the bare ground. And when she asked for a pillow, they slipped a stone under her head, then withdrew so she could sleep. When she awoke, the fancy took her to visit their cloister. So they led her up a hill, and pointing to the horizon with a sweeping gesture, as if the whole world were theirs: "There, Lady, is our cloister!"

The fair visitor declared herself perfectly satisfied. "Truly, today I believed myself in Paradise," she said. And after another long discourse, she took leave of them.

As will have been seen, holy poverty made harsh demands and life was hard at Rivo Torto. We must believe that the farmers and leprosy patients among whom the first Franciscans labored were either poor or stingy; for the brothers often had nothing to eat except scraps begged from door to door. It even happened that for lack of bread they had to eat turnips left in the field.

They would have overdone their penances if their father had permitted them. One night the sleepers in the hut were awakened by groans.

"I'm dying! I'm dying!" moaned a voice.

"Get up, brothers! And make a light!" ordered Francis. He asked who was dying.

"Me!" said the voice.

"What are you dying of, Brother?"

"Of hunger!"

At once, the saint had the table set, and so that the "dying one" should not feel ashamed at eating alone, they all ate with him willingly.

Francis profited by this opportunity to enjoin upon them less severe fasting, urging them not to try to imitate him in this.

"For," he explained, "I who am at the head of the brotherhood have duties that the rest do not have. And besides I am so made that I need only a little coarse food to live."

Francis was also accustomed to sprinkle his food with ashes or cold water. This especially distressed Brother Buonaparte, the convent cook.

"Why shouldn't I feel sad," he complained one day to the saint, "when I see you spoil my dishes I have so carefully prepared, hoping they would do you good!"

"Brother Buonaparte," replied Francis. "Since we both have good intentions, I, in acting the way I do, and you in cooking as well as you can, God will surely not fail to reward us."

But the indiscreet zeal of his sons compelled him many times to come back to this subject. He made it a rule for them not to chastise their bodies except when the body persisted in its laziness and negligence. "In this case," he said, "like well-fed donkeys who refuse to bear their burdens, they must be made to feel the stick."

Unlike the Cathari who received the *consolamentum* and then starved themselves to death to keep from sinning anymore, Francis held life to be a gift from God. "In sickness as in health," he declared, "a religious ought humbly to ask for what he needs. If his request is not granted, let him then patiently bear his infirmities for the love of God. This ill way of winning a martyr's crown."

But the youthful founder was so solicitous of his children's welfare that they all considered him as their "beloved mother"—*mater carissima*. One day Brother Sylvester looked very ill; but no one—so great was the general austerity—noticed it. Francis saw him and said to himself: "I think that some grapes eaten on an empty stomach would do him a great deal of good." And the next morning, rising before dawn, he awakened Sylvester; and while the rest were still asleep, they went to breakfast on fresh grapes in a nearby vineyard.

Another time, it was Brother Leo who felt ill along the way. As a vineyard was close at hand, Francis went and gathered a few clusters of grapes, which quickly restored his friend. But the owner came out from the hedge and began to beat the thief with a stick. As usual, the saint thanked God. However, during the rest of the trip, he would sometimes turn toward his companion and hum the following refrain:

Frater Leo est bene rejectus,
Sed Frater Franciscus est bene percussus;
Frater Leo bene comedit,
Sed Frater Franciscus suo corpore bene solvit.
Brother Leo had grapes to eat,
But Brother Francis he was beat;
Brother Leo had a choice tidbit,
But Brother Francis smarted for it!

The saint was always preaching to his disciples of the good to be drawn from those mortifications that are profitable to the soul without harm to the body. Thus he urged them not to bother about political or scientific news which turns the mind away from more useful preoccupations. When going to Rome where he was to be crowned, the German Emperor Otto IV passed by Rivo Torto in September 1209, the saint shut himself in the hut, enjoining his companions to do likewise. One of them was assigned to place himself in the path of the procession, to remind the new emperor that all earthy glory is fleeting and that his own would not last long. This was a prophecy whose fulfillment was hastened as we know by Innocent II. In January, 1210, he denounced and the following year excommunicated Otto IV, substituting the young Frederick II, his protégé, as head of the empire.

Among the virtues forming the train of Holy Poverty, the *Salutation* particularly mentions humility, patience, and simplicity.

"Oh holy Lady Poverty!" sang Francis. "May God keep you, with your sister, holy Humility."

He who was proud by nature and had once made so many ambitious plans, now deemed himself the meanest of men and aspired to nothing more than to be treated as such. "I am the greatest of sinners," he told Brother Pacifico, who asked him what he thought of himself, adding that if God had granted the same graces to the lowest criminal, he would have profited by it ten times more.

To be sure, many servants of God have talked like this, but Francis really wished to be taken at his word. He was seldom happier than the day when the Bishop of Terni, to congratulate him for his apostolate in the city, publicly declared that once more God had drawn good out of evil, by bringing forth fruits of salvation by so poor and miserable a man, who besides was not uneducated. Delighted to hear things so well put, Francis rushed to the prelate's knees: "How wisely Your Excellency has spoken!" he exclaimed. "You, at least, have given God His due, while leaving me what belongs to me, and of which others unjustly desire to despoil me."

The name which Francis gave to his friars indicated the rank to which he destined them in the world and in the Church. It was the very lowest. In his eyes, their humility ought to equal their poverty. He wanted them to share Christ's humiliations as well as his destitution. "What is the use," he would say to them, "of renouncing the riches of earth, if you intend to keep those of self-love?"

The idea of naming them Friars Minor came to him one day when someone read in his presence the passage of the Rule in which it is said that "the brethren ought to become very little, *minores*, and hold themselves to be inferior to all." Interrupting the reading, he declared that this was the very vocation of his followers and that from then on this is what they would be called. And they well deserved their name, says Thomas of Celano, speaking to the first friars, "for they were truly very little people, humbling themselves before all, and seizing every opportunity for self-abasement and for receiving insults."

If such occasions were lacking, they tried to make them, as did Brother Juniper who went walking in Assisi half-naked, his clothes rolled in a bundle on his head. To be sure, such "follies" did not last; but they were so much to St. Francis's taste that he would have liked to have had many Brother Junipers in his Order.

Soon holy patience, as Francis understood it, likewise appeared to be beyond human strength.

It was the Savior, immolated like an obedient lamb, who was his model; and it was in the Gospel that he had found the formula: "Blessed are you when men shall reproach you and persecute you.... I say to you not to resist the evildoer. If someone strikes you on the right cheek, turn to him the other also. If anyone would take your tunic, let him take your cloak as well."

Giving what you have to someone who wants it, looking on persecutions as blessings, and with no escape from them by recourse to the protection of Rome and ecclesiastical privileges—such was the Little Poor Man's norm of conduct. This it was likewise that he attempted to impose on his whole Order, though in such an undertaking he certainly could not succeed. But Bernard, Giles, Juniper, and a number of others (as we shall see), nevertheless continued to practice "holy patience" according to their father's intention and the letter of the Gospel. "They sought," says Celano, "those places where their reputation for holiness had not yet penetrated, where they hoped to receive much ill-treatment. And how many times did they see themselves insulted, despoiled, scourged, and cast into prison! But, far from defending themselves, they endured it all, thanking God and blessing their tormentors."

The first Franciscans likewise practiced "pure and holy simplicity," which imparts such charm to everything about the Poverello and his companions.

The simple man is he who never dreams of deceiving and who has no fear of being deceived. "I would be a hypocrite," said Francis, "if I did not always act as if I were being watched by the whole world." Fearing to pass for an ascetic, he never failed, when he had been received in a well-to-do home, to enumerate when he left all the dainties he had been served. It was this same scruple about sincerity which led him to accuse himself before his hearers in Poggio Bustone of having used lard in Lent, failing to add that his weak stomach refused everything cooked in oil. Along about this time, his superior made him wear a fox skin over his chest. So he sewed a second skin outside his tunic, so that no one would fail to know how he "pampered" himself.

Himself the soul of honor, Francis was suspicious of none. No one ever honored his fellow man more, trusted men more, nor believed more fully in the given word. "So you are going away thus, you simple man, without anything in writing?" "Do I not have your word, Holy Father?" he replied to Honorius III, who had verbally granted him the Portiuncula Indulgence.

This same childlike candor was to be found among the Franciscans of Rivo Torto. No more could they—so great was their purity of soul—believe in man's malice. They had a licentious priest for confessor, writes Thomas of Celano. But there was no use pointing out his infamy. They did not want to hear anything about it, and continued to address themselves to him more respectfully than before. But when the priest told one of them to beware of hypocrisy, the latter was so distressed that he could not sleep. The others tried in vain to reassure him. "A priest cannot lie," he kept repeating, "so I must be just a hypocrite." And it took Francis to restore his peace of mind.

You recall how the *Sacrum Commercium* disavowed the kind of servants of God who, after promising poverty, lived slothfully within their comfortable monasteries.

But the new "poor men" of Rivo Torto observed the great and holy law of labor. All of them devoted themselves to some form of manual labor. An idler, whom Friar Thomas assures us ate enough for four men, did attempt to sneak into their little band, but he did not stay long. When Francis saw that this big eater refused to go begging, he told him, "Go your way, brother drone! You are good only at eating the honey gathered by the busy bees."

And the parasitic drone left the Order.

We know that Francis himself sometimes hired himself out as a day laborer. Since time immemorial, the people of the valley of Rieti boast that he kept goats in their district. Perhaps he also did carpentry and made household utensils. For St. Bonaventure tells us about the wooden bowl he was working at from the beginning of Lent, and how thinking of it distracted him while he was saying Terce. Although he had put his heart into this task, he did not hesitate to sacrifice it, and threw the vase in the fire to atone for his distraction. The favorite occupation of the first friars, however, was the care of victims of leprosy. "All, whether commoners or nobles, had been told by Francis on their entry into the Order that they would have to work in the lazarets." For no unfortunates on earth were dearer to him. He called them his "Christian brothers," to show that he treated them as equals and as honorable members of the family of Christ.

Francis punished himself once for having humiliated a patient who was particularly repulsive. It was Brother James the Simple who had again brought the man among the friars. "Didn't I tell you," observed Francis, "that it wouldn't do to bring our Christian brothers here?" Scarcely had Francis uttered these words, when fearing to have offended the sick man, he went to the guardian, Peter Catanii. "Give me a stiff penance," he said, "for the fault I have committed."

"Choose your own penance," was Peter's reply.

When mealtime came round, Francis made his "Christian brother" sit down in the place of honor, while he himself drank from the cup which the afflicted man had touched with his suppurating lips and ate from the bowl in which he had dipped his fingers eaten away by ulcers.

The *Fioretti* likewise mentions a certain Brother Bentivoglio who, not to be separated from his patient, put him on his back, and walked at night thus burdened fifteen miles on foot.

The same collection tells the story of a patient believed to be possessed by the devil because of the way he insulted and beat his nurses. To add to this, he cursed dreadfully all the time. The brothers rejoiced to be treated in this way, but finally wound up wondering if it was right for them to take care of such a blasphemer. So they came to consult Francis, who went with them to the lazaret.

"May God give you peace, dear brother!" said he by way of greeting.

"There is no peace for me," replied the sick man, "since I am nothing more than a mass of suffering and rotting flesh."

The saint explained to him that we can turn bodily evils to the saving of our soul by bearing them with resignation.

"How can I stand pain," retorted the despairing man, "that never stops day or night? And that isn't all! For not one of the friars you sent me is any good."

"Well, then! I'll take care of you myself," said Francis.

"All right. But what can you do better than they?"

"I'll do whatever you want me to do."

"Then begin by bathing me, for I smell so, I can't stand myself."

Francis put some water on to heat in which he had steeped some fragrant herbs. Then undressing the patient, he began to rub him gently while a brother poured the perfumed water over his body. Now as the water poured over him, not only did the leprosy disappear, but the man's soul was restored to health. This fellow who always went to extremes began to weep so hard, imploring forgiveness for having blasphemed God and beaten the brothers, that for a fortnight the whole neighborhood rang with his acts of contrition.

But the improvement did not last; and the sick man having received the Last Sacraments, died a holy death, and afterward appeared to St. Francis to announce that he had been saved.

Should we be surprised to learn that happiness reigned among the denizens of Rivo Torto? No longer tormented by vain wishes and desires, and enjoying a pure conscience, these Poor Men "lived perfectly happy, and none of them would have dreamed of complaining," writes Thomas of Celano. For did not their Rule say, "Wherever they may be, let the brethren refrain from murmuring. Let them not appear sad and gloomy like hypocrites; but let them show themselves joyous in the Lord, pleasant and cheerful, as is fitting"?

Pleasant and habitually cheerful, Francis certainly was by nature; and so he always remained, despite the troubles and disappointments he was to encounter. Conforming to the knightly code which insisted on gaiety, this brave knight of Christ thrilled with joy at the thought of being able to partake of his Master's Passion.

Faithful to the Gospel, which bids the persecuted man to rejoice in the midst of trial, he sang when at the beginning of his conversion the robbers dumped him into a snow-filled ditch. He sang all his life, declares the *Speculum*, as if his chief concern were to cultivate happiness within and scatter it around him. And when, in his last months of life, he felt himself growing blind, it was again with transports of joy that he welcomed this final trial.

"O sublime martyr!" exclaims Thomas, "How could you do it, when others found the mere sight of your sufferings a thing almost unbearable?"

This spiritual gladness which feeds on self-denial and voluntarily ignores disappointments, this joyous knightly enthusiasm whose happiness it is to serve the best and most powerful of kings—nothing pleased the Little Poor Man more than to see his friars acting in this way. A brother came back from begging with a song on his lips. Francis ran to meet him, took his sack, kissed him on the shoulder, then grasping his hand, cried, "Blessed be that brother who goes forth to beg without being urged and comes back home in such good spirits!"

"Since they are God's troubadours and minstrels," he continued, "is not the role of the Friars Minor to comfort their neighbor and move him to spiritual gladness?"

Francis said that "spiritual joy is as necessary to the soul as blood is to the body." A gloomy man for him was hardly a citizen of the city of God. Melancholy he dubbed "the Babylonian evil, which plays the devil's game, and renders us vulnerable to his shafts. But for the servant of God who strives to live in joy, the devil's pains go for naught; and he leaves him, finding no entrance to his soul."

This was one of the reasons why he turned his followers away from exaggerated corporal austerities. "Our brother the body," he said to the Penitents of Rivo Torto, "needs a certain ration of food and sleep. If you refuse him this, he will also refuse to serve you, and discouraged, reply, 'How can you expect me to give myself up to vigils, prayer, and good works, when because of you, I am too weak even to stand?'"

So the saint did not want to see long faces. Taking a leaf from St. James, he said that a man must pray when he is sad, and then make haste to become happy again. One day he sent a glum-faced brother back to his cell. "If it is your sins that are troubling you," he told him, "that is something between God and you. Go then and ask His forgiveness, and then come back to us with a smiling face." The case of this gloomy friar was an exception.

The ideal Franciscan is "Brother Juniper, *egregius Dei joculator*, that excellent *jongleur* of God who always had words burning with divine love on his lips." The ideal again is the austere and silent Brother Giles who, we are assured, was always cheerful. When spiritual joy flooded his soul, he would even pick up blades of grass and stones and kiss them. He likewise loved music, and following the example of his blessed father, he would accompany himself—for want of a viol—on two pieces of wood which he rubbed together. To those who expressed astonishment at this, he exclaimed, "Tongue cannot say, nor writing express, nor the heart of man conceive the happiness that God reserves for his friends." So they were happy men, those first disciples of St. Francis; and that is why the *Fioretti*, which recounts their life, is such a joyous book. It may even be that it is the only masterpiece of world literature devoid of all bitterness, in which man truly appears to have found happiness.

As soon as he had returned from Rome, Francis resumed his apostolic activity. Every Saturday night, he walked to Assisi, spent the night in a hut in the Canons' garden, and preached Sunday morning in the Cathedral of San Rufino. As was his custom, he began by wishing peace to his hearers; and often he preached on the union of hearts and the pardon of offenses.

The topic was timely, for more than ever, Assisians were at one another's throats and at sword's point with their neighbors.

It will be recalled how the lords of Assisi, threatened in their privileges, had sought help from Perugia; and that after the battle of St. John's Bridge in which Francis had been taken prisoner, they had refused every attempt at reconciliation. Thereupon the emperor, to keep it on his side, had granted autonomy to the commune of Assisi; and Innocent III, whose vassal Perugia was, had laid its rival under interdict and excommunicated its podesta. But strong in the support of the emperor and loyal to their first magistrate, the citizens of Assisi had only become more adamant toward the exiles and the Perugians. Hostilities had then broken out again, fiercer than before, resulting in general misery in the region. The conflict had gone on for a decade.

On November 9, 1210, the nobles and citizens of Assisi signed a treaty that, in part, read as follows:

> In the name of God and with the grace of the Holy Spirit, in honor of our Lord Jesus Christ, of the Virgin Mary, of the Emperor Otto and of Duke Leopold, the *majores* and *minores* of Assisi pledge themselves by these presents never (except for a previous agreement) to contract any alliance with the Pope, the Emperor, or anyone whatever, and to agree to act together in the future for the best interests of the commune.

In other climes, the nobles renounced their feudal rights in return for a quitrent; the inhabitants of surrounding villages were added to the citizenry; the tax rate was fixed; and from that time onward everyone could go peacefully about his business. Nothing, however, was done for the serfs. Still, the effect of this treaty was to bring back the exiles, and so internal peace was restored to the city.

Modern biographers have attributed to St. Francis a major pacifying role in this event. However, Arnaldo Fortini, the leading authority of the history of Assisi, insists that the pact of 1210 was merely a political truce between the upper and middle classes aimed solely at pursuing the war against Perugia still more effectively; consequently he denies the saint's influence on the pact.

The sojourn at Rivo Torto ended on a singular note. One day the friars were assembled for prayer, when a peasant strolled up to the hut with his donkey.

"In with you! In with you!" he yelled, pushing the donkey ahead of him. "You can see that we couldn't find a better place anywhere than this!"

The peasant made a feint of talking to his beast, but it was plain that his words were directed to the occupants of the shelter. Francis was distressed at such rude behavior and especially deplored the troubling of the community's prayer. But it never occurred to him to resist. He limited himself to remarking, "Truly, brethren, our God-given vocation is not to play the host to donkeys, but to pray and to teach men the way of salvation!" And he left the hut with his companions.

CHAPTER SEVEN

The Life of the First Friars

DRIVEN AWAY FROM Rivo Torto, the friars had to start looking for other quarters. "Dear children," said Francis to them, "since God seems to want to increase our numbers, we must find a little church to say the Office in and bury our dead, and a little house of earth and wattles for us to be together in. So, if it seems good to you, I will go see the bishop about it."

All approved, and Francis set off for the bishop's palace.

Bishop Guido replied that, unfortunately, he had nothing he could give him. The Canons of San Rufino gave the same answer, adding that the best thing for the friars to do was to keep on working in the lazarets, where they were short of nurses. It was the Benedictine Abbot of Mount Subasio who met the desire of the Little Poor Man by giving him the Portiuncula chapel and the plot of earth around it. Francis would not consent to take it as a gift; and to make it clear that it was a loan, every year by way of rent, the friars brought the monks a hamper of loaches that they had caught in the stream.

At the Portiuncula, Francis believed he would really be able to carry out his dream of living the Gospel. Located in the midst of a wood, the hermitage was made up of the chapel of Our Lady of the

Angels, a large thatch-covered cabin which served as the community house, and as many huts as there were religious. The large cabin was of puddled clay; the huts were made of wattles; and the whole was surrounded by a hedge. And that is the way the saint would have liked to see all his residences. Even the churches he always wanted to have "small and built of earth or wood."

As for the kind of life first lived in the brotherhood, whether at the Portiuncula or elsewhere, it can quite well be depicted by sketching the portraits of Brothers Bernard, Rufino, Giles, Masseo, Juniper, and Leo. To speak of these first disciples, who all received their formation from Francis and tried to conform their lives to his example, is to demonstrate what Francis's ideal was, and at the same time evoke the golden age of the Franciscan epic.

We have told of the vocations of Bernard and Giles. The others entered the Order in 1210. All merited to be set up as models for all the Brethren. "The good Friar Minor," said Francis, "ought to love poverty like Brother Bernard and prayer like Brother Rufino, who prays even when he is asleep. He ought to be lost in God as Brother Giles, as courteous as Brother Angelo, and as patient as Brother Juniper, that perfect imitator of Christ crucified. He ought to possess the purity and innocence of Brother Leo, the good manners and common sense of Brother Masseo, and finally, by his charity and detachment from the world, resemble Brother Lucido who never stays more than a month in the same place, asserting that we have no lasting home on earth."

The superior of the brotherhood was, of course, Francis. "His orders were not disputed," wrote Thomas of Celano. "Scarcely had he expressed them, when all rushed to carry them out." But Francis did not spend all his time giving orders. He delegated a part of his authority to a friar who bore the name of "mother," and, like a mother, looked out for the community's needs. The "mother" played the role of Martha and led the active life. Thus the others could, like Mary, give themselves to the contemplative life. From time to time— to reverse the roles and even things up—the "children" became "mothers," and the latter became "children."

This arrangement was kept up for a time in the hermitages, where the number of religious was limited to three or four. But the "mothers" were soon replaced by the "guardians" or local superiors. Their name perhaps came from the fact that they "guarded" the door and watched over their brethren.

The *Fioretti* shows us two guardians, Brother Masseo and Brother Angelo, exercising their charge. A handsomer man or one with a more pleasing personality could nowhere be found than Brother Masseo da Marignano, who, it seems, always brought back the best morsels from the begging tours. Thus he sometimes needed to be humiliated. One day Francis made him whirl around with arms flung wide, until he became dizzy and fell full length on the ground.

Another time he said to him before the assembled community: "Brother Masseo, if the brothers here possess the grace of prayer, you have received the gift of eloquence and know how to talk to people. So to let us practice contemplation, you are to have charge of the door, give out alms and do the cooking. While we eat inside, you will eat outside; and if visitors come, you will be there to say some good words to them without our having to be disturbed."

Brother Masseo bowed his head drew back his hood in sign of obedience; and for several days he was cook, porter, and alms giver. But the others soon began to feel remorse to see all the burden of the work fall on brother Masseo's shoulders, and they came and begged their father to release him. "Until you have done so," they said, "we feel that we will be lukewarm and distracted in our prayers."

They got their request; for, judging that the trial had lasted long enough, Francis restored things as they were before.

But if we are to believe the *Fioretti*, Brother Masseo was again porter and Brother Elias the superior on the day that a youthful pilgrim of a marvelous beauty came to the door of the hermitage and knocked so loud and so long that all in their huts wondered what was going on.

"Young man," said Brother Masseo, "evidently, this is the first time you have come here, or you wouldn't knock that way."

"And how should I knock?" inquired the stranger.

"Like this! First, you knock calmly three times with a little pause between each rap. Then, after the space of an Our Father, if you see that I am not coming, you can knock again."

"But I am in a great hurry," replied the visitor. "Could I speak to Brother Francis?"

Masseo explained that Francis was praying in the woods, and that it was not customary to disturb him when he was receiving such great graces from heaven.

"Then call Brother Elias, who they say is so learned. I should like to ask him something."

But Brother Elias refused to be disturbed; and this put Brother Masseo in an embarrassing position. What was he to say to the stranger? If he told him Elias could not come, that would be a lie, but telling the truth would scandalize the visitor. So while he was debating what to do, the caller pounded louder than ever at the door. Masseo came running. "You didn't pay any attention to what I said," he complained to the angel, who soon afterward vanished.

For the visitor was an angel who, under color of asking Elias why he had banned the use of meat, had come to congratulate the friars for their observance of the Gospel, which, as everyone knows, does not breathe a word of any such prohibition.

For a long time, Brother Masseo prayed God for the gift of humility. "Lord," he prayed constantly, "make me humble, even at the price of losing my two eyes." He was finally heard, without losing his eyes; and ever thereafter so great was his happiness that he expressed it in prayer by a gentle moaning, always the same. When Brother James of Falerone, whom this "cooing" wearied slightly, remarked to him that it was a most monotonous sound, Brother Masseo replied: "Does a man who has found happiness think it necessary to change his tune?"

Brother Masseo, born in Marignano, near Assisi, lived to be very old, and only died, says Wadding, in 1280. Unlike Brother Lucido, Brother Giles, and so many of the first Franciscans, he did not care for traveling and preferred the society of certain of his brethren even to pilgrimages. "I find I gain more," he said, "associating with living saints than with dead ones. For the latter are silent; whereas the others can talk and tell us of the temptations they have overcome, thus forewarning us against the perils that threaten us."

We have seen that the Rule commanded the friars to welcome all visitors, "including thieves and robbers." Now along about the year 1213, Brother Angelo Tarlati, who like his namesake, Angelo Tancredi, was a former knight, was living at the hermitage of Monte Casale. As porter, he one day received a visit from three notorious robbers who, lacking travelers to rob in the neighboring woods, had come to the convent to beg alms. He gave them a very poor reception: "What? Murderers like you? Not satisfied with robbing honest folk of the fruit of their toil, you want to take the little belonging to

God's servants! You, who have no respect for God or man and don't deserve that the earth should hold you! Get out of here, and don't let me see you again!"

Perhaps the fiery guardian called on his sword that in former days he used to thrust through rascals like them. Be that as it may, the robbers withdrew in high anger. But scarcely had they left when Francis returned, laden down with the bread and wine which he had collected as alms. Learning what had happened, he reproached the porter:

> "You have behaved like a man with no religion!" he said. "Does not the Gospel which we have promised to follow declare that it is the sick and not the well who need the doctor? Take this bread and this wine in the name of obedience, and go and find those robbers! Run up hill and down dale until you find them; and as soon as you see them, shout, 'Come, brother robbers! Come and eat the good things Brother Francis begs you to accept!'
>
> "And they will come. Then spread a cloth on the ground and put this bread and this wine on it, to which you will add some eggs and cheese. And serve these unfortunate men with humility and good humor until they are satisfied. Then, and not until then, ask them not to kill anybody any more, adding that serving God is not nearly so hard as their profession. And I do not doubt that the Lord in His mercy will inspire them with better sentiments."

Nor was their conversion long delayed. For from this time on, says the chronicler, they were to be seen every day at the hermitage, bringing on their backs the firewood needed by the friars. And not only did they pledge themselves to gain their living from then on by honest toil, but all three ended up entering the Order, in which they died the death of saints.

The growing brotherhood thus excluded no one; and like our Lord, Francis received sinners gladly. Did he not have the power to turn dross into gold?

Even eccentrics were kindly received by Francis, and his affection for John the Simple and Brother Juniper is well known.

John the Simple was a ploughman, and is believed to have lived in Nottiano, eight miles from Assisi, east of Mount Subasio. While tilling his field, he learned that Francis was sweeping a church in the neighborhood. Leaving his oxen, he went off to find him, took the broom out of his hands and finished the cleaning. Then he sat down beside him by the side of the road and opened his heart to him:

"I have been hearing about you for a long time," he said, "and wanted to meet you. But I didn't know where to find you. Since God has permitted this meeting, what do I have to do to enter your company?"

The saint decided at once that this simple-hearted man would make an excellent friar. "If you want to come with us," he said, "you must first forsake your lawful possessions and give them to the poor, as my other friars have done."

John hastened to unyoke one of his oxen and brought it to St. Francis. "Here," said he, "is my lawful portion of the inheritance; for since the time I have been working for my parents, it seems to me that I have earned this ox. So I want to give it to the poor the way you told me to do."

Now John's parents, poor themselves and with children to take care of, were appalled to learn of their double loss and began to utter cries of distress. Francis took pity on them.

"I do not want to see you weep any more," he said. "Prepare a good meal. We will eat together; and while we are eating, I will tell you something that will make you happy again."

They sat down to table, and presently the saint began to speak to the parents: "It is a great honor for you to have your son decide to enter God's service, for to serve God is to reign. It also means that you will truly become rich, for all the brothers John will find in the Order will become in a sense your own children. You must then be very happy. But to make you still happier, you will do me the favor of keeping, in memory of your son, this ox which according to the Gospel he ought to have given to the poor?"

Now as Francis talked, their tears began to stop, and when the parents learned that John was not going to take his ox when he went away, it was such a relief to them that they were completely consoled.

On receiving the habit, John also took the resolution to imitate his spiritual father in everything. Did Francis stop to pray? At once, Brother John stopped short and began to pray. When Francis knelt, he knelt, and sighed, wept, and raised his arms to heaven the same time St. Francis did, coughed when he coughed, and, in a word, copied his slightest movement. Puzzled, the saint asked him one day the reason for all this.

"Father," he replied, "I have resolved to become holy by following your example in everything. And that is why I wouldn't, for anything in the world, let a single action of yours go by without imitating it."

Francis felt a special affection for John and frequently took him along as his companion. John died early; but often afterward the saint used to speak of him, and always called him "our brother St. John," so sure was he that John was in heaven.

No less edifying and still more picturesque was the famous Brother

Juniper, who entered the Order in 1210, was present at the death of St. Clare in 1253, and died in Rome five years later.

St. Clare, who loved and understood him, had dubbed him "God's *jongleur*," *Domini joculator*. As for Francis, who did not require everyone to be like everybody else, he replied to those who considered Juniper's whimsies out of place, "O brothers! I wish I had a whole forest of junipers like him!"

Brother Juniper enjoyed such a reputation for sanctity that we are told possessed persons would flee across fields to avoid meeting him. Francis himself, when he had to deal with some especially recalcitrant demon, had only to say to it, "I am going to call Juniper," for the demoniac to be immediately delivered.

They tell how, in order to observe the rule of "not resisting evil," Juniper once let himself be taken for a spy at Viterbo and condemned to death without protest. Tied to a horse's tail, they were already dragging him to the gallows, when at the last moment his guardian rushed up and managed to clear up the confusion and rescue the alleged traitor.

It is also reported that in order to practice recollection, Juniper once went six months without saying a word. The first day he kept silent in honor of God the Father, the second day in honor of God the Son, the third in honor of the Holy Spirit, the fourth for love of the Blessed Virgin, and so on. Every day he kept silent in honor of some new saint.

But Juniper when he did speak, expressed himself with deep wisdom, if we are to judge by the two following examples: "Do you know any noblemen whose nobility would keep them from hauling dung, if that would enable him to win a houseful of gold? Then why should we be so hard to please, and why refuse little humiliations that can gain eternal happiness for us?"

To his fellow friars who were discussing how to repel impure thoughts, he indicated his own method: "As for me, as soon as I sense the tempter's approach, I shut myself up in my heart with holy thoughts. Then I shout to the devil who knocks at the door, 'Begone! The inn is full and we're not opening up to anyone!' And when the devil hears this, he at once goes away in defeat."

Juniper was not a man to wish for honors here below, content, like so many others, to give the glory to God. Some devout Romans learned this at their expense the day they set forth to meet him as he was approaching the Eternal City. Seeing some children playing seesaw, Brother Juniper made a show of entering into their game; and with great seriousness, as if he had nothing better to do that day, he began to seesaw until his disappointed admirers withdrew.

The early Rule, following the Gospel, said: "Let the Brethren give to all who ask; and if someone takes away their garment and tunic, let them be stripped without protest." Such precepts made Brother Juniper commit not a few excesses. Like his blessed father, he could not stand seeing a poor man worse clad than he; and sometimes he would give the needy great pieces of cloth cut out of his habit, and sometimes his whole tunic.

His guardian had just reprimanded him about this, when he met a beggar shivering in his rags. "You've come at a bad time," said Juniper to him. "My superior has just forbidden me to give away my tunic. But if you want to take it away from me, I won't stop you."

The beggar needed no second invitation; and lifting up the charitable friar's habit, he pulled it off wrong side out, so that Juniper had to return home in his drawers. Since much fun was made of him on this occasion, he wanted to repeat the experience so as to acquire new merits.

After another such "folly" in which he walked naked from Spoleto to Assisi, the exasperated guardian exclaimed: "O Brother Juniper! I really don't know what penance to give you this time for such scandalous conduct!"

"Father, I'll tell you," replied the culprit. "Just command me to go back where I came from in the same regalia."

After the death of St. Francis, Juniper's charity took a special turn, and the idea often came to him of distributing to the poor the books and other objects that he deemed superfluous in the Franciscan house. The friars had to put their things under lock and key or else have them disappear.

Now how was it, with a reputation like that, that Juniper was entrusted on a feast day with the care of the altar of the Basilica of Assisi? The fact remains that he profited by his charge to detach some costly silver ringlets from the altar-frontal and give them to a beggar woman. Furious, the Minister General stormed so at Juniper that he almost lost his voice. That night, hearing a knock at the door, he opened it to see Brother Juniper standing there with a candle in one hand and a dish in the other.

"Father," said he, "you shouted so a while ago that I thought you must be hoarse. So I've brought you some buttered gruel which will do your throat and chest a lot of good."

The superior refused the remedy and curtly invited Juniper to stop his silly pranks.

"Very well," replied Juniper. "Since you scorn my gruel, which was not made to be thrown away, then please hold the candle for me, and I'll eat it."

Before such simplicity, the Minister was disarmed, and the two religious feasted fraternally together.

Assuredly, this was a superior after St. Francis's own heart. For did not the Rule prescribe that superiors were to be servants to the other friars and take delight in washing their feet? While we are not told that Brother Juniper demanded that particular service, his actions often proved even more embarrassing.

The *Fioretti* tells us that a friar was sick in bed at the Portiuncula.

"What can I do for you?" Brother Juniper asked him.

"I think," replied the patient, "that I would feel much better if only I could eat a bit of pigs' feet."

"Nothing to it!" replied Juniper. "I'll get you some in no time."

Running to the kitchen, he took a large knife, rushed toward a corner of the woods where the pigs were munching acorns, pounced on the finest pig, straddled it, cut off a foot, came back to the convent, and put the foot in a stew. He then carried it to the sick friar, who ate it with much relish and at once felt better.

But soon the owner of the pig arrived, breathing forth fire and brimstone. Even St. Francis was unable to calm him. So he sent for the friar whom he suspected of the crime.

"Was it you, by any chance, who cut off the foot of a pig in the woods?"

"Certainly, Father," replied Juniper triumphantly. "Didn't God create pigs for man's use? And this stew did our patient so much good that if I had had to take the feet off a hundred pigs to cure him, I assure you that the Lord would have been pleased!"

This speech added fuel to the flames of the farmer's wrath, and he went off swearing that they would be hearing from him soon.

"Brother Juniper!" exclaimed Francis. "This time you have really gone too far, and it is up to you to make amends. Go then, and try to calm this man who is beside himself."

"Gladly, Father!"

Brother Juniper caught up with the farmer, threw himself on his neck, pressed him to his heart, fell on his knees, and begged his forgiveness. He spoke to him of the sick friar who was now getting well; and finally got him to agree—to straighten everything out—to sacrifice the rest of his beast and to think no more about it. And all this with so much exuberance, grace, and tears, that the farmer wound up weeping himself, agreed to butcher his pig, and soon after, brought it, with apologies, to the Portiuncula.

Brotherliness flourished in these Franciscan hermitages, as the friars remembered to practice the Rule's advice: "If a mother loves her son according to the flesh, with how much greater reason ought brothers according to the spirit to love one another."

One day when a band of cruel boys were chasing two friars with stones, far from thinking about warding off the blows, each man tried to draw the stones toward himself by placing himself as a shield in front of his companion.

Juniper, we are told, particularly loved Brother Tendalbene, whom he could make laugh or cry at will, and who, in addition, was so patient that he would have let himself be beaten all day without a murmur. When his friend died, Juniper's grief knew no bounds. "Nothing on earth interests me any more," he would go around saying. "Everything else can perish now that my dear Tendalbene is gone."

And as if to destroy this useless world, Juniper took up a stick and began to smash everything in his path. "If I followed my own idea," he would say, "I would take the skull of my dear Brother Tendalbene and divide it in two. One half would make me a bowl to eat from, and the other half a cup to drink from. But my brothers would not be able to understand me, and would probably protest."

Let no one be surprised that we devote so much space to Brother Juniper. We have simply imitated Brother Leo and his friends in their accounts from which all these little stories are taken. Evidently, Juniper was amusing and of a nature to arouse their enthusiasm. But Leo and his partisans had other good reasons for exalting "God's jongleur," whom Francis himself had, as it were, canonized. And was not singing the praises of Brother Juniper to condemn at the same time those friars whose books Juniper stole, and whose conduct resembled less and less the way of life of the first friars?

But it is in Brother Giles that everybody sees the purest example of the primitive Franciscan. "That man is truly my knight of the Round Table," said Francis of him with pride.

Giles lived for a few years at the Portiuncula; then at Cetona, and from about 1234 until his death in 1262, on the outskirts of Perugia, in the hermitage of Monte Ripido.

Giles had at first loved to travel, and had made pilgrimages to Rome, Compostella, and the Holy Land. For Francis had started out by letting those travel whose vocation was not to remain always at home. But whether in the convent or elsewhere, Brother Giles put a quiet fearlessness into observing the Rule—working with his hands, heedless of worldly events, and constantly absorbed in God.

He changed his occupation according to time and place. Sometimes he would hire himself out as a day laborer on farms and in monasteries. At other times he was a scullery assistant in the palace of a cardinal at Rieti. At Acre in the Holy Land, he became a water carrier, going through the city with a pitcher of water on his shoulder and shouting: "Who wants fresh water? Who wants my good water?" Elsewhere he made rush baskets and transported the dead to the cemetery.

Not only did Brother Giles always refuse money for his trouble, but according to the usage then in force at the Portiuncula, he even refused to accept in kind anything he could not use that day. "Like the birds of the air, I have no barns in which to store my wheat," he replied to a farmer who, seeing him glean, offered him a few sheaves. "God preserve me from falling into avarice!" he exclaimed to a woman who, because he was a religious, wanted to pay him more for his faggots than the price agreed upon. At Rome, a man could not find anyone to gather his nuts because the tree was so high. Giles offered to knock them down and go halves. He made the sign of the cross and trembling with giddiness climbed up the tree. When evening came, he had so many nuts that he had to make a sack out of his tunic to carry them away and give them with much joy to the poor.

Little gifted for preaching, Giles liked to keep silent and recommended the practice to others. "The true religious," he declared, "ought to be like wolves, which never show themselves in public unless necessary." He himself sought the solitude of caves and woods and professed that it was better to act than to talk. "Isn't there more merit," he would ask, "in going to St. James of Compostella than in showing others what road to take?" He thought it unfortunate that men did not have long, curving necks like cranes. "Then," he would say, "many words would stick in their throats because of the difficulty they would have getting out."

It is fortunate, though, that the solitary of Perugia sometimes stepped out of his habitual silence. Otherwise, posterity would have been deprived of that little masterpiece, *The Golden Sayings of Brother Giles*.

If, by their pithy form and keenness of observation, these sayings are related to the *Imitation of Christ* and to the *Maxims* and *Thoughts* of the great French moralists, they are nonetheless original by their note of optimism, their humor, and the feeling for nature which pervades them. We are astonished that this humble lay brother who called himself "ignorant" should have possessed such gifts of discernment and of reading men's hearts and the ability to express himself in such precise and familiar terms. He was furthermore a great mystic, who after undergoing mysterious and cruel inner sufferings, was favored by God with graces of a very high order. St. Bonaventure therefore considered him a master of the interior life and drew inspiration with him in his writings on mystical theology.

When people came to consult him, Giles's reply was sometimes brutally frank. To a mother who bewailed the loss of her son, a canon, he said, "Which did you prefer in him, the body or the soul?"

"Alas, it was his body," she replied, "for I had threatened to curse him if he ever became a Friar Minor."

"Then go to the cemetery," Giles retorted, "and find his body you loved so much, and you will see what has become of it."

To two cardinals who requested his prayers, he observed, "Assuredly your Eminences have no need of them, for you have a thousand times more faith and hope than I have."

"And how is that, Brother Giles?" asked one.

"It is," he replied, "because with all your riches and honors you believe and hope to be saved, whereas I, in spite of my poor and despised life, am so afraid of being damned."

He sometimes gave unsolicited advice. Thus it was that he got a certain priest of Perugia to add this little couplet to his sermon: "*Bo! Bo! Bo! Molto dico e poco fo.*" ("Too-rah-loo-rah-loo! Much do I say, but little do I do!")

He also possessed the gift of repartee. One day when he was speaking of the dangers of incontinence, he was interrupted by a married man. "All this does not concern me," he remarked with a smug air, "for I have my wife, and know no other woman."

"Doesn't a man ever get drunk on the wine from his own cask?" retorted Brother Giles.

He had the greatest admiration for his blessed Father Francis. Following his example, he composed verses, sang and danced, and like him played the viol; and he declared that no one should utter Francis's name without licking his lips for joy. "And truly, he had only one defect," he would add, "and that was his poor health. If Francis had been as strong as I am, for instance, no one—not even the whole world taken together—would have been able to keep pace with him."

He regretted that so many of his sons had degenerated. He burst into tears when Brother Leo came to Perugia to tell him about the great convent that Brother Elias was building on the Hill of Hell:

"Let him build it even bigger if he likes! Let him make it as long as from Assisi to Perugia if he insists! I'll never live there! I'll be glad to stay in my own little corner!"

Brother Giles had a chance to give brutal vent to his opinion of the building when he went to Assisi to venerate the relics of St. Francis.

"Really!" he declared to the religious of the Sacro Convento. "Now all you need are wives!"

"Brother Giles! What do you mean by saying a thing like that?"

"I mean that since you have forsaken holy poverty, all that you need to do now is to abandon chastity. You made a vow about that, too!"

When Francis left the Portiuncula to retire into solitude, his choice usually fell on Brothers Angelo, Rufino, Masseo, and Leo and his companions. With one or more of them he would climb to the Carceri, or go to Sant'Urbano near Narni, Fonte Colombo near Rieti, Monte Casale near Borgo San Sepolcro, Le Celle near Cortona,

Sarteano near Chiusi, and finally La Verna in the Casentino, where the great miracle of the stigmata took place. These hermitages, situated among lovely landscapes, are the high places of the Franciscan saga. The Carceri in particular still shows evidence of the life lived there by its first guests. These little "prisons" are caverns in the heart of the forest, on the flanks of Mount Subasio, eighty minutes' walk above Assisi. One may see there, on the brink of a chasm, the grotto where St. Francis prayed and the one where he slept on a tiny stone bed. A little higher up in a cleft in the rock is the one where Brother Sylvester withdrew; he who, "like Moses, knew the happiness of speaking to God like a friend to his friend." A hundred yards away, separated by the torrent, are to be found the grottos of Brothers Rufino and Bernard.

We know that Brother Bernard was sent to Bologna in 1211 to found a convent. At first he was greeted with stones; and to obey the Rule, he would stay for hours to be jeered at on the public square. It was a rich magistrate who was the first to recognize the missionary's holiness and help him carry out his plans. Soon the entire city began to show him marks of veneration. But as nothing could be more displeasing to Bernard, he hurried back to the Portiuncula. "Father," said he to Francis, "you will have to send someone else to Bologna, for it is a place where I myself have more to lose than to gain."

Francis always showed special consideration for his "firstborn son." When he was dying, he blessed him with a special blessing, recommended him to the affection of all, and begged the superiors to let him live wherever he wished. "Of all the brethren," says the Fioretti, "none was so humble as Brother Bernard. He excelled in understanding the most difficult passages of Scripture, and like St. John, merited to soar like an eagle to the very light of divine wisdom."

Once Brother Bernard was rapt in ecstasy and remained motionless, his eyes fixed, from Matins to Nones—even neglecting at the Elevation of the Mass to draw back his hood. He would also forget about mealtime, and stay for days at a time on the mountain conversing with God, causing Brother Giles to say that only swallows and Brother Bernard could live in the air and find their food so far from the earth.

Bernard is believed to have died between 1240 and 1246. When his fellow friars knew that the end was near, many of them hastened to his bedside. Entering his cell, Brother Giles called out to him, *"Sursum corda!* Lift up your heart, Brother Bernard!"

As this old friend wished to remain until the end, Brother Bernard requested that a hut should be built for him in the garden, where, as was his custom, he could indulge in contemplation. A little before breathing his last, this firstborn son of St. Francis raised himself up in bed and said to those around him: "I am not able to speak to you at length. But remember that where I am, you will soon be also; and I tell you that for nothing in this world, or for a thousand worlds like this, would I wish to have lived otherwise than I have done, nor have served any other master than our Lord Jesus Christ."

Brother Rufino, a cousin of St. Clare, belonged to the first nobility of Assisi. Timid, retiring, silent, and perhaps with a slight stammer, he had a horror of speaking in public; and he lived so lost in God that he would often speak incoherently, for instance when he was called away from his prayers to collect alms.

St. Francis, to try his virtue, sent him one day to preach in Assisi. "You will only have to say what God inspires you to say," said the saint.

Rufino declared that not having received the gift of eloquence, he preferred to stay home.

"Since you have not obeyed promptly," said Francis, "I command you, under holy obedience, to go without your habit."

But as soon as Rufino had left, the saint reproached himself for having been so harsh. "What right have you," he thought, "a common Bernardone, to order Brother Rufino, a noble citizen of Assisi, to do outlandish things that will make people think he is crazy? I am going to teach you to perform yourself the things you make others do!"

And removing his tunic, he called Brother Leo and set off with him for the city. When people saw him coming in this outfit, the ridicule that had greeted Rufino broke out afresh. "Their austerities have made them all lose their minds!" people muttered, shaking their heads.

Brother Rufino was just saying the little penitential exhortation of the Rule, when Francis entered the church in which he was preaching. The poor fellow was attempting to shout in order to be heard; but the louder he shouted, the more people laughed. Judging that his punishment had lasted long enough, Francis took his place in the pulpit. Half-clad as he was, he began to picture the Savior's nakedness on the cross in words so pathetic that the laughter of the congregation soon gave way to tears. "And I do not know," adds the author of the *Actus*, "whether so many tears were ever shed before in Assisi as on that day." Putting on their tunics again (which Brother Leo had been careful to bring), Francis and Rufino went back down to the Portiuncula, thanking God for having been associated with the sufferings of his divine Son by this victory over themselves.

The following anecdote, likewise taken from the *Actus Fioretti*, contains a vulgar word, for which we apologize, but whose efficacy Rufino proved in his struggles with the devil.

For it was the devil who, appearing to him at the Carceri in the form of Christ, had been tormenting him for some time about predestination. "Everything that you have done as a Friar Minor is a total loss," said he. "Besides, this Francis you are taking for a guide is damned himself, and my advice to you would be not to have anything more to do with him and to change your state of life."

And Rufino, who did not enjoy either preaching or begging, began to wonder if his vocation were not to become a hermit; and for a time, he avoided St. Francis. But the latter sent Brother Masseo to fetch him. Brother Masseo had a hard time trying to get him to come. As Rufino arrived grumbling, the saint, who had divined everything, caught sight of him and sang out: "Rufino, you dear idiot, just whom have you been trusting?"

Then Francis unmasked the devil's plot and showed Rufino how to get rid of him. "If the devil comes back again, you have only to say 'dung' to him, and he'll leave you alone."

When the devil reappeared, Brother Rufino obediently tossed this simple word at him, and that was all that was needed to put him to rout. And so great was his pique, says the *Fioretti*, that he unleashed a terrible tempest in his flight. Mount Subasio was shaken to its foundations. Stones torn out of the ground were shattered in fragments in the air, and chunks of flaming rock rolled with a terrific roar down the valley. The brothers rushed out of their caves to see what was going on; and so it was that they witnessed the cataclysm, "whose traces" (says the narrator) "are still visible today." Rufino's peace of soul was definitely restored, and till the day of his death at Assisi in 1270, he never again despaired of his salvation. Francis venerated him so highly that he often called him "St. Rufino," and would say, "If it were up to me to canonize him, I would not hesitate to do so right now, so certain am I of his salvation.

Of all the friends and companions of the Poverello, Brother Leo was perhaps the favorite. As he was a priest, the saint chose him as his confessor and secretary. He had dubbed him the *Frate pecorella di Dío*, because of his meekness and candor; and Brother "God's Little Lamb" followed the saint like his shadow, carrying out his slightest wish.

When he was disobedient, says the *Fioretti*, it was because God himself prevented him from obeying by a miracle; as happened in a hermitage wherein the poverty was so great that the friars did not have breviaries. Now Francis wanted to say Matins with Brother Leo.

"Since we have no books," said Francis, "here is the way we will chant the Office today. I will be the first choir, and you will be the second and repeat whatever I say."

"Very well, Father. Let us begin in God's name!"

The saint intoned: "Brother Francis, you have done so much evil and sin in the world that you certainly deserve Hell."

"And God will perform so much good through you that you will surely go to Heaven."

"What? That isn't right at all! Brother God's Little Lamb, you must repeat my words without any change!"

"Very well, Father! Let us begin again in God's name!"

His voice choked with sobs, and beating his breast, the saint resumed: "Brother Francis, the iniquities of which you have been guilty against the Master of Heaven and earth are so great that you deserve to be cursed for all eternity!"

"And you will make, thank God, such progress in virtue that you will merit to be blessed for all eternity!"

"But why don't you say it the way I do?" asked Francis. "God's Little Lamb, I command you under obedience to repeat my exact words. When I say, 'Wicked Francis! Tremble lest you do not find grace before God, you who have so gravely offended the God of goodness and the Father of all consolation!' then you must reply that it is perfectly true that I am unworthy of pardon."

"Very well, Father!" agreed Brother Leo. "I shall reply then that God, whose mercy is still greater than our sins, will surely show mercy to you."

At these words (we read in the *Fioretti*), Francis became a little angry, without, however, losing his patience.

"But, Brother God's Lamb, what has got into you, to be so disobedient and to insist on the very opposite of what I say?"

"Father, God is my witness that I try to repeat your words, but He Himself puts other words on my lips."

This admission disconcerted the saint, who again implored his friend to cry shame on his sins and to threaten him with God's punishment. So Brother Leo attempted an all-out effort to give him satisfaction, exclaiming:

> Brother Francis, not only will God spare you His punishments, but He will shower down His graces upon you and will glorify you for all eternity. For he who humbles himself shall be exalted.... And there is no use in my trying, for I can never say anything else. For the Lord is Truth itself, and He it is who compels me to speak as I do.

It is reserved to Brother Leo to become, together with Thomas of Celano, the great evangelist of St. Francis. As he had been his closest confidant, those zealous for the primitive observance eventually saw in him the only perfect interpreter of the Franciscan spirit. It has been claimed that Brother God's Little Lamb played this role with less serenity than was fitting, and no doubt there is some truth in this. For he did turn into a furious sheep when it came to defending the spiritual heritage of his venerated father. Thus it was when, learning that a marble poor box had been placed in the Basilica of Assisi, he confided to Brother Giles his intention of smashing it.

"Brother Leo," replied the wise Brother Giles, "you had better keep still, if you love life, for Brother Elias is capable of anything."

But Leo set off for Assisi and smashed the famous poor box with a mallet. His reward was to be whipped and imprisoned on orders from the builder of the Sacro Convento. But this treatment must have been sweet to the man who had learned from Francis himself that perfect joy consists in being persecuted.

From that time onward, giving up trying to do battle with too powerful an adversary, Brother Leo, during the long years of life still remaining, limited himself to telling and writing of the wonders he had witnessed. He lived until 1271, and like his friends, Bernard, Rufino, Angelo, and Masseo, was buried in the Basilica of Assisi.

CHAPTER EIGHT

St. Clare and the Order of the Poor Ladies

It was nearly six years after his conversion, says Thomas of Celano, that Francis founded the Order of "Poor Ladies."

It was once common to say that a woman is usually worth what the ideas of the man she admires are worth. So it was with St. Clare, who, better than anyone else in the world, and nearly as well as the Poverello himself, realized his ideal.

Born in 1193 or 1194, she belonged to the rich and noble house of the Offreduccio. She had two younger sisters, Agnes and Beatrice, who both became nuns of San Damiano. Her father was named Favarone di Offreduccio. Among her paternal uncles were Monaldo, feudal chief of the house, and Scipione, the father of Brother Rufino of Assisi. Her mother, Ortolana, must have been an unusual woman to have made—at a time when traveling was fraught with danger—three pilgrimages: to the Holy Land, to Rome, and to San Michele on Mount Gargano. When she was pregnant and praying for a happy delivery, a mysterious vision assured her that her child would be a light for many souls; and that was why Ortolana named her daughter Clare at baptism.

We are told that Clare understood and wrote Latin, that she loved music, and took a special delight in well-turned sermons. She had doubtless had a chance to hear minstrels in her father's house and to read romances of chivalry, for her language likewise is colored by the vocabulary of the literature of chivalry. The white alb which she made for St. Francis and which we see today at Santa Chiara in Assisi attests her skill as a seamstress; and her *Legend* tells how, old and infirm, Clare was propped up by the sisters with cushions so that she could still spin and sew.

Clare possessed a great deal of common sense, a loving and loyal heart, a gentle and prudent persistence, and an unflinching courage. She had the art of making herself loved, and was so persuasive that Francis, the cardinals, and the popes themselves always came round to her way of thinking. Sanctity aside, she was assuredly one of the most noble and charming women known to history.

As a little girl, Clare showed that her thoughts were turned toward God. Hearing her mother tell how the hermit Paul of the desert counted his three hundred daily prayers with pebbles, she began to tell off in the same way the many Our Fathers she prayed.

Clare was very beautiful, and when she was twelve her parents wanted her to marry, but she obtained a delay that she meant to use to prepare other plans. Meanwhile, she wore a cruel hair shirt under her rich clothing, despised money, dearly loved the poor, and deprived herself of the choicest morsels to give them to the needy. When the masons recruited by Francis repaired the Portiuncula, she dipped into her own purse to pay for meat for them, so that they might have more heart for working.

The Friars Minor soon became dear to her, and Francis was to be her guide and model. She had been impressed by the conversion of the "king of youth"; she was thrilled by the knightly bearing of God's songster; and when she attended the services in San Giorgio Church and the Cathedral of San Rufino, what must have been the effect on her—who enjoyed beautiful sermons—of the fiery improvisations of this poet inebriated with God's love! Going to him in secret, she confided to him that her parents were urging marriage upon her, and was encouraged by him never to have any other spouse but Christ.

But the time came when it was evident that further family discussions were useless and that no one would give in. So it was decided that she should take the initiative and flee from her home on Palm Sunday night.

In this year of 1212, Palm Sunday fell on March 18. In the morning, Clare, adorned like a bride, went with her family to San Rufino; but when it came time for the distribution of the palms, her heart failed her. Here she was about to leave her mother and sisters forever, and this was the last time that she would pray with them in the church where she had been baptized. It almost seemed to Clare as though her secret would suffocate her. She could not stir from her pew and the bishop had to descend the sanctuary steps to place the blessed palm in her hands.

That night, with her cousin Pacifica di Guelfuccio won over to her plans, Clare, without so much as farewell, left her home. The two accomplices hastened to the Portiuncula, where, before the altar of Our Lady of the Angels, Francis cut off their hair and clothed them in coarse habits like his own. Then he led them to the monastery of San Paolo belonging to the Benedictine nuns, two miles away in the marshlands of the Isola Romana.

Let it be said in passing that the circumstances of this entry into religion have been censured, and that after seven centuries an English lady of letters is unrelenting toward St. Francis and St. Clare:

"This is an incident which we can hardly record with satisfaction," she writes, deploring that so fair a career should have been begun by this sort of elopement. But if elopements which end in happy marriages are rarely condemned, why not admit that divine love also has its rights, being just as much a reality as human love? And whether the union contracted by St. Clare that night was a happy one, the continuation of this history will permit you to determine.

The young girl's flight stirred up her relatives, who the following day went to the Isola Romana in an attempt to bring the fugitive back home. Clare received them in the chapel, clinging to the altar cloth and showing them her shorn head. The relatives realized that they would not succeed in changing her mind and did not insist. They would at least have liked to keep in the family the property that the girl wished to give to the poor, and they offered to redeem it at the highest rate. But not wanting to have the air of being dispossessed only in appearance, Clare rejected their proposals and the inheritance passed into the hands of strangers.

Upon learning that Agnes was getting ready to imitate her sister, did the nuns of San Paolo fear the renewal of the scenes they had just witnessed? At any rate, accompanied by Brothers Bernard and Philip, Francis hastened to entrust his spiritual daughters to more intrepid Benedictines, taking them to Sant'Angelo Abbey on the slope of Mount Subasio, below the Carceri. It was there a week after Easter that Agnes joined her sister and her friend.

At the flight of this child of fifteen, the family's wrath boiled over, and the uncle Monaldo set off at the head of a dozen horsemen to storm the monastery. To gain admittance, says the *Legend,* he at first showed himself conciliatory. But as soon as he was in the presence of his nieces, he brutally ordered the younger girl to follow him at once. As Agnes refused, one of the horsemen pounced on her and dragged her by her hair to the door. Others came to his assistance and carried her off in their arms by the narrow path winding down the mountain. In her struggles, the poor child left pieces of her dress and locks of her hair on the briars as they went. "Help, dear sister! Help!" she sobbed.

At this appeal, Clare fell to her knees, imploring God to help one who wanted to belong to him. And that was all that was needed, according to the *Legend*, for the girl's body suddenly became so heavy that she seemed fastened to the ground. "Anyone would think she had eaten lead all night!" exclaimed one of the abductors. Then, insane with rage, Monaldo tried to strike her a brutal blow in the face with his fist. At once a horrible pain gripped his arm so that he screamed in agony.

Meanwhile, Clare, running up, confronted these barbarians and commanded them to release her sister. And these ravening wolves, who an instant before were so bloodthirsty and attempting to snatch the pious virgin from the arms of the Lord, became as gentle as lambs, abandoned their prey, and returned peacefully to their homes.

Just as he had done for Clare and Pacifica, St. Francis cut off Agnes's hair with his own hands and received her profession. She now belonged to the jurisdiction of the Church and it was to the Bishop of Assisi that Monaldo would have to appeal to recover his ward. But he probably desisted, for Bishop Guido approved the two sisters and four months later generously gave them San Damiano as a refuge. Here it was that the Order of "Poor Ladies" or "Poor Clares" was born.

We can imagine Clare's happiness at being able to settle in the shadow of the poor shrine recently restored by her friend. She lived there until her death. Agnes spent seven years there, after which she was sent to the monastery of Monticelli near Florence. Her sister, Beatrice, and their mother, Ortolana, also became nuns at San Damiano, and likewise their cousins Balvina and Amata, daughters of Martino di Corano.

Francis always watched affectionately over his "dear little spiritual plant." Chivalrous as always, he had promised never to forsake her, as Clare herself recalled before her death: "When the Blessed Father saw that we feared no poverty, toil, sorrow, humiliation, or the contempt of the world, but rather that we held these in great delight, moved by love he wrote for us a form of life as follows":

> Since by divine inspiration you have made yourselves daughters and handmaids of the Most High and Sovereign King, the Heavenly Father, and have espoused yourselves to the Holy Spirit by the choice of a life according to the perfection of the Holy Gospel: I will and promise for myself and my Friars always to have for you as for them the same diligent care and special solicitude.

Afterward, not only did the religious of the Portiuncula minister to the nuns of San Damiano, but they also shared with the Poor Ladies whatever they collected by begging.

The day came when on the strength of a pontifical decree rightly or wrongly interpreted, the Minister General John Parenti forbade them to preach to the nuns or to hear their confessions. But Clare did not see things that way; and when the collecting friars came back with their loaded sacks, she went to meet them and said, "Go back to your Minister, and tell him from me that since you can no longer feed our souls with your spiritual conferences, it is useless for you still to nourish our bodies with your alms." When Pope Gregory IX heard about this, he revoked the aforesaid decree.

Only one of the sermons preached by St. Francis at San Damiano has come down to us, and it is a sermon without words. It was in 1221. Clare and her community, assembled in choir, awaiting their blessed father. Francis knelt down, and his eyes raised to heaven, prayed for a while. He then had ashes brought, put part of them on his head and sprinkled the rest around him in a circle. Again he paused, recited the *Miserere*, and then left. And that was his whole sermon.

What were the Poverello's reasons for acting in this way? Perhaps, not being in the mood for words that day, God's *jongleur* thought that such a pantomime would be the best possible instruction on the last end of man. Or, perhaps also, feeling his death to be near, he wanted to teach Clare gradually to do without him, and her nuns not to measure their spiritual advancement by the number of sermons they heard.

The fact is that in his eyes the zeal shown by certain friars in recruiting nuns and in assuming their spiritual direction could give rise to abuse. He also feared for them the danger sometimes incurred by familiarity with even the most devout women. He himself, writes Celano, declared that he knew only two women in the world by sight. These were apparently Sister Clare and Brother Jacopa. The fact remains that he did not like to have the name of "Sisters Minor" given to the Poor Ladies, and to those who displayed an exaggerated zeal toward them he said, "The Lord has preserved us from taking wives, but who knows whether it is not the devil who sent us sisters?"

If, for some years, the saint climbed less frequently the path leading from the Portiuncula to San Damiano, it was especially for his own friars' instruction. "Do not believe," he said to those who reproached him, "that my love for Clare and her companions has diminished. But I have tried to be an example to you. Only those ought to minister to the sisters whom long experience has shown to have the Spirit of God." And to get his thought across, he told them the following parable:

> A king had sent two ambassadors to the queen. When they returned, he asked them what they thought of the queen.
>
> "Sire," replied the first ambassador. "You have a very beautiful wife. Happy indeed is he who possesses her like!"
>
> "And what do you think of the queen?" he asked the second.
>
> "I admired," he replied, "the attention with which she listened to your instructions."
>
> "You did not find her beautiful?"
>
> "Sire, it is for you to judge of her beauty. My part was to transmit your message."
>
> The king then gave judgment as follows: "You, whose eyes are chaste" (he said to the one who had just finished speaking), "I will reward you, and you shall ever remain in my service. As for you," (he said to the indiscreet ambassador) "whose unchaste eyes have rested on the queen, go! And never come again to defile my palace with your presence!"
>
> "And if earthly kings are so exacting," added Francis, "what modesty of the eyes does Christ not have a right to expect of those whom He sends to His spouses!"

Apparently, the saint did not mortify his daughters more than strict necessity required. The *Fioretti* relates that he consented one day to invite Clare to dinner at St. Mary of the Angels.

This was a favor that the Abbess of San Damiano had long sought in vain. So she got some mutual friends of the saint and herself to intercede for her. These came to St. Francis and said, "It is too harsh and contrary to divine charity for you and not to fulfill the desire of a virgin so holy and dear to God. Remember that after all she is your little spiritual plant and that it was your exhortations that took her away from the vain illusions of the world."

"Then you think I ought to eat with her?"

"Certainly! And even if she were to ask more, you ought to grant it."

"Well, since that is your opinion, it will be mine, too. And so that she may really have reason to be happy, it will be here at the Portiuncula that we shall dine. For it is a long time that our sister Clare has been a recluse at San Damiano, and nothing could afford her greater pleasure than to see the place once more where she gave herself to the Lord as His spouse."

On the appointed day, Clare arrived, accompanied by a Sister. With deep humility, she first venerated the image of St. Mary of the Angels over the altar where she had taken the veil and had her hair cut off. She then employed the time before dinner in visiting every nook and cranny of the hermitage. Francis, who following his usual custom, had had the food served on the ground, sat down beside her. The others took their respective places, and all made ready to dine. But scarcely had they swallowed the first mouthfuls when Francis began to speak of God, and all fell into an ecstasy.

Soon, however, a crowd came rushing to the convent. It was the inhabitants of Assisi and Bettona and the surrounding district, who, seeing flames over the forest and believing that a great fire had broken out at St. Mary of the Angels, were coming to put it out. But they could see that no damage had been done; and when, entering the "banquet hall," they found Francis and his guests with their hands joined and eyes raised to heaven, they realized that the flames they thought they had seen were the flames of divine love with which these holy persons burned. And they withdrew as edified as they were reassured.

As for Francis, St. Clare, and the other guests, adds the *Fioretti*, they scarcely touched the food at all, being sufficiently nourished by the spiritual consolations they had experienced; and many among them ate nothing at all.

The way of life of the nuns of San Damiano was inspired by the letter of the Gospel and by the Rule of the first Franciscans. The sisters recited the canonical hours, worked with their hands, cared for the sick, and practiced penance and poverty, just as the friars did at the Portiuncula.

Never was there a closer and more harmonious union than that existing between St. Clare and St. Francis. Never were two souls in more perfect accord in their way of looking at things of earth and heaven. One sometimes wonders which of the two copied the other. One would say that there was a kind of spiritual kinship, so alike were their characteristic features and reactions. The Poverello's ideal remained always pure in the heart of his daughter who kept unchanged the deposit of his fairest inspirations and who, like a limpid mirror, reflected his best image. Thus in hours of discouragement and darkness, we sometimes see him coming back to the poor walls of San Damiano—the cradle of his vocation—to seek from his spiritual daughter the comfort and assurance of which he stood in need.

Like the Poverello, Clare was humble, merciful, charming, optimistic, and courteous. At San Damiano, she cared at first for the sick, as Francis had done at the start of his religious life. Later on, in 1220, learning of the martyrdom of the Franciscans in Morocco, and longing to shed her own blood for the faith, she would have gone to the Saracens if she had not been hindered.

She blessed the Creator for having made the world so entrancingly beautiful. She cultivated flowers, loved animals, and counseled the sisters to admire the trees when they went outside the convent.

Clare was also a great contemplative, constantly conversing with God, and every day from noon to Nones, experiencing—from meditating on the Savior's Passion—mysterious torments which filled her eyes with tears. Once, from Thursday to late Friday in Holy Week, she remained so ravished out of herself that a sister had to pluck her by the sleeve to remind her that Francis had forbidden her to pass more than twenty-four hours without taking at least an ounce and a half of food.

The slightest word sufficed to transport her into supernatural realms. One Sunday in Eastertide, she was so struck by the antiphon *Vidi aquam* that she spent the whole day sprinkling her companions with holy water to remind them of the water that flowed from the Savior's side.

Excessively hard on herself, fasting perpetually, rejecting all cooked food, and sleeping on boards, Clare was a mother to her daughters. "Our flesh is not of bronze, nor is our strength that of stone," she wrote in 1229 to Agnes of Bohemia, Abbess of Prague. "So I urge you to be less strenuous in your fasting, so as to render reasonable worship to the Lord, and to season your holocausts with the salt of prudence."

So long as she was not totally incapacitated, she took care of her sick daughters, even of their humblest needs. When her sisters came back from begging, she washed their feet and kissed them reverently. In the winter, she would get up in the middle of the night and tuck in their bedclothes; and in the morning, it was often she who, the first one up, rang the bell and lit the lamps, so as to give extra rest to the nuns who had this duty.

The *Process of Canonization* relates a charming miracle, which shows how quick God was to answer her slightest prayer and also how kind Clare was.

There was a sick nun at San Damiano who was visibly wasting away from lack of appetite. Distressed, the saint asked her if there were not something she would like. "Oh!" exclaimed the nun, who apparently cherished some pleasant memories of her secular life, "I would like to eat some trout from the Topino and some hearth-cakes for Nocera, if I had some! But where are they to be had?"

Clare dropped to her knees, and hardly had she begun her prayer when a knocking was heard at the door. It was a fair youth carrying two packages wrapped in napkins containing the delicacies the sick nun desired. As the hour was late and the weather bad, the sisters invited the youth to spend the night at the guest house used by the Friars Minor. But he refused, and vanished like a phantom.

Painters have popularized this other miracle which is believed to have occurred on a Friday in September 1240, when the imperial army had invaded central Italy, "burning cities, cutting down trees, laying waste vineyards, and torturing women and children."

For Frederick II had enrolled Saracens among his troops, who little heeding the Church's excommunication, fought with no inhibitions against the pope's soldiers, and showed little respect for the nuns who fell into their hands.

Already, declared the *Legend*, this band of ruffians had scaled the walls of San Damiano and entered the cloister, when Clare had the Blessed Sacrament brought, and going toward them, made this prayer: "Lord Jesus, do not permit these defenseless virgins to fall into the hands of these heathen. Protect them; for I, who have nourished them with Your love, can do nothing for them."

She likewise prayed for the city of Assisi, nearly all of whose inhabitants were saved.

Then, continues the biographer: "immediately the boldness of these dogs was changed into fear and they quickly clambered over the walls they had scaled, being routed by the power of her prayers." Not only the sisters but the people of Assisi itself owed their safety to the prayers of St. Clare.

In the first of three letters that she wrote to Agnes of Bohemia, who before becoming Abbess of Prague had been betrothed to Frederick II, Clare exclaimed: "O blessed Poverty, to those who love and embrace her she bestows eternal riches! O holy Poverty, to those who possess and desire her God promises the Kingdom of Heaven! O Poverty, beloved of God, which our Lord, the Creator of the world, has deigned to embrace so completely on earth!"

At this period nothing was more opposed to the usages of the Church than to authorize nuns to do without revenues. Especially for recluses, it was thought that it was tempting God to aspire to live by alms from day to day. In 1215 or 1216, however, Clare obtained from Innocent III what has been termed the *Privilegium paupertatis*; that is, the canonical right to possess neither property nor revenue. Gregory IX attempted to withdraw it, when in 1228, he came to Assisi for the canonization of St. Francis. The former Cardinal Hugolin said to her:

"If it is your vow which prevents you from accepting revenues, I can release you from it."

"Holy Father," she replied, "absolve me from my sins, but from following Christ I have no desire to be dispensed."

Instead she implored the pope officially to recognize for her the right never to have revenues. At this request, Gregory began to laugh. These were not, he observed, the kind of privileges people were accustomed to demand from him. But he finally yielded; and as the formulary of the Pontifical Chancellery possessed no model of similar acts, he himself drew up the original Bull, *Sicut manifestum est*. "As it is manifest," we read in it, "that to be deprived of necessary things does not frighten you...and that He who feeds the birds of the air and clothes the lilies of the field will not fail you in both food and clothing.... We accede to your supplication and authorize you to apostolic favor to live in highest poverty. Likewise by these presents it is granted you never to be constrained to receive possessions."

However, the majority of then existing convents of Poor Ladies renounced the use of this privilege; and others founded afterward imitated them. Thus there were in the Order two observances: that according to which the nuns lived on uncertain alms, and that according to which they lived from assured revenues. Deeming this diversity undesirable, Innocent IV, after deliberation, decided to put an end to it; and by his Bull of August 6, 1247, he imposed a new Rule on the Poor Clares in which the right of all to property and revenues was recognized.

Ill for twenty-nine years, Clare had only six more to live. Her infirmities, arising from her excessive penances, had made her a permanent invalid, nearly always bedfast. But her soul was as serene and ardent as on that night in her youth when Francis received her first vows. She dragged herself to the offices of the community whenever she could; and she enjoined her nuns to remain united to the Friars Minor, and the friars to obey their ministers while practicing the most absolute poverty. Half-helpless, but faithful to the law of labor, Clare continued to make corporals or altar linens for needy priests.

Among the friars who came to see her, the most regular and most welcome visitors were those who preserved the Franciscan spirit of the first days. Like her blessed father, Clare was especially fond of Brother Juniper, of joyous and happy mien, of Brother Leo who had copied out a breviary for her, and of Brother Giles whose improvised sermon one day afforded her so much pleasure.

It was on a day when a great doctor in theology—Adam of Oxford, *not* the famous Alexander of Hales—was preaching at San Damiano. Was it to put an end to too learned considerations or simply to test the preacher's virtue? Whatever it was, Brother Giles interrupted him in the middle of his sermon. "Silence, Master!" he shouted. "That's enough! It's my turn to speak!"

The theologian did not wait to be told twice—and never, it would seem, was Brother Giles so sublime. As for St. Clare, she said to those around her, "How happy our Father Francis would have been to see a master in theology bow thus to a simple lay brother!"

The nearer she came to death, the more she was surrounded by universal veneration. High personages in the Church hastened to her bedside.

September 8, 1252, witnessed the arrival of Cardinal Rainaldo of Segni, protector of the Order, at San Damiano. Clare submitted a Rule of her own to him, which clashed with Innocent IV's Rule. Chapter eight, among others, copied the very words of the Rule of the Friars Minor: "The Sisters," we read, "are to take nothing as their own, whether it be a house, or a place, or anything at all. Instead, they are to be as pilgrims and strangers in this world; and as those who serve the Lord in poverty and lowliness, let them send for alms with full hope in Him. Nor should they feel shame thereby, since for our sakes the Lord Himself came into this world as a poor man. Such indeed is the greatness of this perfect poverty, that it makes you, my dearest Sisters, heirs and queens of the kingdom of heaven, so that though you are in want of this world's goods, you are made rich in virtues. Let this always be your 'portion' here below...and desire never to have aught else under heaven."

Clare won over Cardinal Rainaldo, who promised to interest the Holy Father in her project. Soon Innocent IV himself came twice to visit the sick abbess. He made no attempt to conceal his love and admiration for her. When the invalid besought him to absolve her from her sins, he exclaimed before giving the absolution, "Would to God that I had as little need of it as you!"

The saint now waged her final combat. We can guess with what ardor she implored Christ's vicar to grant to her and her daughters "the privilege of most high poverty." Innocent IV allowed himself to be persuaded, and August 9, 1253 (likely a few days after his second visit), he signed at Perugia the Bull *Solet annuere* which approved the new Rule. The next day a friar hurried from Perugia to San Damiano to bring Clare the longed-for Bull. This was Clare's last joy on earth, for she died the next day.

Although for three weeks she had been unable to take any nourishment whatever, her presence of mind and spiritual strength remained intact. To her sister Agnes who had just returned to San Damiano, she said, "Do not cry, dear Sister. I am not leaving you for long, for you will soon rejoin me." And Agnes did die three months later.

When Brother Juniper approached her bed, Clare asked, "Do you bring me good news from God?" Juniper thereupon began to speak words so burning with divine love that it was like flames leaping up from a burning heart. And his words were a great consolation to the dying Clare.

Also at her bedside were her faithful friends, Leo and Angelo. She asked them to read to her the Passion of the Lord. Upon Brother Rainaldo exhorting her to bear her infirmities with patience, she replied, "Dearest Brother, ever since I have known the grace of my Lord Jesus Christ through His servant Francis, no suffering has troubled me, no penance has been hard, no sickness too arduous."

Clare's daughters gathered round her couch sobbing. She spoke tenderly to them to console them, blessed them for the last time, and enjoined them to walk in the path of holy poverty. She was heard to murmur, "Depart in peace, for thou wilt have a good escort on the journey. Go forth confidently to Him who has protected thee and loved thee as a mother loves her child."

Sister Anastasia asked her whom she was addressing.

"I am speaking to my blessed soul, and he who has been its guide is not far distant." (Doubtless this was St. Francis come to take her to heaven.) "Lord God," spoke Clare again, "blessed be Thou for having created me!" Then she breathed her last.

The funeral took place the next day in the Church of San Damiano with burial later that day at San Giorgio. Innocent IV and numerous cardinals were present. Instead of the Office of the Dead, the pope proposed that the Office of Virgins should be sung in her honor, which would have meant canonizing her before her burial, says the *Legend*. But the Bishop of Ostia, more of a stickler for formalities, protested that it was more seemly to sing the customary Mass of

Requiem and to wait a little before placing Sister Clare on the altars. So they waited two months before opening the formal Process. The canonization took place two years later, August 15, 1255, at Anagni.

CHAPTER NINE

Growth of the Order

A PERIOD OPENS here in which precise dates are scanty. But we do find two sure landmarks—the deed of gift of Mt. Alverna, which will be mentioned later on, and St. Francis's two unsuccessful attempts to visit territory controlled by the Muslims.

It was after the victory of Las Navas that he attempted for the first time to carry out his plan. Never, perhaps, until this year 1212, had men lived in such dread of seeing the Saracens overrun Europe. Innocent III ordered universal prayers and processions and called on all Christendom to take up arms. But many Christians at that time were warring among themselves and others turned a deaf ear, so on July 14, 1212, the Spaniards were alone at Las Navas to wage battle. They won a brilliant victory which stirred all Europe to enthusiasm, and after which men imagined that the Moorish peril had been turned aside forever.

The situation appeared no less favorable in the East, although the crusaders occupied themselves mostly with commerce and with the petty kingdoms they had founded for their own profit. But since the pope had excommunicated them all in a body to bring them to order, people everywhere began to realize once more that the object of the crusade was to deliver the Holy Places; and everybody—even the children—wanted to share in what appeared to be the forthcoming victory. We are told that thirty thousand of these innocents did set out from Touraine and twenty thousand from the Rhineland to recapture the Savior's tomb, and that they all perished on the way or else fell into the hands of slave merchants.

Were the dwellers in the Portiuncula seized by the general enthusiasm, and did Francis believe the moment ripe for going to preach Christ's peace to those whom Christian arms had been unable to conquer? What is certain is that he did decide to leave for the East. Adventure and the unknown were to his liking and the prospect of shedding his blood inflamed his knightly zeal. Besides, had not his recent experiences shown him that with God's help all things are possible to man? Since, following his example, so many Christians had forsaken all in imitation of Christ, why should he not succeed in having those of other faiths likewise open their hearts to the Gospel?

It was likely toward the close of the year 1212 that Francis embarked with a companion on a boat bound for Syria. Unfortunately, contrary winds landed our passengers on the Dalmatian coast. As no further opportunity offered itself that year for continuing their voyage, the two friars determined to return to Italy. They wanted to board a ship about to sail for Ancona, but were barred because they had no money to pay for their passage. So they had to slip secretly on board with the connivance of an obliging sailor. Thomas of Celano gives us to understand that they would have fared ill if a tempest had not suddenly broken out, forcing the overtasked rowers to use up their own provisions faster. The famished sailors were thus only too glad to have recourse to the charity of the two missionaries, whose little store of food had miraculously multiplied.

About two years later, Francis renewed his plans for a spiritual crusade in Muslim lands, choosing this time Morocco. "He dreamed of nothing else," writes Celano, "than of converting the Miramolin and his satellites." Accompanied by Bernard of Quintavalle, he headed for Spain, "walking so fast," (so great was his haste to reach his destination) "that his companion often had trouble keeping up with him. But God intervened, and sickness compelled him to give up his journey."

Friar Thomas adds in passing that at this time he himself entered the Order, but he tells us nothing more of this second abortive expedition. According to well-founded local tradition, we may believe that on this occasion Francis made a pilgrimage to St. James of Compostella and returned to the Portiuncula by way of France.

Before embarking for the East, however, Francis had undertaken several apostolic missions in the north of Umbria and in Tuscany. These had resulted in recruiting a goodly number of new friars. At Pisa he received Brothers Albert and Agnello who later on filled important offices in the Order. At Florence he received John Parenti, who was to become Minister General from 1227 to 1232. The latter discovered his vocation in a most curious manner. A former student of law at the University of Bologna, now a judge at Civita Castellana, from a window one day he observed a swineherd having a hard time getting his pigs to enter a city gate, and he heard the man shout to them: "Go through the gate, pigs, the way judges go into hell!"

These words set John Parenti to thinking, and he lost no time in abandoning a profession so generally looked down upon.

It is not known whether it was before or after Francis left for Syria that he spent a Lent in an island of Lake Trasimene. He insisted on staying there alone, eating only half a loaf of bread. He would have preferred to eat nothing at all, remarks the *Fioretti,* if out of humility he had not wished to leave to the Savior the glory of having gone without any food for forty days.

When this Lent was over, Francis passed through the neighboring regions. It was probably at Cortona that he enrolled in the brotherhood a man of gentle birth who extended hospitality to Francis and his companion one day, and whom the saint praised for his courtesy.

This Messer Guido, says the *Fioretti*, could have done no more were he entertaining angels from heaven. He warmly embraced the two friars, washed and kissed their feet, caused a great fire to be lit and an excellent repast brought to them, and as they ate served them himself with a beaming countenance. He then said to Francis, "Father, from now on I want to provide for your needs, for God has given me great wealth. I must show Him my gratitude by sharing it with the poor. So now whenever you need cloaks or tunics, do not think of buying them, for I will pay for them."

When alone again with his companion, Francis said to him, "I tell you I have rarely seen so courteous a man, and nothing would please me more than to have him as a friar. He is grateful to God for his blessing, generous to the poor, and most courteous to others. Now courtesy, brother, is one of God's finest attributes; for God makes His sun to shine and His rain to fall on sinners and just alike. And courtesy is truly the sister of Charity, for it extinguishes hatred and maintains love among men. So we must come back this way again some day, in case the Lord should inspire this perfect gentleman to join with us in His service."

And Messer Guido did enter the Order. He spent all his life at Le Celie, near Cortona, in a cave in a valley by a stream, only leaving this retreat from time to time to preach penitence to the people in the neighborhood.

From the Cortona country, Francis went through the region extending to the southwest of Lake Trasimene, founding among others the hermitages of Cetona and Sarteano. On a journey through the marches of Ancona, he received as many as thirty recruits at once in the city of Ascoli Piceno.

So the friars increased rapidly. Before the close of 1215 they had spread over not only north and central Italy, but to southern France and Spain.

They were to be met along the road, walking two by two, recollected and joyful, while their little hermitages were found on the outskirts of the towns or in the surrounding mountains. They did not live withdrawn from the people, since it was from them that they received their subsistence. The people on their part loved the friars for their voluntary destitution, as one loves children for their weakness. They were edified by the spectacle of their life in which religion appeared devoid of ambition and greed, and they did not stint their friendship or their bread.

As the friars furthermore proved to be good and obedient Catholics, and never preached without the permission of the parish priests, and practiced poverty for its own sake and not to fight the Church or recall simoniacal priests to their duty, the clergy likewise favored them.

Only the Bishop of Imola, it would seem, refused Francis permission to preach. "Brother," he replied curtly. "I am here for that purpose, and I don't need anyone to tell me what to do."

With a courteous bow, Francis withdrew—but he was back an hour later. "Are you back again?" boomed the bishop. "What do you want now?"

"Your Excellency," replied Francis, "when a father drives his son out the door, there is nothing left for him to do but to come back in through the window. So I, as your loving son, have not hesitated to come back to see you."

Deeply moved, the bishop embraced him, and gave him and his friars permission to preach in his diocese as often as they wished.

The time to ridicule and insult was over. From now on the Little Poor Man stole all men's hearts. Instead of sowing—like so many of the reformers—the seeds of rebellion and hatred, he built up, showed the tasks that needed to be done, and nourished souls eager for perfection and holiness. Men blessed this herald of a spiritual springtime. Even robbers, touched by his respect and trust, were friendly inclined. As for the Patarini and other heretics, he did not try to win verbal victories over them; and these disputers usually left him in peace. Often his arrival in a town resembled a triumphal entry. The church bells were rung and people went to meet him shouting, "*Ecco il santo!*" ("The saint is here!")

Enthusiasm like this, comments the *Fioretti*, astonished good Brother Masseo, who one day expressed his thoughts to the saint in this way: "Why after you? Why after you, rather than another?" he kept repeating.

"What do you mean, Brother Masseo?" asked Francis.

"Father, there's something I don't understand."

"What is it, Brother?"

"I was wondering why everybody runs after you, trying to see and hear you, and have you direct them, when you are neither handsome, nor learned, and not even of noble birth. Why you, rather than others?"

At these words, the *Fioretti* tells us, Francis could not conceal his joy. At first, he stood motionless, his face upturned to heaven. Then, falling on his knees, he thanked God and explained: "Why me? Why me? Do you want me to tell you, Brother Masseo? Well, know that all this comes from the All-Seeing God who, looking down and finding nothing viler on earth, quite naturally fixed His gaze on me. For to make His work shine forth in men's eyes, the Lord takes what is ignorant, weak, and despicable, in preference to what is learned, strong, and noble; so that the creature may have no cause to glory, but the glory may go to the sole Author of all good."

When people insisted on touching Francis's garments in veneration, he would say, "Don't canonize me too soon, for a 'saint' like me might still bring sons and daughters into the world!"

At the hillside hermitage of Sarteano, he suffered, according to Thomas of Celano, "violent temptations of the flesh." He was praying one night in his cell when the devil suggested that he ought to give up his austerities. The tempter said that God did not ask men to destroy themselves, and that it was therefore better for him to lead the common life and have a home and family, rather than to keep on with so miserable a life as a celibate. At once, the saint arose and laid aside his garment, saying:

Since the tunic belongs to the Order and does not deserve to be torn, I will respect it. But you, brother ass," he continued, addressing his body, "are going to be whipped to teach you better behavior." And he began to scourge himself with a rope. As the temptation did not go away, he went outside, took some snow, and began, in the bright moonlight, to make seven snow figures in a row in front of him. Then going from one to the other, he said to himself aloud, "There you are, Francis! The family you want to raise is complete. This one here is your wife. These four smaller ones are the children she has given you, two sons and two daughters, as you see. These two big ones are your servant and your maid. And now it is to you, the father, that they all look for support. So hurry and get them something to wear, for they are all naked and are going to freeze to death in this bitter cold.... What?... You hesitate?... You think there are too many of them?... Then remain in God's service, friend, and don't think about anything else!"

Meanwhile the devil had fled and the temptation vanished. So Francis, thanking God, returned to his cell. But a friar who had been praying that same night on the mountain in the moonlight had seen and heard everything, which greatly vexed the saint when he learned of it. So Francis forbade the friar ever to speak of this scene to anyone.

Toward the end of spring in 1213, Francis went to Romagna and reached the foot of the castle of Montefeltro (now San Leo) perched on a spur of the Apennines near San Marino.

Now on this day, the *Fioretti* reports, a relative of the lord of the place had been made a knight and a number of noblemen were present at the ceremony. When Francis heard of the festivities, he decided to attend with his companion. On his arrival he went into the square where all the noblemen were assembled. Climbing up on a little wall and beginning to speak, he took as his theme a couplet from a poem of chivalry:

> *Tanto è il bene ch'aspetto*
> *Ch'ogni pena m'è diletto.*
> I aspire to so great a treasure
> That all pain for me is pleasure.

Using these verses, he pictured the suffering that the apostles, martyrs, virgins, and confessors had endured to obtain an eternal reward, and developed thoughts so sublime that he stirred the enthusiasm of the knights present.

But the most deeply impressed of them all was Count Roland, lord of Chiusi-in-Casentino, who was inspired with a generous plan which he wished to tell Francis about at once. Francis tactfully protested that "politeness required Roland first to dine with his hosts and friends."

When the banquet was over, Roland told the saint of his plans. A mile and a half from his castle at Chiusi, atop Mount La Verna, he possessed an ideal site for the practice of contemplation and penance. "If you are willing to accept it for yourself and your friars," he added, "I freely and gladly offer it to you."

Unfortunately, Francis could not go there at the moment. "But as soon as I get back to the Portiuncula," said he, "I will send my friars, and if they find the place suitable, we will build a hermitage there in God's name."

And everything went as Count Roland wished; for an authentic deed signed by his sons in 1274 states that the gift of Mount La Verna was made to the brothers on May 8, 1213.

Did the Little Poor Man see something supernatural in this acquisition? Did Providence, which had not permitted him to land in the territory of the Saracens, mean for him to forsake the active ministry for prayer and contemplation? This is the question that Francis now asked himself once more and for which besought guidance and light.

He called Brother Masseo, according to the *Fioretti*, and said to him, "Go to Sister Clare, and ask her to pray to God to know whether I should preach part of the time, or spend all my days in prayer. Then go and ask the same thing of Brother Sylvester."

Brother Masseo went first to San Damiano where he transmitted Francis's message to Clare. Then he climbed up to the Carceri where Brother Sylvester was leading a hermit's life. Sylvester had a reputation for always getting a prompt answer to his prayers; and indeed, heaven let him know at once that it was Francis's vocation to be occupied both with his own salvation and with the sanctification of others. Sylvester told this to Brother Masseo, who at once started back to San Damiano, where St. Clare informed him that she had received the same reply from God.

Brother Masseo then went down again to the Portiuncula where Francis was waiting for him. After washing his feet, the saint had a good meal served him, and only afterward, kneeling bareheaded, his arms stretched out crosswise, he asked him, "What does my Lord Jesus Christ desire of me?"

The faithful messenger then disclosed his twofold and identical message. "Good! Let us go forth in God's name!" exclaimed Francis, rising. And taking with him Brother Angelo and Brother Masseo, he headed for Cannara, two leagues distance from Assisi, and began to preach.

Of all the sermons that St. Francis preached on this journey, the one to the birds is certainly one of the most beautiful ever preached on earth.

"Because everything comes from the same source," writes St. Bonaventure, Francis sensed the kinship which exists between men, animals, plants, the sea, and the stars. And is not the outlook of him who takes no thought of the bonds linking all creatures together and themselves to God most incomplete? Did not Christ himself speak of the goodness of the heavenly Father who gives the sparrow its food and the lily of the fields its brilliant garb? And before sin came into the world, did not men, beasts, and the elements live in harmony? But no one in the West ever experienced or expressed as did St. Francis such a feeling of the universal brotherhood of all creation. His heart is the way one pictures Adam's in the Garden of Eden; and it is to be believed that the very beasts perceived it, for they always showed such gratitude for the honor he paid them.

So, with his companions, Francis went beyond Cannara and going toward Bevagna, he reached—after a half an hour's walk—the place known today as Pian dell'Arca. "There were some trees there," relates the *Fioretti*, "so filled with birds that never had the like been seen in these parts; and there was likewise a multitude in the neighboring field."

Marveling at this spectacle and filled with the Holy Spirit, Francis said to his companions, "Stay here by the road and wait for me, while I preach to our sisters, the birds."

He entered the field, and scarcely had he commenced his sermon, when all the birds clustered round to listen. They remained motionless, even though the saint's habit brushed against them lightly as he passed.

My little sisters, the birds," he said to them, "many are the bonds which unite us to God. And your duty is to praise Him everywhere and always, because He has let you free to fly wherever you will, and has given you a double- and three-fold covering and the beautiful colored plumage you wear.

Praise Him likewise for the food He provides for you without your working for it, for the songs He has taught you, for your numbers that His blessing has multiplied, for your species which He preserved in the ark of olden times, and for the realm of the air He has reserved for you.

God sustains you without your having to sow or reap. He gives you fountains and streams to drink from, mountains and hills in which to take refuge, and tall trees in which to build your nests. Although you do not know how to sew or spin, He gives to you and your little ones the clothing you need.

How the Creator must love you to grant you such favors! So, my sister birds, do not be ungrateful, but continually praise Him who showers blessing upon you.

At these words, all the birds began to open their beaks and spread their wings; and stretching out their necks, they reverently bowed their heads, showing by their songs and actions the great joy they felt. Francis rejoiced with them, charmed and delighted at their numbers, their variety, and the loving familiarity they showed. At last, he made the sign of the cross over them and dismissed them. Then all the birds rose together and fled off, in the form of the cross he had made over them, in four groups toward the distant horizon.

The Poverello's whole life is filled with similar incidents. The theologian St. Bonaventure reports no fewer than fifteen of them, according special mention to the hare of Greccio which followed Francis like a little dog, the kingfisher and the fish in Lake Rieti which came regularly to ask his blessing, the pheasant of Siena that refused to eat for sorrow after its friend died, the cicada at the Portiuncula that came at his call and, lighting on his hand, sang God's praises with him, and finally the devoted sheep that also lived at St. Mary of the Angels, accompanying its master to the Office, prostrating itself at the Elevation, and saluting with its gentle bleatings the statue of the Blessed Virgin.

Other biographers of the Poverello revert continually to this feeling he had for the beauty of the world and for the love he bore toward every living creature. "How are we to express," exclaims Celano, "the tenderness he showed as he discovered in them the Creator's power and goodness! How are we to depict the joy he felt at seeing the sun, moon, and stars, and the pleasure he took in contemplating the beauty of the flowers and inhaling their fragrance!"

To the gardener of the Portiuncula he recommended taking part of the space devoted to vegetables for flowers; and when he came across flowers growing in the fields, he would stop for a while and talk to them. "One could say that His heart, by a unique privilege, had penetrated the secret of all things created."

When he walked on stones, he did it with a kind of reverence, thinking of Christ whom St. Paul compares to a rock. When he washed his hands, he would choose a place where the water would not be trampled underfoot afterward. Out of regard for his "brother fire," he would not let still-smoking firebrands be tossed aside, candles snuffed, or lights and hearth-fires extinguished. He forbade his friars who went to the woods to chop down trees, wishing to give every growing thing a chance to live out its life.

Francis cherished the tiniest forms of life. He would pick up worms lying on the road and put them to one side to keep them from being crushed. In the winter he had warm wine and honey brought to the bees to help them through the cold months. He built nests for doves so that they might increase and multiply; and one day in the march of Ancona he gave his new cloak to redeem two lambs being carried off to the butcher.

But Francis had his preferences, so Brother Giles informs us; and he did not quite forgive the ants for what appeared to him their feverish haste and exaggerated foresight. His unstinted praise went to the birds, who took no thought for the morrow but trusted from day to day in Providence. His favorite bird was the crested lark, called *lodola capellata* in Italian. "Sister lark with her little hood," he would say, "looks a little like us, and with her earth-colored plumage, she urges us to be satisfied with our poor and coarse habits. She is humble enough to seek her food in dust and dung. Soaring high (as she usually does) and praising the Lord with her song in the air, she teaches us to despise earthly things and to make our dwelling even now in Heaven."

Now of all the beasts that have had a place in the Franciscan legend, there is none more famous than the wolf of Gubbio whose edifying history is related by the *Fioretti*. While his "conversion" may have taken place in the last years of the saint's life, the reader will permit us to anticipate events a little and report it here.

Once Francis had stopped for the night, at the monastery of San Verecondo north of Assisi. Next morning when, mounted on a donkey, he was preparing to set off for Gubbio, the peasants warned him that the country was infested with ferocious wolves. But the saint replied, "What have my donkey and I done to my brother wolves for them to seek to devour us?" And he started off.

When he arrived at Gubbio people could talk of nothing else but the wolves. There was one wolf especially that claimed their attention. Of an extraordinary size and ferocity, always famished and furious, it ate not only animals, but men and women. People were so terrified that they went out from town armed from head to foot. But this fierce brute was accustomed to dining on the best-armed people, and the time came when hardly anybody dared venture outdoors. Now God, in order to make manifest his servant's sanctity, inspired him to confront the raging wolf; and although everyone implored him not to, Francis set forth with his companion.

The people of Gubbio climbed up on roof and rampart to see what was going to happen. Terrified, they soon saw the wolf lunging toward St. Francis with gaping jaws! But with the sign of the cross, Francis stopped it. "Come here, brother wolf!" he ordered. "In Christ's name, I forbid you to be wicked."

At these words, the wolf put its head down, and came and lay at Francis's feet.

"Brother wolf," continued the saint. "I am very sorry to hear of the dreadful crimes you have committed in these parts, going even so far as to kill creatures created in God's image. You deserve death by torture like the worst of murderers, and I understand why the people of Gubbio detest you. But I want to reconcile you with them, so that they will not be afraid of you anymore and you will not have to fear anything from them or their dogs."

The wolf made signs to show that these words were most pleasing to it. St. Francis continued: "If you agree to make peace, brother wolf, I will tell the people to feed you as long as you live, for I know that it was hunger that drove you to commit so many crimes. Do you promise never to harm man or beast again?"

The wolf bowed its head to show that it agreed, and to seal the pact, placed its right paw in the saint's outstretched hand. Francis then led the animal into town. The wolf followed its benefactor like a lamb. The pair halted on the public square where the people of Gubbio were gathered.

Francis then preached a fine sermon in which he showed how our sins draw down God's punishment in this world and plunge us into hell in the next—a fate much more fearful than the jaws of the fiercest wolf. He urged his hearers to do penance, adding: "My brother wolf here promises never to harm you again, if you will promise to feed him as long as he lives. I have received his pledge and I stand surety that he will keep his word."

As one man, the assembly swore that it would take care of the wolf. Again the wolf knelt, bowed its head, wiggled its ears and wagged its tail, and by placing its right paw in the saint's hand, once more indicated that it would keep the pact.

And this it never failed to do during the two years that it continued to live. The town took care of it, and the wolf came and went freely without molesting anyone, and without even the dogs barking at it. It died of old age, and the *Fioretti* declares that grief was universal at its death. For the people had become attached to it, and when they saw it peacefully trotting around town, they thought of St. Francis, whose memory was so dear to the inhabitants of Gubbio.

CHAPTER TEN

The Meeting With St. Dominic

ALTHOUGH THE EARLY biographers make no mention of it, historians generally admit that Francis was present at the Fourth Lateran Council. The assembly opened on November 11, 1215, at St. John Lateran, before a huge gathering. Representatives of the spiritual and temporal powers of the whole of Europe and of the Near East were present; and it was before four hundred bishops and archbishops, eight hundred abbots and prelates, besides the ambassadors from all ruling sovereigns, that Pope Innocent III pronounced the opening address.

Did the pope have a feeling that only a few months remained to him for carrying out the great idea of his reign? Certainly, His Holiness spoke as if he were soon to appear before God, declaring in particular that it was for no temporal ambition that he had convoked the Council, but moved by the sole desire of reforming the Church and recovering the Holy Land from the Muslims.

In his eyes the two enterprises were indissolubly linked. Since Christians at that time still looked on the repossession of Christ's tomb as a point of honor, the pope hoped that a victorious crusade would somehow restore Europe to a state of grace and renewed fervor, thanks to which the abuses favorable to the success of the

157

heretics might be abolished and the reform of the Church brought about.

After depicting the profanation of the Holy Places by the Saracens, the pontiff deplored the scandals dishonoring Christ's flock, threatening it with God's punishments if it did not reform. He recalled Ezekiel's famous vision in which the Lord God, his patience exhausted, cries out in a loud voice:

> "Approach, you who watch over the city, every one of you with his weapon of destruction in his hand." And I saw six men approaching from the upper gate which faces the north, every one of them with his deadly weapon in his hand. In the midst of them stood a man clad in linen with a writer's inkhorn at his belt.... And the Lord said to him: "Go through Jerusalem and mark with the sign of the TAU the foreheads of all those men who weep and lament over the abominations which are done in it." And He said to the others: "Pass through the city after him, and smite. Let not your eyes spare, *nor* show any pity. But spare and slay not those upon whom you shall see the TAU."

"And who are," continued the pope, "the six men charged with the divine vengeance? They are you, fathers of the Council, who with all the arms at your disposal—excommunication, depositions, suspension and interdict—shall smite without pity those unmarked with the atoning cross who persist in dishonoring the city of Christendom."

These words inspired the deliberations and resolutions of the Council. After condemning the errors of the Cathari and pantheists, the assembly decreed the establishment of schools of theology to remedy the ignorance of the priests, and commanded the faithful to confess and receive Communion at least once a year. It compelled Jews to wear a distinguishing badge, and strengthened the decrees against heretics and other unbelievers. Lastly, it enacted measures designed to curb the greed and ambition of the Roman prelates, measures whose benefits would, it was hoped, extend to the lower ranks of the clergy. But, as we know, these decrees remained a dead letter. Almost the same is to be said of the crusade set for the year 1217, but which lacking the support of the monarchs of Europe, had no important result.

Did the pope foresee these failures? It would seem so, to judge from the disillusioned tone of certain passages in his discourse.

How is it, then, that men date from his pontificate the religious reform destined to stave off for a few centuries the already menacing schisms and secessions? It was because this reform, given legal status in the canons of the Council, was instituted and implemented from this time onward, thanks chiefly to the Dominican and Franciscan Orders, both beneficiaries of papal favor and officially recognized at this time.

The Friars Minor obtained a stronger legal status during the Council. The latter having decreed that every new Order must adopt either the Rule of St. Benedict or St. Augustine, Innocent III declared that this measure did not include the Franciscans whose Rule he had approved five years previously. The Dominicans, however, adopted the Rule of St. Augustine and the Constitutions of Premontre and were approved the following year.

Some writers believe that it was the Council that persuaded Francis that he had a role to play in the reform of the Church. In support of this thesis, they allege the cult given by the Poverello from that time on to the letter TAU.

"The TAU," the pope had said, "has exactly the same form as the cross on which our Lord was crucified on Calvary. And only those," he added, "will be marked with this sign and will obtain mercy, who have mortified their flesh and conformed their life to that of the Crucified Savior."

Could one better preach the return to the Gospel demanded by contemporary reformers or more clearly condemn the lust for gold, honors, and pleasure with which they reproached the clergy? Incontestably, these words and many others manifest the Church's willingness for self-regeneration, and for absorbing the reform movements of the period.

How could Francis, who saw God's hand in everything, be other than impressed by this proclamation which expressed so well his ideal of life and his dream of an apostolate?

The fact is that the TAU, which the pope made the emblem of the reform, became from then on Francis's own blazon. He used it as a signature, painted it on his door, and placed it on his writings. Even his friends, it would seem, noticed the new use that he made of the saving talisman. For instance, there was Brother Pacifico who, before the Council, had seen his venerated father in a vision, pierced by a cross with four arms, and who in another vision after 1215 saw him marked with a TAU on his forehead.

We can hardly say that all this merely proves the Poverello's devotion to the Savior's Passion. Others have seen in it the proof that Francis felt as though the pope's appeal had been meant for him personally, and considered himself from that time onward as officially enrolled among the knights of the penitential crusade. Henceforth, he would be one of the scribes with the inkhorn charged with marking the foreheads of the elect, and his disciples would be invested with a sort of ecclesiastical ministry—to the point that instead of following their evangelical vocation as wandering penitents, these *jongleurs* of God would henceforth heed and obey the directives of the pope and Roman Curia.

It was perhaps his meeting with St. Dominic that served to confirm Francis in such sentiments. Twelve years older than the founder of the Franciscans, the Spaniard Dominic de Guzman had been until past forty a canon of the cathedral of Osma in the kingdom of Leon. He had always been devoted to study and to the practice of virtue. His true vocation was born in the course of a journey made to Rome in 1205 in company with Diego, his bishop. Innocent III, who had just appointed the Cistercians to convert the Albigensians, invited the two Spaniards to join them. The Cistercian methods had small chance of success. The people, seeing the papal legates appear with great pomp, followed by a train of mules loaded with baggage, had all the more reason for admiring the austerity of the Cathari apostles and for letting themselves be indoctrinated by them. The Cistercians soon gave up the attempt. The Bishop of Osma died in the midst of his labors, and it was Dominic who then became head of the mission. He recruited a few priests who were determined to make their doctrines their rule of life, and with them he continued his preaching. These "preachers" practiced rigorous penance, went barefoot, and organized debates sometimes lasting several days.

As we know, the Cathari refused to listen to reason; and as they were deemed to be endangering the whole social structure, it was decided to settle the affair by force of arms, and in 1209 to organize against them the famous crusade known as the Albigensian Crusade. In 1215 St. Dominic momentarily left the theater of war to attend the Council; and it was apparently on this occasion that he met for the first time the young founder of the Friars Minor.

In a dream, according to the Dominican chronicler, he had seen himself presented by the Virgin to our Lord, accompanied by a stranger who, like himself, was charged with converting the world. When the next day he perceived Francis in a street in Rome, he recognized in him the unknown man of his dream. He stopped Francis, narrated his vision to him, and embracing him, said, "Let us be comrades, and nothing on earth can prevail against us."

Unlike the Poverello, who knew nothing of what men learn in schools or of administration, Dominic was as endowed with a genius for organization as he was able in explaining the doctrine of St. Paul and in learnedly refuting heretics. His plans were in complete harmony with the pope's program; and in founding an Order which overcame the ignorance of the people by preaching, and that of the clergy by the establishment of schools of theology, he fully realized the views of Innocent III, if, indeed, he was not simply carrying out his instructions. Moreover, he enjoyed the entire confidence of Cardinal Hugolin, the most influential man of the Curia, and it was at the latter's residence that his most important interview with Francis took place.

A word must be said of this prelate whose influence was exercised in the Church for more than half a century, and whom we shall see appearing again on every page of this biography. A relative of Innocent III, to whom he owed his career, and whose ideas he had embraced, Hugolin became in 1216 the collaborator of Honorius III until the day when he himself, under the name of Gregory IX, was in turn elected pope. His pontificate, which lasted from 1227 to 1241, is one of the most amazing in history. The inflexible old man still led the fight in person against Frederick II, perhaps the most dreaded adversary the Roman Curia has ever known.

Handsome, brave, robust, and eloquent, possessed of unparalleled energy and skill, a great traveler and a scholar, this statesman was likewise a man of God. He seemed happy only in the society of monks, on whom he chiefly counted to reform the Church. His life was austere and his soul open to mystic inspiration; and in his decisions, the latter frequently outweighed the calculations of human policy.

Hugolin had a warm and faithful heart. "Dearest sister in Christ," he wrote to St. Clare, "ever since I have been compelled to leave you, I have been so sad and weep so much that I should die of grief, if prayer, my habitual remedy, were not my consolation."

He had no less affection for St. Francis, whom he venerated as one sent by God, and to whom he tried always not to cause pain. If he did not hold all Francis's views as capable of realization, he did at least, as long as the saint was alive, unceasingly seek with great tenderness to adapt his ideal to whatever he judged to be in the best interest of the Church and of souls.

Thus it was at the residence of Cardinal Hugolin and evidently in accord with him, that St. Dominic made the following proposition one day to the Little Poor Man. "Brother Francis," said he, grasping his hands, "I would like to see your Order and mine combined and living under the same Rule in the Church."

The administrative advantages envisaged by the papal statesman and by the perspicacious founder of the Preaching Friars are readily divined. Besides, they doubtless were able to observe some of the lack of organization in the Franciscan brotherhood, and foresaw that its leader might soon be out of his depth. Thomas of Celano does not tell us how Francis got out of this proposition, but it was skillfully evaded.

Francis likewise rejected another proposal the Cardinal made to the two saints in the same interview. "Since," said he, "the pastors in the early Church were poor and consumed by charity rather than by greed, why shouldn't we choose bishops from among your friars?" Here again it was his interest in Church reform that inspired the collaborator of Innocent III.

The two founders vied with each other, to let the other have the honor of replying first. Finally, Dominic spoke up. "My Lord," he said, "the dignity of their state should suffice my friars, and for my part I will not permit them to seek any other."

Francis then replied: "Your Lordship, my brothers are called *Fratres minors*, that they may not attempt to become *majors*. Their vocation teaches them ever to remain in a humble condition. Keep them in it, even against their will, if you would have them be useful to the Church. And never, I beg of you, permit them to become prelates."

Such was the way the saint conceived of the cooperation of his friars in the task of restoring the Christian spirit.

Before separating, writes Thomas of Celano, Dominic and Francis affectionately recommended themselves to each other. Dominic begged Francis to give him his cord as a souvenir. He obtained it only after much urging and put it on under his second tunic. As the Little Poor Man withdrew, Dominic said to those around him, "I tell you truthfully that there is not a religious who would not profit by following in the footsteps of so holy a man."

The two saints sometimes saw each other after that and continued to love each other.

But as soon as they were dead, their sons became bishops just like other priests; and it is plain that in Friar Thomas's eyes, some were too eager to do so, for he does not spare his reproaches. "Sons of

saints!" he exclaimed in 1245. "How can you unblushingly give full
rein to ambition and turn aside from the road leading to the eternal
city? You whose fathers wished only to know the path of humility!"

He likewise chided the jealous and the quarrelsome: "If the honors
you run after show that you are bastard sons," he wrote, "the envy
that you bear one another shows the depth of your degradation.
Whereas your fathers tenderly loved one another, you cannot even
bear the sight of one another. Why do you not turn your arms against
the demons, instead of biting and devouring one another? Your
sermons would surely bear more fruit if people knew you to be more
charitable, and they would have more faith in your words if they did
not sense the hate with which your hearts are filled." But the writer,
realizing that his rhetoric has carried him away, adds, "There are
friars here and there who do edify, and these words are not addressed
to them. I mean to speak only of bad religious, who, to my way of
thinking, ought to be expelled from their Order before they corrupt
others."

In conclusion, he turns to God, imploring him to make Dominicans
and Franciscans "kindly disposed toward each other."·

Certainly, in the main, one can say that his prayer has been heard
and that, to borrow Lacordaire's oratorical style, "the kiss of Dominic
and Francis has been transmitted from generation to generation on
the lips of their posterity."

There was a time, however, in which questions of scholasticism or
prestige incited some of these religious to such rivalry that the popes
themselves were obliged to intervene. But today when everybody
yields the pleasure of solving the unsolvable to everybody else, and
zeal for God's glory rarely moves people to annoy their neighbors,
Preachers and Minors are united in fellowship. And the memory of

the ancient quarrels is so blotted out that a century ago Fr. Lacordaire was able to pen in good faith that "never has the breath of jealousy sullied the spotless crystal of their centuries-old friendship."

CHAPTER ELEVEN

The Indulgence of the Portiuncula

ON SATURDAY, JULY 16, 1216, Jacques de Vitry arrived in Perugia where the Roman Curia was then in residence. Newly named Bishop of St. John D'Acre, he was about to take possession of his diocese and had therefore come to receive episcopal consecration, only to learn on arrival that Innocent III had died that very morning.

Men's manners were rude in those times, and the ambitious acted undeterred by convention. "There is no one who dies as solitary and forsaken as a pope," remarks the contemporary Thomas of Eccleston. Innocent III had indeed barely entered his death agony when all his courtiers forsook him to go off to their own affairs. But Francis, declares the same chronicler, had hastened from Assisi to pay final homage to the great pontiff who had understood his vocation and approved his work.

The pope's body was borne in an open coffin to the cathedral where the funeral was to take place the next day. "That was the day," writes Jacques de Vitry, "when I really understood the nothingness of earthly grandeur. Incredibly, the preceding night, thieves had entered and stripped the Pope of everything of value he had on. With my own eyes I saw his half-naked body lying in the middle of the church, already smelling."

He then describes the impression made on him by the Roman Curia the few weeks he was there. "The members are so taken up by temporal affairs and by lawsuits," he writes, "and so preoccupied by everything having to do with kings and states that one can scarcely touch upon questions pertaining to religion. All this caused me much grief.

"Happily," he continues, "I found in my travels one spectacle of quite another sort." And he goes on to describe to his correspondents in Lorraine the things he has just seen in Umbria six years after the journey to Rome of the first Friars Minor and four years after the clothing of St. Clare. We should give full weight to this unique on-the-spot evidence (in October 1216) of a traveler who had no reason for embellishing Franciscan origins. Nothing better confirms the writings of Thomas of Celano and the *Three Companions.*

"The thing that has consoled me," declared Jacques de Vitry, "is the sight of so many men and women who have abandoned their wealth and forsaken the world for love of Christ. These men, who bear the name of Friars Minor, are held in highest esteem by the Pope and cardinals. Utterly uninterested in temporal concerns, they devote all their efforts to withdrawing from the world souls in danger and inducing them to follow them. By the grace of God they have already achieved great success and made numerous converts; for their followers recruit others, and their hearers increase of themselves. As for their mode of life, it is that of the primitive Church, where, as the Scripture says, the multitude of believers had but one heart and soul. During the day they are to be found in the cities and villages, preaching or working. At night they return to their hermitages to retire into a solitary spot to pray.

"The women dwell together in refuges near the cities, living by the work of their hands without accepting any gifts. And they are so humble that any veneration shown them confuses and displeases them.

The new bishop next describes the Chapters of the Friars Minor:

> Once a year the men of this Order assemble at a place agreed upon to rejoice in the Lord and to eat together. There, taking counsel of upright men, they adopt and promulgate holy laws which are then approved by the pope. Then, separating for another year, they scatter throughout Lombardy, Tuscany, and even to Apulia and Sicily.
>
> Recently Brother Nicholas, a holy and religious man, and compatriot of the Pope, left the Curia to join them. But he was recalled by the Supreme Pontiff who could not get along without him. My own opinion is that God has determined to make use of these poor and simple men to save a multitude of souls before the end of the world, and to denounce by their example the remissness of our prelates, who like dumb dogs refuse to bark.

The vacancy of the apostolic see lasted only two days. "It is true," says Ciaconius, "that to hasten the election, the Perugians had decided to lock up the members of the Curia and to progressively decrease their rations." Of the nineteen cardinals present, two were apparently going to cause a stalemate: Guido, Bishop of Palestrina, and Hugolin dei Conti, whom we know already. To hasten matters, the electors charged these two favorites with the task of electing a candidate. They chose Honorius, a man of advanced age and in poor health, but who nevertheless lived until 1227. "An excellent and pious old man has just been elected pope," wrote Jacques de Vitry, "and he is furthermore a plain and benevolent man who has given almost all his fortune to the poor."

Francis must have thrilled with joy at learning of the election of a pope so filled with love for God and the poor. The Lord himself, he thought, has taken in hand the cause of the holy Gospel; the great projects announced by Innocent III would now be realized; the new crusade already being preached would restore Christ's tomb to Christians; and prospects for the reform of the Church appeared most bright.

Did these fair hopes play a part in determining the extraordinary step that Francis made a few weeks later? For it was at this time that he came to ask of Honorius III the famous Indulgence of the Portiuncula or Great Pardon of Assisi.

In his Lateran discourse, Innocent III had pointed out as marked with the TAU three kinds of predestined men: those who would consent to take the cross, those unable to go on the Crusade who would busy themselves at combating heresy, and, finally, those sinners who would work at the task of self-reform. Did these words stir up a desire in St. Francis to put the whole world in the state of grace, by making it easy for those who could not set out for the Orient or who were too poor to gain an indulgence, to share in the universal redemption? Whatever it was, on a summer's day in 1216, he took Brother Masseo with him and set out for Perugia.

"The previous night," writes Bartholi, "Christ and His Mother, surrounded by heavenly spirits, had appeared to him in the chapel of St. Mary of the Angels."

"Francis," said the Lord, "ask of Me whatever you will for the glory of God and the salvation of men."

"Lord," replied the saint, "I pray You by the intercession of the Virgin, Advocate of mankind and present here, to grant an indulgence to all those who visit this church."

The Blessed Virgin bowed before her Son to show that she seconded the request, and her petition was granted. Christ next bade Francis to go to Perugia to obtain the desired favor from the pope.

As soon as he was in Honorius's presence, Francis said to him: "I recently repaired for Your Holiness a church dedicated to Mary, God's Blessed Mother. I now come on behalf of those who shall visit this church on the day of its dedication, to solicit an indulgence which they may be able to gain without an offering."

"It is fitting that those who desire an indulgence should make an offering," observed the pope. "And how many years' indulgence do you desire? One year? Three years?"

"Holy Father, what are three years?"

"Do you want six years? Seven years even?"

"It is not years, but souls I desire!"

"What do you mean by 'souls'?"

"My meaning is that everyone who shall enter this church, confessed and absolved, should receive remission of all his sins, both as to their guilt and penalty."

"But this is a thing unheard of, and quite contrary to the usages of the Roman Curia!"

"But, Holy Father! It is not of myself that I speak, but I have been sent by Jesus Christ our Lord!"

"Well, then! I grant it to you. In the Lord's name let it be done as you desire!"

At these words the cardinals present begged the pope to take back his words, pointing out that such a favor would be hurtful to the indulgences of the Holy Land and Rome, which from then on would be counted as nothing. But the pope refused to recall his words. His counselors besought him to at least restrict as much as possible this unheard-of favor.

Addressing himself to Francis then, Honorius said, "The indulgence is granted in perpetuity, but only once a year; that is, from the first vespers of the day to those of the following day."

Promptly withdrawing, Francis bowed and was already started for the door when the pope recalled him. "So you are leaving, simple little man, without any document?"

"Your word is enough for me, Holy Father! If this indulgence is willed by God, He will manifest it Himself. My charter is the Virgin Mary, my notary is Christ, and the holy angels are my witnesses."

So he set out with Brother Masseo for the Portiuncula.

The travelers had been walking for an hour when they came to the village of Collestrada, above a knoll halfway between Assisi and Perugia. There Francis, worn out with fatigue, fell asleep. When he awoke he received a revelation which he disclosed to his companion. "Brother Masseo," he said, "know that what has been granted me on earth has just been ratified in Heaven."

The dedication of the chapel took place on the following second of August. Borrowing the words used by Solomon at the inauguration of the Jerusalem temple, the liturgy of the feast seemed chosen for the occasion. "Lord God," it reads, "is it to be thought that You should indeed dwell on earth? Behold, the heavens themselves cannot contain You, and how much less this house which I have built! Let Your eyes, however, be open day and night upon this house. And when strangers come from distant lands to pray there, listen to them, O Lord, and send them away forgiven."

Before the bishops of Assisi, Perugia, Todi, Spoleto, Gubbio, Nocera, and Foligno, Francis, looking down at the crowd from a wooden pulpit, told them the great news.

"I desire to send you all to Paradise," he cried, "by announcing to you the indulgence which has been granted me by Pope Honorius. Know then that all those present, and those who shall come in the future to pray to this church, will receive the remission of their sins. I should have liked to have had this indulgence granted for a week, but I have only succeeding in getting it for one day."

Such is, according to the documents to be considered presently, the origin of the famous Pardon of Assisi. We must confess that the indulgence aroused strong opposition.

Things were not like they are now, when every Catholic can gain plenary indulgences without loosening his purse strings or going outside his parish. At this period, only pilgrims to the Holy Land, to Rome, and to St. James in Galicia could obtain such favors. However rich they might be in relics, other shrines were infinitely less well endowed, having only a few days or few years of indulgences to offer visitors.

Placed thus on the same footing with the three most celebrated pilgrimages in Christendom, the Portiuncula promptly lowered the status of those innumerable sanctuaries from which monks and clergy derived fame and subsistence. That they should have exerted every effort to fight it is understandable. Do we not see them—on the roads or at the ports—going out to meet pilgrims bound for Assisi, to "prove" to them that the Franciscan privilege was false and urge them to go back?

Today the only moot question is no longer whether the indulgence be valid—for this the Church has many times confirmed—but if it owes its origin to the initiative of St. Francis.

For some critics the saint's trip to Perugia with the verbal concession wrung from Pope Honorius is a legend. For others it is a proven historical fact.

The first group allege the silence of the ancient biographers, who they say would not have failed, had the story been true, to report so glorious a fact. Neither Thomas of Celano, St. Bonaventure, nor *The Three Companions* make any mention of it. It is only some fifty years after the event that testimony in its favor appears. What credence then is to be placed in evidence so tardy?

Advocates of authenticity reply that the silence of the first biographers was necessary; and that therefore it has no weight against evidence which, for all its lateness, is no less conclusive. If these early authors remained silent, say they, it was because they had every reason to do so.

It must be recalled that Francis had obtained the indulgence against the wishes of the cardinals, who considered it harmful to the success of the crusade; and had the indulgence been noised abroad, these prelates would most assuredly have had it revoked. The saint knew it; and with his horror of entering into conflict with the clergy and of soliciting privileges of the Roman Curia, religiously refrained from requesting confirmation from the apostolic chancery. Furthermore, according to Coppoli, he forbade Brother Leo to mention it, leaving its later revelation to God. It is germane to add that the Franciscans themselves, charged with collecting crusade funds, were opposed to any mention of a favor capable of jeopardizing the effects of their preaching. Were not these sufficient reasons for the silence of biographers writing at that time?

But time marched on; the era of the crusades had closed; and the Friars Minor had become powerful enough in the Church to shout from the housetops a secret already out. In 1277, acting on orders from Jerome of Ascoli, Minister General and future pope, Brother Angelo, and Provincial of Umbria, began to collect notarized testimony capable of confounding the adversaries of the Great Pardon.

Among the witnesses named, we find Benedict and Rainerio of Arezzo, Pietro Zalfani, and Giacomo Coppoli. The two friars, Benedict and Rainerio, testified that Brother Masseo had told them the history of the indulgence many times in the words we have reported above. Signor Pietro Zalfani of Assisi, who had been present as a youth at the dedication of St. Mary of the Angels, gave a summary of St. Francis's address on this occasion. Signor Giacomo Coppoli of Perugia attested that he had heard from the lips of Brother Leo the story of the circumstances under which the indulgence had been granted.

It is noteworthy that at the period of these depositions the Great Pardon had already become very popular, and soon pilgrims from all over Italy were converging on St. Mary of the Angels. It was at this time, around 1308, that owing to redoubled attacks from the enemies of the Portiuncula, Teobaldo Offreducci, Bishop of Assisi, had a solemn diploma drawn up, with the idea of putting an end to objections.

This official act was evidently most vexing for the adversaries of the indulgence, as it still is for modern critics who deny its authenticity. The document reports in detail how the great favor was obtained. It reproduces the sworn testimony of those witnesses already named, to which is added that of Brother Marino, a nephew of Brother Masseo. Then it inveighs (with a bit of name-calling) against the envious, the jealous, and the ignorant, who "with their foul mouths" dare to impugn a privilege recognized in Italy just as much as it is in France or Spain; a privilege which for so many years (the document continues) has been openly preached before the Roman Curia, to which Pope Boniface VIII has just shown himself favorable anew, and of which the cardinals themselves are eager to avail themselves to obtain pardon for their sins.

Teobaldo Offreducci's diploma did not reduce the diehards to silence. But their attacks were unavailing, since from this time onward, August second of every year brought to St. Mary of the Angels a multitude of pilgrims from all over Europe to obtain "without having to make an offering, the remission of the penalty due to their sins."

Later on, as we know, the popes generously extended the same favor to many churches in the entire world; and since that time only the learned continue to dispute the Franciscan indulgence.

CHAPTER TWELVE

Missions in Christian Lands

FOLLOWING THE EXAMPLE of King Arthur, who every year at Pentecost assembled the knights of the Round Table in chapter, Francis early formed the custom of holding capitular assemblies. These took place at the Portiuncula, giving Francis an opportunity to see his first companions again, to become acquainted with friars who had recently entered the Order, to give paternal advice to all, and to add to the Rule, after a general consultation, some new regulation deemed necessary.

In the beginning, these meetings were quite closely spaced. They were held at Pentecost and Michaelmas; but in time they took place less frequently; and commencing with 1221, they were held only every three years.

The most celebrated of them all is the "Chapter of Mats," described by the *Fioretti*. Present were five thousand friars divided in the plain around St. Mary of the Angels into silent groups of sixty, a hundred, or three hundred men, whose sole occupation was prayer, charitably rendering service to each other, or conversing of spiritual things, a group so disciplined that it could have been taken for an army encamped. As it was summer, some of the friars slept outdoors, others in huts of reed, and all of them slept on the bare ground or on straw, with a stone or piece of wood for a pillow. It was these many temporary shelters set up in the fields that gave this famous chapter its name.

Hugolin, affirms the *Fioretti*, came every day without fail to St. Mary of the Angels. We can picture the immense procession of Friars Minor going to meet the prelate. From Perugia, where the Curia was staying, a brilliant escort of clerks and nobles, in addition to St. Dominic and seven Friars Preachers, accompanied him. Hugolin was moved to tears at sight of the Poverello and his thousands of sons, their ascetic faces beaming with virile joy and zeal. Recalling, perhaps, the pope's words at the Lateran Council, he exclaimed, "Here is the army of Christ's knights all ready for battle!"

Then, with one of those instinctive gestures of the born leader, the cardinal dismounted, and casting aside his sumptuous cloak and his shoes, walked barefoot to the chapel to say Mass. Francis preached the sermon, taking as his subject these verses he knew so well:

> We have promised great things,
> And still greater have been promised to us.
> Let us keep the promises we have made;
> Let us long for the fulfillment of those made to us;
> Pleasure is fleeting, but its punishment eternal;
> Suffering is light, but the glory to come is infinite.

The saint exhorted his friars to obey the Church and to pray for all Christendom. He urged them to be patient in adversity, pure as angels, to live at peace with God and man, and be humble and gracious toward all. He moreover counseled them to despise the world and to love the poverty taught by the Gospel. In conclusion, he said, "I command all of you here present to be diligent in prayer and praise to God without care for your bodily nourishment, for Christ has expressly promised to provide for you." The order was immediately carried out, and one and all went off to pray.

St. Dominic did not fail to observe that all this was most imprudent, and he expected disaster to befall these thousands of hungry and heedless men. But the Lord showed that feeding his poor belonged to him; for a long procession of donkeys and mules was soon seen arriving at St. Mary of the Angels, laden with bread and wine, beans, cheese, and all sorts of victuals that the inhabitants of Perugia, Spoleto, Foligno, Assisi, and the surrounding regions were bringing to Francis and his sons. They even brought plates, goblets, and all other necessary dishes. Not only did no one go hungry, but when the chapter was over, a number of friars had to stay at the Portiuncula to finish the food that remained.

Meanwhile, Dominic had recognized the intervention of Providence in all this; and after apologizing for having taxed Francis with blundering, he promised to observe evangelical poverty henceforth himself and to make its practice mandatory on his sons.

"Now the zeal of the Friars Minor," declares the *Fioretti* in conclusion, "incited them to too many corporal austerities. Some of them who wore hair shirts and iron chains about their waists had become unable to pray; some friars had even died. When Francis heard about these things, this most mild and prudent father commanded those using such instruments of penance to take them off at once and put them in a pile. And no fewer than five hundred of these instruments were counted—a great heap which the Saint ordered to be left there. After which, encouraging his sons once more in good works and telling them to pass through the world without stain, he sent them back to their provinces filled with joy, with God's blessing and his own."

If we cannot identify this "Chapter of Mats," of which the account in the *Fioretti* is confusing and full of errors, we do have four General Chapters for which we have accurate information. The first two were held in 1217 and 1219 and decided upon the establishment of foreign missions. The two others took place in 1221 and 1224, and coincided, as we shall see, with the most painful period in the life of the Little Poor Man.

The rapid extension of the Brotherhood called for the introduction of the elements, at least, of organization. With this the Chapter of 1217 was concerned. It divided the Order into "provinces." These took the name of the region in which they were established and had a "Minister Provincial" at their head. In the course of time, certain important provinces were subdivided into "custodies" presided over by a "custos." On the lowest level were the residences, hermitages, and friaries, under the jurisdiction of the "guardians."

Those innovations did not prevent the founder from wishing to preserve in his religious family the spirit of quasi-equality that had prevailed in the beginning. Nothing in the titles of the superiors was to include the idea of authority or ambition. Avoiding the designations of "masters" or "priors" so as not to give the impression that they were above the others, Francis had given them the name of "ministers," "custodians," or "guardians," to indicate that they were at the service of the friars rather than at their head. In his eyes, as we have seen, their role was that of a mother caring for her children. "I have chosen him as mother," he said of Brother Elias, named Minister General. "He is the pious mother of the Province of France," he said in the same way of Brother Pacifico, designated as Minister Provincial in that country.

And this is the way in which the superiors were pledged to justify their titles. "Let them remember," said Francis, "the words of the Lord, 'I am come not to be served, but to serve.' They ought, then, to be the servants of the other friars, visit them frequently, instruct, encourage, and watch over them, like a shepherd over his sheep. And let the Brothers obey them in all things not contrary to our vocation. And in their actions, let all be inspired by the holy Gospel, which commands us not to do to others what we would not wish done to us, and to do to others what we would wish them to do to us. In fine, let the Minister remember that the souls of the Brothers have been entrusted to him, and that if one of them should perish by his fault, it is of him that our Lord will demand an accounting."

It was following the Chapter of 1217 that the first departure of the friars who were to establish the Order outside of Italy took place. In calling for volunteers of this knightly expedition, Francis had not concealed its dangers. No one, for example, had either sent for them or was expecting them in the lands where he was sending them; they themselves were ignorant of the language and customs of those far-off regions; they were going forth without money and without authorization to receive it; and in accordance with their father's will, they were likewise leaving without letter of recommendation from pope, bishop, or prince—a factor laying them wide open to suspicion.

As was his custom, the saint had resolved to set the example. "As it is not fitting," he said, "for me to send you into privation and insult without exposing myself to them also, I beg of you to ask God which direction I ought to take for His greater glory." When he was enlightened on this point, he told them his decision: "In the name of our Lord, Jesus Christ, of His glorious Mother, and of all the saints," said Francis joyously, "I choose the province of France. For the French are especially dear to me, because they have a greater reverence than other people for the Holy Eucharist."

As the volunteers who had responded to his appeal stood before him, Francis enjoined them: "Always go two by two, walk in all humility and modesty, praying much, and refraining from vain speech and observing silence from sunrise to Terce. Even while traveling, behave as if you were in your hermitage and carry your cell with you. For your cell is your body which goes with you everywhere, and the hermit who occupies it is your soul, whose constant care should be to remain united to God in thought and prayer."

With these words, he blessed them, and then with Brother Masseo set out toward the north. The author of the *Fioretti* gives us a poetic account of the incident that marked the beginning of the journey:

> Arriving at some village along the road, they were hungry and so separated to beg their bread. To those who did not know him, Francis was of unassuming appearance, so that all that he collected that day were a few old crusts. Brother Masseo, meanwhile, with his more impressive appearance, had received some large pieces of fresh bread. When the two travelers, who had agreed to meet near a fountain, compared their collection, Francis could not contain his joy at his companion's success:
>
> "Brother Masseo! Brother we are unworthy of such abundance and of such a treasure!"
>
> "'But dear father, how can you speak of abundance in the face of such poverty? Not only do I see here neither table nor servants, but we lack even a bowl and a knife!"
>
> "Our incomparable wealth," replied Francis, "consists precisely in our not owing to man's ingenuity but to God's providence alone this alms of bread, this fine stone which serves as our table, and this clear fountain where we may

quench our thirst. So we ought to pray God to love ever more the noble treasure of holy poverty."

Joyfully they ate their bread and drank from the fountain. Then, singing hymns, they arose and went on their way. Suddenly, Francis was inspired to change their itinerary, "Dear beloved Brother," said he to his companion, "let us first go to Rome and pray the Apostles Peter and Paul to obtain for us the inestimable grace of holy poverty."

They turned back, and once more Francis began to sing the praises of his beloved lady:

"It is blessed Poverty, Brother Masseo, who makes us trample under foot earthly and transient things. She it is who removes the obstacles which prevent us from attaining God. It is she again who permits us even on earth to converse with angels; and finally, it is she who unites us to the risen Christ returning to His Father, raising us up to Heaven even in this life.

"Truly, Brother Masseo, coarse vessels like ourselves are unworthy to contain such divine riches. So let us go and pray the holy Apostles, perfect lovers of this Gospel pearl, to obtain the favor we desire. And by their intercession, may Christ, the teacher and most exalted example of holy Poverty, vouchsafe to make us true observers and humble disciples of this dear and most loveable virtue."

Perhaps the *Fioretti* was right when it says that the Little Poor Man wanted to go to Rome before setting out for France. For he had often gone and knelt at the tomb of the apostles when on the eve of making an important decision.

In any case, it was at Florence that he met Cardinal Hugolin who was preaching the Crusade in Tuscany. The cardinal, knowing the opposition which the brotherhood still aroused and the inner perils threatening it, said to his friend: "You must not cross the Alps while there are prelates in the Curia who persist in looking with disfavor on your Order. Do not go, if you want cardinals who, like me, are favorable to it, to be able to defend it successfully."

"But would it not be shameful to send my friars far off, and to stay here myself sheltered from the perils they must face?"

"You were wrong to let them go off to those distant regions where they risk starving to death."

"My Lord," replied the saint, "God wants my friars to spread out over the whole world; and not only will Christian lands give them a good reception, but even infidels will receive them and be converted by their words."

If the cardinal, says the *Speculum*, did agree that this was the vocation of the Friars Minor, he nonetheless persuaded Francis not to leave Italy. Instead, it was Brother Pacifico who introduced the Franciscan Order in France.

Brother Pacifico was a former troubadour who had been crowned poet laureate by the emperor, and had ever since borne the name of the "King of Verses." "A poor strayed soul," writes Celano, "the king of those who compose light songs, attached to the chariot of iniquity by the thongs of vanity, he walked in darkness until that day wherein Divine Goodness deigned to bring him back to righteousness."

He had gone to visit one of his relatives in religion at a convent of former Benedictine nuns who became Poor Ladies near San Servino in the march of Ancona, when he heard St. Francis preach. At once he was conquered by the seraphic poet, and as Francis continued to exhort him to do good, "A truce on words!" cried the poet laureate. "What I ask of you is to take me away from men immediately so that I can belong to the Great Emperor!"

Francis gave him the habit of the Order and called him Pacifico because of the peace that from that moment filled his heart. Pacifico was to have much to do to preserve this peace in the trials that awaited him in Paris.

There the friars who were lodging in a dependency of the Abbey St. Denis were taken at first for Albigensians with subversive designs. Unfortified by references, all that they could show was their Rule, which they presented to Bishop Peter of Nemours and to the theologians of the Sorbonne. These conceded the Rule to be Catholic, but wrote to the pope, nevertheless, for further information. On June 11, 1219, Honorius replied that the Franciscans were excellent Catholics, deserving to be well treated. This attestation did not prevent certain bishops from continuing to harass them, and a Bull of May 29, 1220, was required to proclaim anew that the friars offered no danger to public security.

The King of Verses left France in 1223 or 1224, and was succeeded by Gregory of Naples. The latter undertook to build on the place called "Vauvert" (on the present site of the Luxembourg) a vast and beautiful convent, little in keeping with holy poverty. Francis learned of his ostentatious dwelling and ordered it destroyed. He was not obeyed; but in 1229 the barely finished building collapsed; and as hell was held responsible, the demon who carried on operations there was thenceforth held in horror by the Parisians. Later on, the "demon Vauvert" became by corruption the *diable vert*. The convent itself, rebuilt larger than before, soon sheltered men like Alexander of Hales, St. Bonaventure, Roger Bacon, Duns Scotus, and Occam;

and for a century, together with the rival convent of the Dominicans, was the most important intellectual center of Christianity.

It is especially to the contemporary chroniclers Jordan of Giano and Thomas of Eccleston that we owe our knowledge of the fate of the friars sent to other countries.

Those who went inside Portugal were treated as undesirables up to the time the royal family granted them their protection. Queen Urraca saw at once that they were good servants of God; and, thanks to her, King Alfonso II permitted them to settle in Lisbon and Guimarrens. The Infanta Sancia was no less favorable to them. She made them welcome in her own district of Alenquer; and such was her solicitude for them that she always kept a few spare habits in her palace for friars returning from travel who needed a change.

It was at the convent of Alenquer that a very recollected friar was living whom the noble Maria of Garcia desired to have as her spiritual director. But he fled her with as much obstinacy as she put into pursuing him.

"Bring me," he said to her one day, "a bundle of straw and we will set it on fire." (The unduly devout lady would have brought him the moon.)

When the bundle had been reduced to ashes, the friar said to her, "Know that God's servant gains no more from consorting with women than straw does from consorting with fire." And this ended their relations.

Directed by Elias, the friars also set out for Syria. This, according to Jordan, took place in 1217. Few details are given, beyond the entry in Syria of Caesar of Speyer.

The mission to Hungary is described more at length. The friars had embarked with a Hungarian bishop returning to his homeland;

but he apparently abandoned the mission too soon to its fate, for our missionaries were cruelly treated in that land. Apparently, they were taken for religious charlatans, come in penitential garb to exploit the devotion of the people. They were driven from the cities; and in the country, farmers set their dogs on them, and herdsmen chased them, jabbing them in the back with their pointed sticks.

"Perhaps it is our clothes they want," said one of the friars, and to obey the Gospel, they took off their cloaks. As people continued to beat them, they took off their habits. Evidently, this too was not enough, for they had to give up their breeches.

"I know one of them," writes Jordan, "who lost his breeches fifteen times. The idea finally came to him of smearing them with cow dung. Only then did the disgusted shepherds leave them alone." Understandably, all were in a hurry to leave this inhospitable country.

Still worse was the reception accorded the friars in Germany. They arrived, says Jordan, under the leadership of John of Penna, to the number of about sixty, none of whom knew German. Having learned the word "Ja," they answered "Ja" the first night when people asked if they were hungry; and this time they were well fed. But the trouble was that they likewise replied "Ja" the next day when people inquired if they were those cursed heretics who, after corrupting Lombardy, had come now to infect Germany. The rumor spread that the plague of the Cathari was invading the empire. So the friars were arrested, imprisoned, bound naked to the pillory, and flogged until they bled. They speedily agreed that this country was no place for them; and leaving hurriedly, they went back and told the Italians that no people in the world were more dreadful than the Germans, and that anyone returning to them was plainly hankering for martyrdom.

As Jordan notes, the missions of 1217 "thus came to naught." It is true, he added with the author of Ecclesiastes, that the hour of success had not yet come and that there was a time for everything under the sun.

The moment soon came for Germany to show herself more merciful toward the Friars Minor.

"I was present at the Chapter," writes Jordan, "in which a few years later [1221] Francis, seated at the feet of Brother Elias and too feeble to speak himself, plucked Elias by his habit and whispered something in his ear. 'Brethren,' said Elias, 'the Brother (for Francis was so called in the Order) wishes to observe that we have forgotten to mention the Germans. There are, he says, many good Christians among them, like those we often see pass by here with long staffs and big boots, going to the tomb of the Apostles. The Brother is aware that those among you who went to Germany a while back were harshly treated; so he does not want to force anyone to go there. But if there are any who desire to go of their own free will, he will bless them more than if they were to set sail for missions beyond the seas. Let those, then, who want to go to Germany step to one side.'"

At this appeal, about ninety friars took seats apart, to await further directions.

"I recall," continues Jordan, "that at this period there were two things for which I especially prayed God daily; first, not to fall into the Albigensian heresy, and secondly, not to die a victim of Teutonic fury. A witness to the courage of these ninety heroes, I, who regretted failing to make the acquaintance of the Brothers beheaded at Morocco, did not wish to miss the opportunity of seeing the future martyrs.

"So I went up to them, and going from one man to another, I asked them their names. One of them told me that he was Brother Palmerius, adding, 'You are coming with us too!' and laughing, made me sit down beside him. He was a deacon, a native of Monte Gargano, a pleasant fellow, who later on became guardian of the friary of Magdeburg. I thought this one of his usual jokes. 'No! No! I replied, 'I just came over to make your acquaintance.' But my struggles were in vain, and Palmerius and his friends kept me in their midst.

"They were just finishing reading the list of religious, divided by provinces, and I had just learned that the provincial of Germany was Caesar of Speyer, when the latter approached our group to choose the men he was going to take with him. His attention was called to me. 'Not at all!' I protested. 'I have never wanted to go to Germany! Besides, it's a cold country and bad for my health.' These protests made an impression on the new provincial and on those around me. So they took me to Brother Elias to have him settle the matter. 'Brother,' said the Minister General, 'I command you under holy obedience to make up your mind and tell us whether or not you want to go to Germany.'

"On hearing holy obedience mentioned, great was my perplexity. On the one hand, I did not want to say 'No,' and thus follow my own will. On the other hand, I feared by saying 'Yes' to expose myself rashly to martyrdom and to deny the Faith under torture. So I went to consult my friend, that holy friar I told about above who had lost his breeches so many times in Hungary. He advised me to tell Brother Elias that I had no preference, and that I would obey whatever he commanded. This I did; and Brother Elias ordered me to accompany Brother Caesar. We set off to the number of twenty-seven, twelve clerics and fifteen lay brothers; and that is how I was one of those who introduced the Order in Germany."

The travelers were soon en route by way of Trent, Bolanzo, Sterzing, and Mittenwald. They went in small groups, so as not to give the impression of an invasion. Among them were John of Piano de Carpine who later went to central Asia, our friend Thomas of Celano, who seems to have returned very soon to Italy, and several eloquent preachers. Sometimes the missionaries were hospitably received by prelates; and at other times they were met at the door by an evasive *God berad!* ("May God provide"), which reduced them to eating forgotten turnips in the fields.

Eventually, they became most successful, however, in their enterprise, won the friendship of the people, made many recruits, and founded friaries all over Germany, emigrating into Bohemia, Poland, Romania, and as far as Norway.

It would appear that Brother Juniper had some imitators among them; for one day in the year 1222 the religious of Salzburg, on receiving a letter from Brother Caesar directing them to be present at the provincial Chapter "if they wished," they were plunged by these last words into deep consternation. Did their superior doubt their obedience and had he lost confidence in them? So, by common consent, they set out and walked two hundred and fifty miles on foot to Speyer to clear up this mystery and protest their submission. The Minister Provincial, delighted to see them again, smilingly promised to write more clearly in future.

Brother Jordan likewise frankly admits his own troubles and blunders. At Erfurt, where he was guardian, and where for a number of years the community was living in what had been an abandoned church and nunnery, the magistrates came to him and offered to build a cloister. "A cloister?" replied Jordan. "I have never seen one. I don't even know what it is. But if you want to do us a favor, just build us a little house near a stream where it will be easy for us to wash our feet every day."

A few years later, returning from Italy where Thomas of Celano had presented him with some relics of St. Francis, he had to stop at the friary of Eisenach. The porter surprisingly refused to let him in and told him to go to the door of the church. As he was waiting outside in some astonishment, he finally saw his fellow friars arriving, who then escorted him into the church with candles and hymns. Unable to comprehend why he had merited such a reception, he suddenly remembered the relics he was carrying. "And I," he writes, "who up till then had not been such a great admirer of St. Francis, was compelled to admit that if people arranged ceremonies like that in his honor, then he really must be a saint."

Finally, Jordan's *Chronicle* relates the journey he made with a companion to Rome to bring the grievances of the Saxon friars against Brother Elias to the pope.

This was in 1238. Gregory IX had not yet risen when the two friars unceremoniously burst into his bedchamber. The pope ordered them to leave. But rushing up to his bed, Jordan began burrowing under the bedclothes, and, extracting the pope's foot, covered it with kisses as he murmured, "Oh, Holy Father, do not drive us away, I beg of you, for we do not have any such precious relics in Saxony!"

The former Cardinal Hugolin, who knew his Friars Minor, could not help laughing. "He sat up in bed," writes Jordan, "listened to us kindly, and after saying that we did well to appeal to him, he promised to put a stop to the actions of Brother Elias." The latter was removed from office the following year.

The establishment of the friars in England encountered fewer difficulties than elsewhere. It is true that it took place somewhat later, after the Chapter of 1223; so we are anticipating a little in speaking of it here.

The *Chronicle* of Thomas of Eccleston describes the beginnings of this English province, whose fervor brought so much joy to St. Francis. The founders were nine in number, including their head, Blessed Agnellus Pisa, who all embarked on a boat belonging to the Benedictines of Fécamp, landing at Dover on September 10, 1224. Some settled at Canterbury, and others at London, and still others at Oxford, where a number of students and illustrious professors soon joined them. All showed as much zeal for study as for holy poverty.

They took a hand themselves in the construction of the friary at Oxford; and some high prelate or other, who had recently entered the Order, could be seen carrying stones and mortar like a mason's apprentice. Those taking courses at the university had to walk a long way through the snow barefoot and wade through swamps up to their knees.

The chapel of the friary of Canterbury was done by a carpenter in a day. At first, only three friars were in residence, one of whom was so crippled that the other two had to carry him to the choir at night to chant Matins. But so merry were they in their extreme poverty that the Office was sometimes interrupted by the infectious gales of laughter that would sweep over them.

Eccleston speaks at length of Brother Solomon, the first novice recruited in England. This young man, who up to then had been noted for his elegance, took the bowl and went begging according to the Rule. When he knocked at his sister's door, she herself opened it. She handed him some bread, turned her face away, and exclaimed: "Cursed be the hour I ever saw you thus!" But he took the bread with great joy and went off.

Brother Solomon was happy at being treated by his family as St. Francis had been. Entrusted with the care of the sick, he begged for them flour and figs which he put in his hood, and faggots which he carried under his arm. Once, in winter time, he took so ill that the other friars feared he would die. To add to their distress, they had no wood for a fire to warm him. Then, writes Eccleston, holy charity suggested to them the same stratagem used by pigs in a like extremity. They clustered close around him and rubbed themselves against him until they succeeded in reviving him.

The old chronicler also holds up as an example the holy friar Geoffrey of Salisbury to whom Lord Alexander of Bassingbourn came one day for confession. As the latter rattled off his sins without compunction, Brother Geoffrey began to weep so much that Lord Alexander was also moved to tears, became genuinely converted, and finally decided to enter the Order.

The Franciscans prospered wondrously in England. Less than ten years after their arrival, they had in their ranks men like Adam Marsh, John of Reading, Haymo of Faversham, and Richard of Cornwall; and twenty years later, they possessed no less than forty-nine friaries in the country. They were known at first by the name of "Brethren of the Order of the Apostles," so greatly did their way of life evoke in the eyes of the people that of the humble founders of the Church.

CHAPTER THIRTEEN

Missions in Pagan Lands

IT IS PLAIN that toward the year 1219, where we are now, the relations of the Little Poor Man with his followers were no longer the same. Up to this time, almost everyone had followed him as a venerated father and infallible oracle. But from now on, many would oppose his ideal and attempt to evade his authority.

It was inevitable that, growing and spreading as it did, the Brotherhood should become less homogeneous and less fervent. The friars who had received their training at Rivo Torto were now submerged in the mass. The immense majority of the Order was composed of religious who had not been formed by St. Francis. A great many hardly knew him. The superiors or ministers were recruited for the most part among the outstanding and influential clerics, to many of whom it was repugnant to be led by "a man without learning," a man indeed considered an impractical and even dangerous visionary by some prelates in high places.

Certainly, in coming to the Chapter of 1219, these ministers did not bring with them a definite reform slate; but they nonetheless made no effort to conceal their dissatisfaction and their own inclinations. What they wanted, in fine, was for the Order to bear a closer resemblance to other religious congregations, to be able to devote themselves to study, to practice a poverty less strict, and to profit by ecclesiastical favors.

They had a good opportunity, for instance, to show how the friars, for lack of official references, had been expelled from countries of the Empire and were threatened with a similar fate in France. Now, if Francis did not reproach others for having recourse to Bulls, exemptions, and privileges, he himself would have none of them. It was not his idea to be either protected or preserved. Had not his beloved Christ been compelled to flee before his enemies? Had he availed himself of immunity and protection at the scourging and crucifixion?

So, far from displeasing him, persecution which made him like to our Lord delighted him. This was the concept he instilled into Brother Leo, giving him the most astounding definition of perfect joy that men had heard since the Gospel passage: Blessed are they who suffer persecution. The famous dialogue must have taken place about this time. Together with the *Canticle of the Sun*, it constitutes St. Francis's masterpiece. To the religiously minded of all time, the Poverello repeats that it is not in performing wonders, but in sacrifice and suffering that man's true nobility and earthly happiness consist.

"Brother Leo, God's Little Sheep, take your pen. I am going to dictate something to you," declared Francis.

"I am ready, Father."

"You are going to write what perfect joy is."

"Gladly, Father!"

"Well, then, supposing a messenger comes and tells us that all the doctors of Paris have entered the Order. Write that this would not give us perfect joy. And supposing that the same messenger were to tell us that all the bishops, archbishops, and prelates of the whole world, and likewise the kings of France and England, have become

Friars Minor, that would still be no reason for having perfect joy. And supposing that my friars had gone to the infidels and converted them to the last man...."

"Yes, Father?"

"Even then, Brother Leo, this would still not be perfect joy. If the Friars Minor had the gift of miracles and could make cripples straight, give light to the blind and hearing to the deaf, speech to the dumb, and life to men four days dead, if they were to speak all languages and know the secrets of men's consciences and of the future, and were to know by heart everything that has been written since the beginning of the world until now, and were to know the course of the stars, the location of buried treasure, the natures of birds, fishes, rocks, and all creatures, understand and write it on your paper, Brother Leo, that this would still not be perfect joy."

"Father! For the love of God, please tell me then just what is perfect joy?"

"I'll tell you. Supposing that in the winter, coming back from Perugia, I arrive in pitch darkness at the Portiuncula. Icicles are clinging to my habit and making my legs bleed. Covered with mud and snow, starving and freezing, I shout and knock for a long time. 'Who is there?' asks the porter when he finally decides to come. 'It is I, Brother Francis.' But he doesn't recognize my voice. 'Off with you, prankster!' he replies. 'This is no time for jokes!' I insist, but he won't listen. 'Will you be off, you rascal? There are enough of us without you! And there is no use in your coming here. Smart men like us don't need idiots like you around. Go, try your luck at the Crosiers' hospice!'

"Once more, I beg him not to leave me outside on a night like that, and implore him to open up. He opens up, all right. 'Just you wait, impudent cur! I'll teach you some manners!' And, grabbing a knobby club, he jumps on me, seizes me by the hood, and drags me through the snow, beating me and wounding me with all the knobs in his cudgel.... Well, Leo, if I am able to bear all this for love of God, not only with patience but with happiness, convinced that I deserve no other treatment, know, remember, and write down on your paper, God's Little Sheep, that at last I have found perfect joy."

Among the friars present at St. Mary of the Angels in 1219, there were a certain number who would have preferred joys less perfect, convents less poverty-stricken, and in general more comfort and security. Was it this year that Francis, on arriving at the Chapter, was surprised to discover a stone edifice suddenly sprung up alongside St. Mary of the Angels? At any rate, he was indignant. What? In this dear Portiuncula that was to serve as a model to the whole brotherhood, they had dared to make a mock of holy poverty? It was in vain that the culprits explained that this new building was owing to the solicitude of the Assisians. Climbing at once on the roof, and calling on his friars to help, the saint began hurling down the tiles. It was plain to be seen that this was only the beginning; and to keep the whole building from being torn down, the friars shouted to the knights of Assisi, who stood close by, ready to intervene.

"Brother," they remonstrated. "In the name of the commune we represent, and which is the owner of the building, we implore you to stop!"

"Since this house belongs to you," Francis replied, "I have no right to touch it." And sick at heart, he broke off his work.

A still more painful scene occurred one day when "several wise and learned friars got Cardinal Hugolin to urge Francis to be guided by the wiser brethren." To their way of thinking, it was from the way of life of Sts. Benedict, Augustine, or Bernard that inspiration for revising the statutes of the Brotherhood should be taken. The cardinal carried their request to the saint. Francis made no reply, but taking the prelate by the hand, he presented himself with him before the Chapter.

"Brothers! Brothers!" he cried, overcome by emotion, "the way that I have entered is one of humility and simplicity! If it is a new way, know that it was taught me by God Himself, and that I will follow no other. So do not speak to me about the Rules of St. Benedict, St. Augustine, or St. Bernard. The Lord wishes me to be a new kind of fool in this world, and will not lead me by any other way. As for you, may He confound you with your wisdom and learning, and make the ministers of His wrath compel you to return to your vocation, should you dare to leave it!"

These maledictions terrified the assembly and even the cardinal; and this time, at least, no one dared to insist.

The Chapter of 1219 maintained the decisions relative to the division of the Order in provinces. Their number was even increased, since France from then on had three provinces. Friars were appointed to go to Christian lands where they had not yet penetrated or to return to those from which they had been driven. But the great innovation of this Chapter was the creation of missions in pagan lands.

Brother Giles left for Tunis, where the Christians of the city, fearing that his zeal might compromise them, thrust him in a boat to force his return. Great was his disappointment at seeing the crown of martyrdom escape him; but he consoled himself when it was given him to realize that certain vexations of the devil outdid all other tortures in cruelty. Other friars, whom we shall meet soon again, headed for Morocco. Francis himself, ever eager to shed his blood for Christ, chose to go to Egypt.

After appointing two vicars to replace him at the head of the Brotherhood, Francis left the Portiuncula at the beginning of June and went to Ancona to take passage on one of the ships conveying crusaders to the East.

A large number of friars accompanied him, but not all of them could be accommodated. Francis said to them, "Since the sailors refuse to take all of you, and since I, who love you all equally, haven't the heart to make a choice, let us ask God to manifest His will to us." Calling a young boy who was playing on the wharf, he asked him to point out twelve friars at random, and it was with them that he embarked. Among them were Peter Catanii, the former jurist, Illuminato of Rieti and Leonard, two former knights, and Brother Barbaro, one of the first disciples.

They set sail on June 24, 1219, St. John's Day, and first put into port at the island of Cyprus. They reached St. John d'Acre about the middle of July, and a few days later Damietta in the Nile delta, which had been under siege by the crusaders for a year. Duke Leopold of Austria, their leader, had all sorts of men under his command. If some had taken the cross out of holy zeal, many were mere adventurers, attracted to the Orient by the hope of pillage and pleasure. The license and disunity reigning in this army was sufficient explanation of its previous failures.

When, on the morning of August 29, Francis learned that the army was going to attempt a decisive assault, he said to his companion, "The Lord has revealed to me that the Christians are running into a new defeat. Should I warn them? If I speak, they will call me crazy. If I keep still, my conscience will reproach me. What do you think, Brother?"

"The judgment of men matters little!" replied his companion. "After all, this will not be the first time you have been taken for a madman! Unburden your conscience then, and tell them the truth!"

The leaders mocked Francis's warnings and the attack took place. The result was, as we know, a disaster in which the crusaders lost over four thousand men, killed or captured. Francis had not the heart to witness the battle; but he sent messengers three times for news. When his companion came to him to announce the defeat, he wept much, says Thomas of Celano, especially over the Spanish knights whose bravery had led nearly all of them to their deaths.

The saint remained there for several months. At first, his apostolate among the crusaders had marvelous results. He was hailed as a prophet ever since, in opposition to the leader, he had dared to predict defeat. His courage and knightly bearing filled the warriors with admiration and his guilelessness and charm won their hearts. "He is so amiable that he is venerated by all," wrote Jacques de Vitry to his friends in Lorraine.

The celebrated chronicler who at that period occupied the episcopal see of St. John D'Acre and made frequent visits to the crusaders' camp, added that many abandoned the profession of arms or the secular priesthood to become Friars Minor. "This Order which is spreading through the whole world," he wrote further, "imitates the primitive Church and the life of the Apostles in all things. Colin the Englishman, our clerk, has entered their ranks, with two others, Master Michael and Dom Matthew, to whom I had entrusted the parish of the Holy Cross. Only with difficulty do I hold back the Chanter and Henry and others." Jacques de Vitry also announced to his correspondents that "Brother Francis has not feared to leave the Christian army to go to the enemy camp to preach the faith."

The idea of converting the Saracens must have appeared singularly fantastic to men who up to then had thought only of cutting their throats. It is true that the Moors asked only to do likewise; for, quite apart from an eternal reward, every Muslim who brought a Christian head to the Sultan received a golden bezant from him. Cardinal Pelagio, who now arrived in Damietta with reinforcements, was far from encouraging Francis in his project. If not actually forbidding the undertaking, he at least declined all personal responsibility, charging Francis not to compromise thereby the Christian name and Christian interests.

The saint took Brother Illuminato with him and set out toward the enemy lines, singing, "Though I walk in the midst of the shadow of death, I will fear no evil, for Thou art with me." To comfort his less reassured companion, Francis showed him two ewes peacefully grazing in this perilous spot. "Courage, Brother!" he cried joyously. "Put your trust in Him who sends us forth like sheep in the midst of wolves."

However, the Saracens appeared, jumped on the two religious, and began to beat them. "Soldan! Soldan!" shouted Francis as long as he was able. The soldiers thought that they were dealing with envoys and brought them in chains to their camp. Francis explained in French that he desired to see the Sultan and convert him to the Gospel. Had he said this anywhere else, it would have meant instant death; but the court of Al-Malik al-Kamil included skeptics who liked to discuss the respective merits of the Koran and the Gospel, and who likewise were chivalrous in their deportment.

The Sultan also doubtless saw in the arrival of the Friars Minor an opportunity for diversion and ordered the evangelizers to be shown in. It is said that in order to cause them embarrassment, he had a carpet strewn with crosses laid down in the room in front of him. "If they walk on it," he said, "I will accuse them of insulting their God. If they refuse, I will reproach them for not wishing to approach me and of insulting me."

Francis walked unhesitatingly over the carpet, and as the prince observed that he was trampling the Christian cross underfoot, the saint replied: "You must know that there were several crosses on Calvary, the cross of Christ and those of the two thieves, the first is ours, which we adore. As for the others, we gladly leave them to you, and have no scruples about treading on them, whenever it please you to strew them on the ground."

Al-Malik al-Kamil soon conceived a warm friendship for the Poverello and invited him to stay with him. "I would do so gladly," replied the saint, "if you would consent to become converted to Christ together with your people." And he even offered, writes St. Bonaventure, to undergo the ordeal by fire in his presence.

"Let a great furnace be lit," said he. "Your priests and I will enter it; and you shall judge by what you see which of our two religions is the holiest and truest."

"I greatly fear that my priest will refuse to accompany you into the furnace," observed the Sultan.

And indeed, at the simple announcement of this proposal, the venerable dean of that priestly group hastily disappeared. "Since that is the way things are," said Francis, "I will enter the fire alone. If I perish, you must lay it to my sins. But if God's power protects me, do you promise to acknowledge Christ as the true God and Savior?"

The Sultan alleged the impossibility of his changing his religion without alienating his people. But as his desire to keep this charming messenger at his court was as strong as ever, he offered him rich presents. These were, as we may well imagine, refused. "Take them at least to give to the poor!" he urged. But Francis accepted, it appears, only a horn which later on he used to summon people when he was about to preach.

He departed very sad as soon as he perceived the uselessness of his efforts. The Sultan had him conducted in state back to the Christian camp. "Remember me in your prayers," he begged as Francis left, "and may God, by your intercession, reveal to me which belief is more pleasing to Him."

Thanks to the reinforcements of Cardinal Pelagio, Damietta fell on November 5, 1219. Francis was present at the taking of the city; but this victory of the crusaders drew more tears from him than did their recent defeat. The streets were strewn with corpses and the houses filled with victims of the plague. The captors fought like wolves over the immense booty, selling the captives at auction, except the young women reserved for their pleasure.

When Francis saw that Damietta had become a pandemonium in which his voice was lost in the clamor of unleashed instincts, the saint left the country and took ship for St. John d'Acre. There he met Brother Elias, Provincial of Syria, and among Elias's recruits, Caesar of Speyer who had fled Germany to escape the relatives of those whom he had enrolled in the crusade and the husbands of the women he had converted.

It was also at St. John d'Acre that Francis learned that five of his sons had just shed their blood for the faith. They were Brothers Otho, Bernard, Peter, Accursus, and Adjutus, who had left the Portiuncula at the same time he did; and who, as we have seen, set out for Morocco by way of Spain.

Truly these five had left no stone unturned to obtain the grace of martyrdom. Arriving first in Seville, which was still in the power of the Moors, they had entered the mosque and began to preach against the Koran. It was a good place to meet Muslims, but a bad one in which to insult Mohammed. They were hustled out and beaten by the followers of the prophet. They then went to the royal palace.

"Who are you?" the king asked them.

"We belong to the regions of Rome."

"And what are you doing here?"

"We have come to preach faith in Jesus Christ to you, so that you will renounce Mohammad, that wicked slave of the devil, and obtain everlasting life like us."

The prince, beside himself with fury, ordered them to be beheaded; but seeing the joy his sentence caused them, he took pity on them and attempted to win them by presents. "May your money go to perdition with you!" they replied.

They were taken in chains to the summit of a tower, from which they shouted down to the passersby that Mohammad was an imposter. They were then shut up in the public prison where they still attempted to convert their jailors and fellow prisoners.

They were again brought before the king, who gave them the choice of returning to Italy or of being deported to Morocco. "Do whatever pleases you," they replied, "and may God's will be done!" It was decided that they should go to Morocco.

Shortly after their arrival, the Amir al-Muminin Yusuf, who commanded in Africa in the king's name, had them brought before him, half-naked and in chains. "Who are you?" he asked.

"We are disciples of Brother Francis, who has sent his friars throughout the world to teach all men the way of truth."

"And what is this way?"

Brother Otho, who was a priest, began to recite the Creed; and he was starting to comment on it, when the Miramolin stopped him, saying, "It is surely the devil who speaks by your mouth." He thereupon handed them over to his torturers.

These used their cruelest devices against their victims. All night long the poor friars were flogged until they bled, dragged by the throat over pebbles, and doused with boiling oil and vinegar, while, their hearts failing them, they exhorted one another in a loud voice to persevere in the love of Christ.

The following day, January 16, 1220, the Miramolin summoned them at dawn to learn if they persisted in despising the Koran. All proclaimed that there is no other truth than the holy Gospels. The prince threatened them with death. "Our bodies are in your power," they replied, "but our souls are in the power of God."

These were their last words, for Abu-Jacob thereupon had his sword brought and cut off their heads in the presence of his women attendants.

When these facts were reported to Francis, he is said to have exclaimed, "Now I can truly say that I have five Friars Minor." But when the account of their martyrdom was read before him, he interrupted the reading as soon as he perceived that a few words praising him had been inserted.

Syria, at this period, was partly Christian and partly Muslim. Thanks to a permit received from Conradin, Sultan of Damascus and brother of Al-Malik al-Kamil, Francis could travel anywhere in the country without paying tribute. He made use of this privilege, says Angelo Clareno, to visit the Holy Places. How we would like to have a contemporary account of those who saw him or accompanied him to Palestine—showing us the Little Poor Man celebrating Christmas in Bethlehem, weeping on Good Friday at Gethsemane and Calvary, and communicating on Easter morning at the Holy Sepulchre! But, unfortunately, the records are silent about these months in the life of St. Francis.

They only break the silence again to state that during the summer of 1220, an emissary from the Portiuncula named Brother Stephen arrived in Syria bearing bad news. His message was that the vicars were leading the Order to ruin, and that the faithful friars implored their father, if he was still of this world, to come back at once and save his work.

CHAPTER FOURTEEN

Crisis in the Order

A CRUCIAL PERIOD now faced the Brotherhood of the Little Poor Man, which was rife with every kind of dissension and dispute. Among the causes of such a crisis must be emphasized the lack of organization in the Order and the increasing diversity of aims of its members.

Inspired by the three Gospel texts in the missal of Assisi: "If you would be perfect, renounce all that you possess. Take nothing with you for your journey. Let him who would be My disciple deny himself and carry his cross," the Rule of 1209, taken as it stood without authorized commentary, was less a piece of monastic legislation than a code for spiritual living. Thus the friars had at first enjoyed great freedom, some living as hermits, others as pilgrims, day laborers, nurses, or wandering preachers. Moreover, their vow of obedience was somewhat unique, since any precedence among them on a stable basis simply did not exist; and their superiors were as likely to be recruited from illiterate laymen as from clerics versed in canon law.

If such a way of life proved agreeable to a few heroic penitents stimulated by the presence of the most radiant of the saints, it could no longer be so to thousands of widely scattered religious, among them a number of clerics and scholars who found too hard or too narrow the primitive ideal of Rivo Torto. Thus the fire had been smoldering under the ashes, and already disunion reigned in the Order when Francis embarked for Egypt.

His extended absence had permitted the fomenters of new ideas to push their advantage, especially since they could count on the compliance of the two vicars. For those to whom the saint had turned over his powers were definitely their men. Their names were Matthew of Narni and Gregory of Naples, one of them charged to remain at the Portiuncula and receive new friars, and the other to go from friary to friary to settle problems that arose. Of the first we know nothing, except that he thought as did his colleague. As for Gregory, an ardent advocate of studies and a great friend of Brother Elias, he was according to Eccleston, a good preacher and administrator. Later, however, as Minister of France (1223–1233) he showed himself to be so cruel and authoritarian that he was removed and condemned to imprisonment.

Meanwhile, the task of both was a thorny one. For how were they to govern an Order in which independence and even vagabondage were so esteemed? To be sure, it was often for reasons of piety that the "Lord's wandering minstrels" were moved to travel about. We see one of them, among others, who garbed himself as a pilgrim, resolved to play the madman for the rest of his life, and so reap a rich harvest of insults. But some among them showed themselves less edifying on their travels; those, for instance, who sought the society of women, "eating with them out of the same bowl," not to speak of greater familiarities. There were also those who followed weird impulses which had no relation to their vocation. Such was John Capella (if it were really he) who set off for Rome with a band of leprosy patients of both sexes, proposing to unite them in a mixed congregation and already soliciting papal approval for his scheme.

These abuses and many others evidently gave the vicars cause for intervention. As the rumor of Francis's death spread, they further imagined that it was up to them to impart to the Brotherhood the organization it lacked, and they seized this opportunity to make their own views prevail.

Having called together a chapter composed of the most influential friars, they promulgated constitutions inspired by the legislation of other Orders. They tightened up on discipline, multiplied fasts, and prescribed many privations foreign to the Rule. These measures were owing perhaps to the desires of many well-meaning clerics who clamored for a more regulated life. Here and there in the guise of residences, vast and solid buildings were seen to rise. The Provincial Peter Staccia established a house of studies in Bologna like the one possessed by the Dominicans. Finally, in order to be less hampered in their apostolate, the friars solicited favors from the Roman Curia. Thus it was that the missionaries to France received papal letters commending them to the bishops of the country, and Brother Philip, the visitor of the Poor Ladies, obtained a bull of excommunication against anyone attacking his protégées.

All this, so contrary to the intentions of the founder, transformed the character of the Brotherhood too radically not to call forth protests from the earlier friars. Many among them revolted. They had cause to rue it, however, for Gregory of Naples was firm and meant to be obeyed. "Certain recalcitrants were afflicted with unjust penances, others were driven from the community like men of evil life, and still others, in order to flee from the wrath of their persecutors, escaped and wandered hither and yon, bewailing the absence of their beloved shepherd and guide."

Then it was that one of these unfortunates escaped unbeknown to the vicars and had the good fortune to meet Francis in Syria. He handed him a copy of the new ordinances and implored him to hasten to the rescue of his perishing Order.

The saint was at table with Peter Catanii when Brother Stephen appeared. Meat was being served. Now according to the new constitutions it was a day of abstinence.

"Master Peter," inquired Francis, "what are we to do?"

"Master Francis," replied Peter, "we shall do whatever pleases you, for it is up to you to command."

"Then let us eat meat, in keeping with the liberty given us by the holy Gospel."

Francis left at once, taking with him Caesar of Speyer, Peter Catanii, the friend of his early days, and Brother Elias, who had just revealed his talents as Provincial of Syria. These were three superior men who would, he believed, assist him in restoring the unity of his religious family.

At Venice, where they disembarked, the travelers separated. Francis, who had acquired new infirmities in the Orient, wanted to take a few days rest before returning to the Portiuncula.

One might have said that even the wild creatures in this country were glad to see him again. A flock of larks, singing loudly, flew about him in a thicket. "Brother," he remarked to his companion, "since our sisters the larks praise their Creator so gladly, let us join them." And they paused to recite their hours. But as if anxious to emulate the friars, the birds made such a racket that they could not hear each other pray. "Sister larks," said the saint, "would you have the goodness to stop a moment?" And the birds stopped their concert until Francis and his companion had finished reciting their breviary.

CRISIS IN THE ORDER

The saint headed for Bologna. Being ill, he rode astride a donkey that Brother Leonard was leading by the bridle. Now, tired himself, Leonard who, as we have seen, was born of a noble family, had an inner moment of bad humor. "Some things are very queer on this earth!" he thought. "For instance, who would have thought that I, whose parents would not have dreamed of associating with the Bernardones, would one day be walking along on foot, while their son rides at ease?"

"You are quite right, brother," observed Francis, dismounting. "It is plain that since you are a nobleman, it is not right that I should ride the donkey and you go on foot."

Surprised at being found out, Leonard fell at Francis's feet and begged his pardon.

The saint could soon gauge for himself the importance of the revolution under way. As he neared Bologna, he learned that the friars were occupying a great house belonging to them—the one where Peter Staccia had established his convent of studies. He summoned the minister and said to him: "Are you trying to destroy my Order, forgetting that it is my will that the friars spend less time in study than in prayer?" And having compelled all the religious, even those who were sick, to vacate their property on the spot, he imposed a curse on Peter Staccia and withdrew. It was in vain that Peter ran after him to have him take back his curse. He replied that it was too late, and that it had been confirmed by Christ himself. And this was so true, writes the author of the *Actus*, that the guilty friar "soon surrendered his soul to the devil in the midst of a horrible stench."

When the faithful friars learned of their father's return, "joy filled their hearts, as though a new light shone upon them." They came out of hiding, thinking all would now be straightened out. But the saint judged otherwise. What had happened showed that the innovators were supported by those higher up, and that he alone would be unable to restore peace.

In a dream, he saw a black hen no bigger than a dove, with many more chicks around her than she could shelter under her wings. "This hen," he said to himself on awakening, "is certainly me with my short stature and dark skin. The dove she resembles is a symbol of the simplicity I must practice to obey the Gospel. The chickens are my virtuous friars whose number is now too great for a little man like me to defend. So I am going to entrust them to the Church of Rome, which is alone able to protect them."

Without going near the Portiuncula or wishing to encounter the rebels, he went to Rome. Refusing out of humility to knock at the pope's door, he waited for a long time on the threshold. When the pope appeared, he threw himself at his feet, saying, "God grant you peace, Holy Father!"

"God bless you, my son," replied Honorius III.

"Your Holiness," continued Francis, "your dignity is too great and you are too absorbed in great matters for the poor to have recourse to you as often as they would like."

Doubtless, the benevolent pontiff remarked that there was no lack of cardinals to whom one could address himself at need.

"Exactly! There are too many of them, Holy Father! Please designate just one of them for me to take your place and to treat with me about the interests of my Order!"

"Whom do you want me to appoint?"

"The Bishop of Ostia," replied Francis, who had complete confidence in the friendship and piety of the powerful cardinal. For had he not, to show his sympathy for the friars, even doffed the purple sometimes and put on their habit?

The pope agreed to the Little Poor Man's request, and Hugolin, named "protector, governor, and corrector of the Brotherhood," became the representative of the Holy See for the business of the Order. From that time onward he became the saint's permanent advisor as well as the supreme arbiter between the rival parties of his religious family; and it was he, who after trying to restore peace, helped to give it its definitive statutes.

The skill and authority of the man whom Francis now called his "apostolic lord" soon made itself felt; and this in a way to reassure the founder without at the same time discouraging his adversaries.

Brother Philip had to give up visiting the Poor Ladies, and the letters of excommunication he had obtained were annulled. John Capella was obliged to dissolve his mixed congregation of leprosy patients and return to his convent. A Bull of September 22, 1220, forbade the lovers of travel to circulate in the future without letters of obedience; and as much to weed out undesirables as to form the rest to discipline, a year's novitiate was required of those desiring to enter the Order. Finally, it was decided to prepare without delay for the Chapter of 1221, while Francis was to busy himself with working out a new Rule which would—so it was hoped—meet with general approval.

Meanwhile, the rebellious vicars, dismissed from office, had had to give way to Peter Catanii, who had already replaced Francis on many occasions in his absence. Unfortunately, Peter died prematurely on March 10, 1221. And his death can be said to have been an event with far-reaching consequences, when we consider that this old and loyal disciple of the Poverello was succeeded by Brother Elias, the least Franciscan of men, who governed the brotherhood for thirteen years.

Except from 1227 to 1232, Elias Bombarone exercised the functions of Minister General from 1221 to 1239.

Despite all the research that has been made about him, Brother Elias remains a mysterious figure. Born, it would appear, in or near Assisi, he had been by turns a mattress maker, schoolteacher, and notary before entering the Order. Ambitious and charming, a man of universal talent, he was born to be outstanding in the highest offices. Although a simple lay brother, he was reputed to be very learned, and "no one," says Eccleston, "was more famous in his time in all Christendom." We see the Bishop of Lincoln, the famous Robert Grosseteste, seeking his friendship, Italian cities asking him to arbi-trate their conflicts, and Bela IV, King of Hungary, sending him a golden cup to win his favor. Enjoying the confidence of the two masters of the world, the pope and the emperor, he long played the role of peacemaker between them, and St. Clare herself was attached to him.

He doubtless had his virtuous moments, since Francis and Hugolin had placed him at the head of the Brotherhood, and he always had a goodly number of partisans. It may also be said to his credit that he loved and venerated the Poverello, that he did everything possible to alleviate the sufferings of his last years, and to glorify him after his death.

The two superimposed churches that he erected on the rock of Mount Subasio to enclose the saint's tomb constitute one of the architectural marvels of Europe. He flanked them with a sort of convent-fortress, which he made his general headquarters and which he offered as a refuge to the popes in case of need; and they did sometimes store their treasures in it. And when we consider that less than twelve years were required to complete all these works, we must agree that Brother Elias was a remarkable man indeed.

We have seen that Brother Giles, Brother Leo, and their friends looked upon the basilica and the Sacro Convento of Assisi as a complete betrayal of the Franciscan ideal. But in the eyes of the Vicar General and his party these glorious edifices were to be symbolic of the role and status to which the Friars Minor could aspire in future. Elias, for his part, constantly worked at increasing vocations to the Brotherhood. He divided the Order into seventy-two provinces, allegedly to honor the seventy-two disciples of our Lord, but with an eye to humiliating the Dominicans whose manpower was less. He multiplied missions in pagan lands, promoted study, and urged the friars to mix in politics, and to establish important foundations everywhere.

Evidently, it was only gradually that Elias was able to reveal his characteristic role and to carry out his plans. In the first years of his generalship he was still restrained by filial piety and prudence. But with Francis dead, he threw off all reserve. He never went anywhere save on horseback, dined at a separate table, ate choice viands, kept a special cook for his own use, and a dozen servants, dismissed and replaced provincials according to his good pleasure, scattered and persecuted those religious faithful to the spirit of the Portiuncula, and, too occupied with his building projects and embassies to visit the transalpine provinces, he sent substitutes charged with imposing his will with an iron hand and carrying out his vengeances. Supine submission was the only road to his favor. By his orders, Caesar of Speyer, his former disciple and companion in the Holy Land, was thrown in a dungeon where he succumbed to ill treatment. Even Brother Bernard of Quintavalle had to flee to Assisi to escape the same fate.

From 1235 on, the friars of Germany, France, and Italy beseeched Cardinal Hugolin, now pope, to put an end to this insufferable dictatorship. But Gregory IX waited until 1239 to give them satisfaction. It is true that at this date his own dealings with the emperor were irreparably ruined and that Brother Elias inclined too much to the Ghibelline side to be of further service to the Holy See.

The former general was formally excommunicated when he took refuge with Frederick II who continued to make use of him. In 1244, under Innocent IV, he tried to reenter the Order and regain his power, but his attempt only netted him an additional excommunication. Elias lived for some time longer at the imperial court; then with a dozen faithful followers he retired to the humble and charming hermitage of Le Celle near Cortona. The entire city was devoted to him and venerated him as a saint. Elias built a new church in honor of St. Francis at Cortona, and died on April 4, 1253, reconciled at the last moment with the Church by a secular priest.

Although Francis had abandoned the charge of Minister General to Brother Elias, he nonetheless remained for all the true father and lawgiver of the Brotherhood. It was as such that, assisted by Caesar of Speyer, a man well versed in the Scriptures, he revised the Rule of the Chapter of 1221. It comprised twenty-three chapters interspersed with numerous texts taken from the New Testament and inspired (as we shall see) by the purest spirit of Rivo Torto.

It naturally took into account the Bull *Cum secundum*, which had inaugurated a year's novitiate (chap. III), and proscribed the practice of vagabondage (chap. V). It likewise profited from the experience acquired in the course of the preceding ten years, and here and there alluded to the abuses revealed by recent events. Thus chapters III and IX condemn all distinction between permitted and forbidden food; chapter XII forbids the friars unchaste looks and association with women; and chapter V authorizes disobedience to superiors whose orders run contrary to the Franciscan vocation.

But for the rest, far from mitigating the text of 1210, the Rule of 1221 merely reproduced, developed, and commented on it in the sense of a perfect and literal observation of the Gospel.

Neither in common nor as individuals are the friars to own anything. They are to have no beasts of burden at their convents or elsewhere (chap. XV). They are not "to claim or defend" their tiny hermitages against "anyone whatever" (chap. VII). As for money, it is not only forbidden them to possess it, but even to make use of it in any way: "They are not to value it any more than pebbles," and if (which God forbid) one of them should transgress the prohibition, let him be considered by all as a false friar, a thief, a traitor, and a Judas carrying the purse (chap. VIII).

Their social rank is that of the poor, and they shall hold to it in imitation of our Lord, his Mother, and his disciples, who lived (Francis assures us) on public charity. Their habit is to consist of a tunic that can be patched, a hood, a cord, and drawers (chap. II). They are not to travel on horseback but on foot (chap. XV), carrying nothing with them, neither sack nor wallet, nor bread, nor silver, nor staff; and they are not to resist evil, but let themselves be despoiled without protest (chap. XIV). Chapter VII recalls the obligation of manual labor and the comportment of religious in domestic service. Chapter IX treats at length the solicitation of alms to which the friars will be obliged to resort, since it is forbidden them to lay up anything in store, and because their labor will not always suffice for their living. Let them not be ashamed to beg, since, following our Lord's example, they have voluntarily embraced poverty, and alms are a right and a legacy acquired by Christ's merits for all the poor. But let them rejoice to find themselves in the company of those whom men despise, the poor, the weak, the infirm, the victims of leprosy, and the beggars by the wayside.

The Rule also mentions the Chapters of Pentecost (chap. XVIII), the ministers whom it constantly calls the servants of the other friars (chaps. IV, V, XVI, XVIII), the superiors who are forbidden to take the name of prior (chap. VI), the preachers and the exhortation to penance which each may make when and wherever he pleases (chap. XXI); those who go to the Saracens and others, who have two ways in which to do good: the first, by comporting themselves as Christians without arguing or quarrelling with anyone, and the second, by preaching the Word of God (chap. XVI). Finally, the friars are commanded to confess to each other if there are no priests, while waiting to do so to an approved confessor (chap. XX); and all are to behave in word and in deed as good Catholics, under pain of being driven from the Brotherhood (chap. XIX).

All this let us note, was required of clerics as well as of laics; for, except for the Divine Office, for which the former were to recite the Breviary, and the latter to say Pater Nosters, the legislator made no distinction between them. And it was in referring to the Divine Office that he forbade clerics to have any books except those needed to recite their hours.

The tone of the Rule recalls that of the Gospels, wherein precepts and prohibitions are mixed with love-inspired encouragement and counsel. Here is Chapter Ten, "Concerning the Sick Brethren":

> In whatever place a Brother shall fall sick, the others shall not leave him without taking care to have one of the friars or more, if need be, appointed who will serve him as they would

wish to be served themselves. But in case of great necessity, they can entrust him to some other person who will assume his care. And I ask the friar who is sick to give thanks to the Creator for all things, and to desire to be whatever God wills for him, whether healthy or sick, because all whom God has predestined to eternal life He prepares by the goad of suffering and infirmity and the spirit of compunction, as the Lord says: Those whom I love I rebuke and chastise [see Revelation 3:19] But if the sick friar lets himself be troubled or angered whether against God or the other friars, or is too demanding of medicines in the vain desire of saving the flesh which is soon to die and which is the enemy of the soul, this comes to him from the evil one; and he is a carnal [self-centered] man and is acting no more like one of the friars, since he loves the body more than the soul."

The last two chapters alone make up a third of the Rule. There is first of all a long "admonition" (chap. XXII), made up almost entirely of Gospel texts, in which the Little Poor Man warns his children never to look back. He says:

Consider this word of the Lord, "Love your enemies and do good to them that hate you." It is because our Lord Jesus Christ called a traitor "friend," and of His own free will gave Himself up to His executioners that we must, in imitation of Him, look upon as friends those from whom we have received suffering and injustice, humiliations, torments, martyrdom, and death. We ought to love them with our whole heart, for they obtain for us everlasting life.

The only thing that remains for us to do, now that we have forsaken the world, is eagerly to do God's will and please

Him.... Let us not then be one of those stony places where the divine seed falls without bearing fruit.... Let the dead bury the dead. Let us beware of the wiles of the devil, who by the affairs and cares of this life desires to stifle in our hearts the Lord's words and precepts... In the name of that holy charity which is God, I beseech all the brethren to lay aside every obstacle, every care and encumbrance, that they may serve, love, honor, and adore God with pure hearts and minds.... Let us build within a tabernacle and dwelling for Him.... Let us pray: Our Father who art in Heaven. Let us have recourse to Christ, the Shepherd and Bishop of our souls...who Himself vouchsafed to pray to His Father for us, saying, 'Holy Father, keep in Your name those whom You have given Me. I do not pray that You take them out of the world, but that You keep them from evil...for where I am, Father, I will that they may be with Me and behold Your Glory in Your kingdom.

The twenty-third and last chapter is a long prayer, a sort of heavenly hymn as worthy of admiration as the most beautiful prefaces of the ancient liturgy. It constitutes perhaps the most perfect example of the way in which Francis spoke to God and of God when he let his heart speak. We must be content to quote only a few extracts:

Almighty and Sovereign God, holy and just Father, King of Heaven and earth, we give You thanks because by Your only begotten Son and in the Holy Spirit You have created all things spiritual and corporeal, and have made us in Your image and likeness.... We thank You that, having created us through Your Son, You caused Him to be born of the glorious and blessed Virgin Mary, and willed that we poor captives be redeemed by His Cross, blood, and death.

And because we all, miserable sinners, are not worthy to name You, we humbly pray that our Lord Jesus Christ, Your beloved Son, may give You thanks, together with the Holy Spirit the Comforter, for all Your benefits. Alleluia. And you, glorious and blessed Mary, Mother of God, ever Virgin...and all saints present, past, and to come, we humbly beseech you to give thanks to God most high, to His most dear Son, our Lord Jesus Christ, and to the Holy Spirit, the Paraclete, forever and ever. Amen! Alleluia!

And all those who would serve Almighty God in the Holy, Catholic, and Apostolic Church, the priests, deacons, subdeacons, acolytes, exorcists, lectors, porters, and all clerics, and all religious both men and women, kings, princes, workers, tillers of the soil, servants, masters, virgins, the chaste, married people, laymen, men, women, babes, youth, old people, the sick and the well, the humble and the great, all people, families, tribes, and nations, all men on earth present and to come, we humbly beg and beseech them—all of us Friars Minor, useless servants—humbly beg and beseech them to pray for us the grace of perseverance in the true Faith and in penitence, without which no man can be saved.

Let us all love with our whole heart, powers, and strength the Lord God who has given us our bodies, our souls, and our lives. Let our one desire and purpose, then, be to seek to love and enjoy our Creator and Savior, alone true God, complete and perfect good, alone merciful and mild, from whom comes all forgiveness, grace, and glory.... May nothing cause us to adore, serve, praise, bless, glorify, exalt, extol, and give thanks to the Most High God, Father, Son, and Holy Spirit, Creator of all things, the Savior of those who believe, hope, and love Him, God unchanging, invisible, unutterable, ineffable, incomprehensible, unfathomable, blessed, laudable, glorious, exalted, great, sublime, clement, lovable, delectable, wholly and absolutely desirable forever and ever.

This long document closed with this supreme adjuration:

In the name of the Lord I ask all the friars to know the tenor and meaning of these words and to recall them often. And I pray all in deep humility, to cherish, observe and keep this Rule of Life. And on behalf of Almighty God and of our Holy Father the Pope, I, Brother Francis, formally prescribe and ordain that no one shall add to or take away from it anything whatever, and that the Brethren shall never have another Rule.... *Amen.*

Such is the Rule that Francis brought to the Chapter of 1221. There was in it, as we see, none of the compromises hoped for by the ministers. Rather, it seemed to be a veritable challenge. The Little Poor Man did not expect approval for it to come without a struggle; but at this period he was still hopeful and willing to fight, as is proved by the text which served as the theme of his opening sermon: "*Benedictus Dominus Deus qui docet manus meas ad proelium.* Blessed be the Lord, my God, who teaches my hands to make war."

The Chapter, which united at least three thousand friars and lasted seven days, was presided over by Cardinal Rainerio Capocci, replacing Hugolin, unable to attend. And the Cardinal must have congratulated himself on his inability to be present; for his attempts at arbitration, brought out into the open, would have had no chance of success. Carried away by the holy founder, the majority of the friars would have rallied to his intransigence, while the opposing party would not have consented to disband. And thus the gulf separating the adversaries would have been widened still more.

The documents made no mention of the discussion that took place on the Rule. If there was any, there is no doubt that the ministers and Brother Elias were agreed not to push matters to a conclusion. For it was better to separate with nothing decided, and to leave it to the Cardinal-Protector to prepare—by private negotiations—a satisfactory solution. And so it was done.

But before seeing how Hugolin resolved the conflict, we must first relate in chronological order the institution of the Third Order, which was in part his work, and the founding of the first Franciscan school, to which he likewise gave his support.

CHAPTER FIFTEEN

The Third Order

IT ALMOST BEGAN to look as though Francis was going to transform Umbria into a second Egypt of the Desert Fathers. He made God so lovable and the spiritual world so real that there were times when all his hearers wanted to forsake the world to assure their salvation.

Jacques de Vitry was alarmed at this epidemic of vocations: "There is a great danger," he wrote in March 1220, "in thus accepting pell-mell the perfect and the imperfect. The latter should at least go through a trial period before being admitted into religion." The saint himself complained of the quantity of his new candidates. "There are too many Friars Minor!" he murmured. "May the time come when the people instead of meeting them at every turn may complain that they see too few of them!"

It was both to divert the stream of candidates and to permit laypeople to live in a holy way in the world that he instituted the Order of Penance.

"Do not be in such haste," he said to the people of Cannara who wanted to leave everything to follow him. "I promise to provide something for you."

For already he was thinking of the Third Order, if we are to believe the *Fioretti*. The new institution did not receive its canonical statute until 1221, but many laypeople had not waited until this date to lead a Franciscan life. Among these early tertiaries may be mentioned Count Orlando of Chuisi, the donor of Mount La Verna, Praxedis, the Roman recluse to whom Francis gave a habit and cord, and, finally, the Lady Jacopa de' Settesoli, widow of the knight Graziano Frangipani.

It was apparently in 1212, a few months after the clothing of St. Clare, that the Poverello made the acquaintance of "Brother Jacopa," who became his great and faithful friend. Jacopa, who was then about twenty-two years of age, belonged to high-ranking Roman nobility, descending on her father's side from the Norman knights who had invaded Sicily, and allied on her husband's side, according to legend, to Flavius Anicius, who saved the people of Rome from famine by giving them bread: hence their name of *Frangens panem*. The name of Settesoli came from the domain of Septizonium which the Frangipani had acquired in 1145 from the Camaldolese monks.

On becoming a widow, Jacopa would no doubt have embraced the religious life, if the guardianship of her two sons and the safeguarding of their patrimony had not prevented her. A deed of May 13, 1217, shows her generously renouncing a claim against the Holy See in order to put an end to a lawsuit pending between the papal steward and her minor children. She was an able woman, well deserving, because of her virile energy, the name of "Brother Jacopa" by which Francis made her famous in history.

The Poverello was often her guest during his visits to the Eternal City; and at her house he used to eat a tasteful confection called *"mostacciuoli,"* which he asked for again (as we shall see) on his death bed. This mixture of almonds, sugar, and other ingredients crushed in a mortar was perhaps what we call today "sugared almonds." Jacopa also appears to have seen to renewing the saint's wardrobe.

In gratitude for her loving care, Francis made her a present of a lamb "that he used to let follow him," says St. Bonaventure, "in honor of the most meek Lamb of God." And the amiable Doctor adds that this "lamb seemed to have been formed by him to the spiritual life," so pious had it become and solicitous of the perfection of others. "It would follow its mistress to church, stay near her while she prayed, and go back home with her. If Jacopa forgot to wake up in the morning, the lamb would come and give her little butts with his head and bleat in her ear to constrain her to go to her devotions."

When the Poverello was about to leave this world, he expressed the desire that Clare and Jacopa might see him for the last time. After Francis's death, the noble Roman lady went back to Assisi to reside, to be near those who had known him, and to relive past memories with them.

As ever it happens to those whom death seems to forget, Jacopa knew the sorrow of surviving those whom she loved—her two sons and all her grandchildren. She also knew other sufferings, for she saw the Frangipani allied to the enemies of the papacy and persecution raining down upon the most faithful followers of holy poverty. Her brightest hours were assuredly those she spent conversing with Brother Leo, Brother Rufino, and their friends. She also used to visit Brother Giles, the hermit of Monte Ripido. Once she was a witness to the way Giles refuted the paradoxes proposed to him one day by a theologian on the subject of predestination. Drawing from his sleeve a tiny zither with willow strings, Brother Giles began to reel off in verse—as he scraped away at his instrument—a dozen syllogisms whose conclusion was always the same, namely that man either freely saves himself or freely damns himself. Then, having sung enough, the holy *jongleur* went into one of his habitual ecstasies.

Some historians believe that Brother Jacopa died in 1239, while others hold she was still living in 1273 and that she died past ninety. She was buried in the basilica of Assisi, not far from her master. The following epitaph was inscribed on her tomb: *HIC REQUIESCIT JACOBA SANCTA NOBILISQUE ROMANA;* and on the half-effaced fresco surmounting the tomb we still see her, led by an angel and bringing the dying Francis the hair-cloth garment in which he was buried.

By common consent, the "Letter to all the Faithful," written about 1226, constitutes a sort of rough sketch or draft of the future Third Order Rule. It is a circular addressed to the whole world, urging all men to a better practice of the Gospel. It begins:

> To all Christians, religious, clerics and laymen, men and women, to all inhabitants of the earth, Brother Francis, their servant and subject, offers respectful greeting, and desires for them the true peace of Heaven and sincere charity in the Lord.

The saint first declared his intentions: "Since I am the servant of all, I am obliged to serve all and to communicate to all the sweet smelling words of my Lord. So, since I cannot visit each of you because of my infirmities and bodily weakness, I have purposed to repeat to you in this letter—which will be my messenger—the words of our Lord Jesus Christ, who is the Word of the Father, and the words of the Holy Spirit, which are spirit and life."

Next follow several pages containing, along with numerous Gospel texts, the favorite themes developed by the saint in his sermons; which may be paraphrased as follows: It was for the salvation of us all that the Word of God became incarnate in the womb of the Virgin Mary, and that after having lived in poverty with his Mother, he offered himself as a victim on the cross. Yet few, alas, consent to taste and see how the Lord is sweet and his burden light, and many prefer darkness to light. But they deserve to be called blessed who love the Lord and do what the Gospel teaches. And what does it teach? To love God with a pure heart, to worship him in spirit and in truth, and to pray without ceasing, preferring for this the Lord's Prayer, and to receive the Lord's Body and Blood in Communion. We ought, moreover, to be good Catholics, to visit churches, and to confess our sins to the priests, who though sinners themselves, are nonetheless God's ministers and deserving of our respect. The Gospel likewise commands us to love our neighbor as ourselves. Let us then do good instead of evil to our brothers. If our function be to judge, let us judge mercifully; if it be to command, with indulgence, deeming ourselves the servants of others. If our role be to obey, let us obey humbly, unless the thing commanded should be a sin. Let us avoid excesses of the table; let us do penance; let us give generously to the poor. In fine, let us be simple, humble, and pure, rather than wise and prudent according to the flesh.

Here is an eloquent passage:

> And upon all those who shall have done these things and persevered in them, the Spirit of the Lord will rest and live and dwell within them; for they shall be the sons of the Heavenly Father, whose works they do, and the spouses, brothers, and mothers of our Lord Jesus Christ. We are His spouses when the faithful soul is united to Jesus Christ by the Holy Spirit. We are His brothers when we do the will of His Father who is in Heaven. We are His mothers when we bear Him in our heart and body by charity and the sincerity

of our conscience and bring Him forth by holy deeds, meet to enlighten our neighbor. Oh, how glorious, how holy, how grand it is to have a Father in Heaven! How holy, how beautiful, and how sweet it is to have a spouse in Heaven! How holy and how blissful, pleasing, and humble, peaceful and sweet and heartwarming and supremely desirable it is to have such a Brother who has given His life for His sheep!

As for those who do not live according to the Gospel, they are blind men who shun the light and lose their souls. To arouse them, Francis depicts vividly the story of a miser's death:

The body is sick, death draws near, while the friends and relatives of the sick man urge him to make his will. His wife and children make a show of tears. The sick man, seeing their tears, is moved. "All I have," he sighs, "I leave to you." Truly, is he not cursed who entrusts his soul and body, and all he has to such hands? Cursed is he who puts his trust in man, says the Lord. Now the heirs call a priest who says to the dying man:

"Do you wish to receive a penance for your sins?" "Yes," he replies. "Do you agree to make reparation with your money for the wrongs and injustices you have committed to the detriment of others?" "No" he replies. "How so?" "Because I have given everything I have to my friends and relatives." Whereupon, he becomes unable to speak and dies that way, the poor wretch! The devil tears his soul from his body with such cruelty that you would have to be that man to have any idea of it. Everything that he thought he possessed in power and resources is taken away from him. His relatives and friends divide up his fortune, while cursing him for not leaving them more. And already the worms have begun to devour his flesh; and thus does he succeed in ruining himself body and soul in this short life and in gaining hell, where he will be tormented forever.

The saint ends with these words:

> To all those who receive this letter, I, Brother Francis, your little servant, most humbly beg and beseech you in the charity which is God, to receive humbly and lovingly these sweet words of our Lord Jesus Christ and to keep them perfectly. Let those who are unable to read, have these words read to them frequently, and remember them and devoutly practice them until death, for they are spirit and life. If they do otherwise, they must render account thereof before the judgment seat of Christ. But those who receive them gladly and delight to meditate on them and to copy them to help others, if they persevere therein till the end, may they be blessed by the Father, Son, and Holy Spirit. Amen.

Was this letter to all the faithful especially addressed to tertiaries? Certainly Orlando, Praxedis, and Jacopa might find in it a sort of reminder composed for them by their spiritual father. The people of Cannara could likewise believe that their beloved preacher was keeping his promise to think of them, when he sent them so beautiful a sermon. It was no less true, however, that for seculars desirous of living the Franciscan life something more was needed. They required a real Rule and special statutes, like those of the Friars Minor and the Poor Ladies they desired to resemble.

No one could better satisfy their aspirations than Cardinal Hugolin, always ready to promote the ideas of St. Francis in the interests of the Church. As a papal legate in Lombardy, he had seen the work of the Humiliati, who teemed in those regions and had, as we have said, a third order whose members lived like real religious.

It was from these Lombard tertiaries, it would seem, that the cardinal took his inspiration for drawing up, with St. Francis, the Third Order Rule of 1221. While it is true that the original text is lost, critics agree in finding the exact reproduction of it in documents dating a few years later. It consisted of thirteen chapters, part of them dealing with the personal sanctification of tertiaries, part with their social life, and the rest with the organization of fraternities.

Of the personal sanctification of the tertiaries. The brothers and sisters, says the Rule, ought to dress modestly, in keeping with the state of penance they have embraced. Chapter I determines the material, form, color, and cost of this clothing. Fur worn by the penitents is to be modest lambskin; their wallets and belts are to be made of plain leather without silk bindings. Avoiding banquets, spectacles, dances, and other too worldly amusements, they are to be content with two meals a day, observe abstinence four times a week, and fast every Friday and sometimes on Wednesday, besides the Lent before Easter. The "visitator" will grant dispensations, however, to the feeble, to laborers, and to pregnant women.

If they know how to read, the tertiaries are to recite daily the seven canonical hours. If not, they are to say fifty-four Our Fathers and Glorys, and during the Lents, unless prevented, all are to assist at Matins. They are to examine their conscience every night, confess and receive Communion three times a year; and every month they are to meet to attend Mass, listen to a sermon, and take part in prayers said in common.

Social life. The penitents are to take care to pay the prescribed tithes, to pay the debts they have contracted, and to make restitution for goods unjustly acquired. They shall be obliged to exhort members of their families to serve God, to urge the sick to repent, and to denounce to the ministers or the visitator any members of the fraternity who may cause scandal. They will attend the funerals of fellow tertiaries and recite for them a certain number of psalms or Our Fathers with the *Requiem aeternum.* At each monthly meeting they are to contribute a sum for the poor and the sick. These are not to be neglected, for the ministers are to see that they are comforted with visits and receive all necessary assistance.

It is further incumbent upon each tertiary to make his will within three months of his profession, to become reconciled with his enemies, and not to make new ones. Finally, the brothers are forbidden to bear arms or to take any solemn oath without the consent of the pope.

Organization of the fraternity. This is directed by a visitator, two ministers, and several minor officers. The visitator possesses supreme authority. He shall be told of infringements of the Rule, grant necessary dispensations, and expel incorrigibles. Both ministers are elected annually by the outgoing ministers with the advice of the members. They shall make inquiry as to the orthodoxy of postulants, and shall pledge the newly professed before a notary to observe the Rule faithfully until death, shall convoke the penitents to the monthly meeting, distribute the alms, and take care of the sick.

Finally, the minor officers are brothers whose role it is to assist the ministers, collect monthly dues, assist the poor, and act as messengers and secretaries.

Such in substance were the statutes of the new institute. The text itself was a simple statement of regulations and of prohibitions, in plain words and without Scripture references, very similar in form to the constitutions drawn up by Hugolin for the Poor Clares. It contained none of that enthusiasm and idealism that Francis brought to everything he did and said; and it is evident that he took little part in drawing up this canonical and administrative document—he who could not open his mouth without quoting the Gospel and uttering the Savior's name.

The article which best revealed the intervention of the future Gregory IX was assuredly the one referring to the oath. Already the great statesman Innocent III had inserted it into the Rule of the Lombard tertiaries. It was without doubt a revolutionary feature in that period of history.

The whole political structure of the Middle Ages rested on the oath. A man swore an oath to his suzerain or to his commune. Then whatever happened, however unjust or arbitrary the war in which the suzerain or the commune was involved, he was bound to take up arms and espouse their quarrel. Thus, to have control of the oath meant that the Holy See could wield an unheard-of power against its adversaries. In that way, by opposing wars which it judged to be unjust and by favoring the others, it could break the resistance of the communes, resist the civil power, and hold the emperor himself in check. And that is what happened, as soon as the tertiaries spread throughout the peninsula. Thanks to them, the papacy found everywhere valuable auxiliaries, whose help enabled it to drive the Ghibellines to the wall.

Great also were the social consequences of the new institution. The obligation of its members to make their will deprived the suzerain of the benefits of intestate successions. The establishment, in each fraternity, of a common treasury facilitated the redemption of the tallage and the emancipation of the serfs. The fraternal mingling within the penitential communities of peasants and nobles brought the various classes of society closer together. All this, without taking into consideration the canonical immunity which freed the tertiaries from lay jurisdiction, and the voting system whereby they named and replaced their superiors—all this gradually undermined the feudal order and tended at the same time to better the poor man's lot.

It is almost impossible to know the exact extent of Francis's awareness of all these novelties. Apparently, it was enough for him that the Rule prescribed and promoted the observance of the Gospel for it to be according to his own heart. Likewise, it was doubtless enough for those to whom it was addressed to know that it came from him for them to be eager to receive and obey it. So they put on the cord, placed Franciscan visitators at their head, and considered themselves henceforth sons of the Poverello.

It was in Florence, in 1221, during a sojourn of Francis with Hugolin, that the first fraternity was canonically erected. And wherever Franciscans and Poor Clares were to be found, the Third Order was set up. Its members soon spread all over the world, either grouped in fraternities or keeping their Rule as isolated tertiaries. In the course of centuries, the Church raised a hundred and twenty-nine of them to her altars. Among them, we find kings like St. Louis of France and St. Ferdinand of Castile, princesses like St. Elizabeth of Hungary, former sinners like Margaret of Cortona and Angela of Foligno, innocent children like St. Rose of Viterbo, numerous popes, simple priests like the Curé d'Ars, a merchant of combs like Blessed Peter of Siena who died a centenarian in 1289 and merited a place in the *Divine Comedy*, and men still more illustrious, such as Petrarch, Raphael, Michelangelo, Murillo, Galvani, Volta, Christopher Columbus, Palestrina, and Liszt. Fifty-three members of the Third

Order Secular of St. Francis are canonized saints, and seventy-six have been formally beatified by the Church. Of the latter, eleven are being considered for canonization, while an additional thirty-seven tertiaries are candidates for beatification.

Among these holy personages, it is fitting to mention here especially the one who is their common patron, Blessed Luchesio, the first tertiary. Perhaps a boyhood friend of St. Francis, he went at first into business and politics at San Casciano in the region of Siena. His life at that period cannot be said to have been the most edifying; for as a wheat merchant, he hoarded grain in times of plenty for resale at a high price in times of scarcity. Politically, he was active in the Guelf faction. Buona Donna, his wife, as beautiful as she was intelligent, shared his ambitions and tastes. But when Siena fell into the hands of the Ghibellines, they both fled to Poggibonsi in the territory of Florence, where the adherents of the pope were still masters. There, Francis's exhortations completed the conversion of this couple, whom the blessings of exile had already visibly transformed.

Already distributing their goods to the poor and reserving for themselves only four acres of land, they put on the penitents' habit, and from then on their lives were dedicated to the poor. They received them into their home and shared the vegetables from their garden with them. If the sick were too feeble to come, Luchesio cared for them in their own houses. He brought some of them home with him; and often his neighbors would see him coming back with a couple of them, one perched on the back of his donkey and the other one on his own back. He went to the Maremma (the marshes between the mountains and the sea) and as far as the Tyrrhenian seashore when malaria was raging in those districts. And if his own resources were exhausted, he would appeal to public charity, begging from door to door for his protégés; and because of the charm of his personality, generally obtaining all that he asked.

God permitted that this couple, who had been one in life, should not be separated in death. When, in April 1260, Buona Donna fell ill, Luchesio was so affected that the malady from which he himself was suffering suddenly grew worse. He still kept on his feet to assist his wife to receive the last sacraments. Then he clasped her hand, saying: "Dear wife, we have always loved each other on earth. So why don't we go to Heaven together? Just wait for me a little, Buona." Going back to bed, he called back his friend, Fr. Hildebrand, who gave him the last sacraments. Then seeing that Buona Donna had expired, he made the sign of the cross, pronounced the names of Our Lady and St. Francis for the last time, and surrendered his soul to God.

CHAPTER SIXTEEN

The First Franciscan School

SOME RECENT WRITERS have advanced the thesis that Francis encouraged his sons to study; but this idea appears to many as somewhat startling, and in general it is the opposite opinion that has prevailed.

Yet let no man believe that, following the envious and the ignorant, the Poverello despised learning and scholarship. On the contrary, he had such a reverence for books that if he saw a scrap of writing on the ground, he would pick it up and put it in a safe place. "Who knows," he would say, "whether this paper does not have God's name on it or some praise addressed to him?"

To those who observed that this was not usually the case with pagan writings, he would reply, "I pick them up, because even they contain letters that can spell the Creator's glorious name. Whatever is good in them does not belong to the infidels any more than to other men, but to God, the only Source of good."

As for the scholars, the courteous Little Poor Man asked nothing better than to bow before their superiority and to show his esteem for them. He would have us venerate the theologians who dispense God's Word to us; he dubbed the illustrious Anthony of Padua his "bishop"; he called the Doctor of Laws, Peter Catanii, "messere"; and was so devoid of prejudice with regard to the erudite that he called upon some of them—such as Elias, Pacifico, Peter Staccia, and Gregory of Naples—to fill the highest positions in his Order.

Nevertheless, regardless of how noble and beneficial learning appeared to him, Francis did not consider it useful for his friars. In vain would one have objected to him that it was a necessity for whoever would scan God's mysteries. Francis knew that man is incapable of solving the insolvable, and that it is by prayer and humility alone that he merits the supernatural light that permits him to draw near to God. "I used to be tempted myself," he would say, "to have books. But the Gospel showed me God's will. I opened it and came upon these words: 'To you it is given to know the mystery of the kingdom of God; but to the rest, all things are revealed in parables.'"

He had also observed that scholars, never being done with their studies, devoted time to them that could be better employed elsewhere. "In the Day of Judgment," he would declare, "they will present themselves empty-handed to the Supreme Judge." He added that it was better to practice virtue than to be able to talk about it. "It was for shedding their blood fighting against the infidels," he liked to repeat, "that the Emperor Charlemagne, Roland, Oliver, and the other paladins deserved to live in men's memories. But today's heroes would rather gain glory by telling of such deeds than in trying to imitate them."

Especially did he see in learning a stumbling block to the poverty and humility of his Order. If he knew some modest and reserved scholars, he no doubt knew still more whom self-esteem had made obstinate and proud; and this made him say that "there are many whom learning makes so puffed up and proud that they are utterly incapable of humble submission." He knew likewise that comfortable buildings were needed to house libraries and men of study. Now how could Francis, who wanted only "little houses made of branches and mud," reconcile these requirements with the cult of holy poverty?

With the satisfaction of self-love and the public esteem it generates, together with the expense involved, Francis feared, then, lest study should imperil the vocation of his friars and raise them above the rank in which he had placed them. His intention was that they should forego study just as they had renounced large churches, beautiful monasteries, and ecclesiastical honors—that they should leave to others the more appealing ways of being useful to one's neighbor. Besides, as he said to a novice, "there are so many who seek to become scholars" that the friars for their part can very well do without this, since "God will bless them for making themselves sterile out of love for Him."

As this novice had been authorized by Elias to have a psalter, he came to Francis to have the permission confirmed. "Once you have a psalter," replied Francis, "you will want a breviary. And when you have a breviary, no longer deigning to disturb yourself, you will say haughtily to your brother, 'Brother, please fetch my breviary!'" Then taking up a handful of ashes, he began to rub his head with them, saying: "I—a breviary! I—a breviary!"

A few months later, the novice came to him again to talk about the longed-for book. "Go and do as the minister says!" exclaimed Francis, exasperated. At once repenting, he ran after the novice. "Come back, brother, and show me the place where I spoke to you!" Then, throwing himself on his knees and beating his breast, he said to the novice, "*Mea culpa!* Forgive me for answering you as I did; for according to the Rule, a real Friar Minor ought to be content with his habit, cord, and drawers, and possess nothing else."

So to the friars who were unlettered, Francis recommended that they should not seek schooling. But many educated men had been admitted to the Brotherhood and continued to flock in. Now, must these, for lack of books, forget what they had learned and become ignorant once more?

Francis would have liked that the learned sacrificed their learning, just as the nobles renounced the privileges of birth, so that ridding themselves of every trace of superiority, both should strive to acquire "holy simplicity, the daughter of grace, sister of wisdom, and mother of justice." Nothing, writes Thomas of Celano, was dearer to him than this virtue, "which, content with its God, despises everything else," and is therefore greatly superior to learning. The saint explained his meaning by the following parable:

> Once upon a time there was a great assembly, to which the religious of the whole world were convened to hear two sermons. The first was to be preached by a scholar, the second by an ignorant man. Before opening his mouth, the scholar said to himself: "This is not the time to show off what I know; for there are men here who know more than I do, and whom I shall not be able to astonish. So I shall speak simply." Garbed in sackcloth, he ascended the pulpit and humbly limited himself to a few maxims on the brevity of life, the utility of patience, and the everlasting happiness promised to the elect in Heaven.
>
> The assembly found this discourse perfect and was deeply edified by it. Only the unlearned man, whose time had come to speak, was a trifle disappointed—the only sermon he felt capable of preaching had just been stolen from him. "Well!" he said to himself, "if the savants are now going to speak like simple men, then I shall adopt the style of the savants, and like them, give a brilliant commentary on the Scriptures."

He knew a few verses of the Psalms. He chose one of them, relying on divine inspiration to explain them. And God came so mightily to his aid that his hearers were filled with admiration by his eloquence.

And Francis added:

> This assembly is our Order, whose variety is pleasing to our Heavenly Father. In it the learned and the ignorant alike ought to share of their best with one another: the first, by placing themselves like the simple in the one school of the Holy Spirit; the second, by imitating the humility of the learned, who have forgone places of prominence in the world to share our despised state.

But, you may ask, without study, how could the friars be expected to give themselves to preaching and the apostolate? Wasn't St. Francis contradicting himself here and demanding the impossible? Not at all! To grasp this point we must recall the way Francis understood the apostolate; and let us especially consider what distinguished his Brotherhood from that of the Friars Preachers.

To be sure, Francis's Order, like that of St. Dominic, was an apostolic Order. But his methods for converting souls were not at all like those used by his friend. For Dominic had founded an Order corresponding to the need of the Church at that time for preachers versed in dogma and the Scriptures. The monks of those times did not preach; and the bishops and parish priests whose office it was to do so, generally refrained: the first because they were cloistered or too busy with their temporal concerns, the second because they were too ignorant, and both of them were too often discredited by their conduct from preaching effectively about virtue. Here and there bishops farmed out the preaching to laymen, who turned over to them part of the proceeds. But these substitutes were not trustworthy, and were rightly discredited by the hierarchy.

They likewise deplored the scarcity of professors of theology, since too many clerics preferred to devote themselves to jurisprudence, which opened up to them more lucrative careers. Even the great University of Bologna had no chair of Sacred Theology at this period. In vain, the Third Lateran Council in 1179 had ordered that there should be a professor of grammar in every diocese, and in every archdiocese a professor of theology, to instruct the clerics; but this decree, as to the second part at least, remained a dead letter.

It was the Friars Preachers who supplied the Church with the preachers and doctors she lacked. They were authorized to "recite the canonical hours in a brief and rapid manner, so as to allow more time for study;" and were obliged, "whether travelling or at the monastery, to study day and night." And Dominic succeeded so well in his purpose that half a century after his death his Order possessed around seven hundred doctors of theology; whereas in 1220 one could not have found more than a hundred in all Christendom.

Quite other was to be the type of activity of the Franciscans. Their very name defined their role. Far from entrusting to them the influential mission of teaching alongside the bishops, Francis had called them "Minors" to indicate that they were to remain in the lowliest place, to imitate the crucified life of the Savior and observe the Gospel literally. For occupations, he assigned them manual labor and the care of lepers; and in the conversion of sinners, it was on their prayers and their example that he counted most. "Many," he declared, "are the friars who, devoting their energies to study rather than to prayer, attribute the good they do to the sermons they preach. They thus appropriate to themselves what belongs to others. My true knights of the Round Table are those who weep in solitude for their own sins and the sins of others. To them the Savior will show on the Last Day all the souls saved by their prayers."

Let us add that as a good troubadour, Francis also trusted in poetry and music to "touch men's hearts and bring them to spiritual joy." We shall see later that after composing the "Canticle of Brother Sun," "he taught it to his companions and dreamed of sending them all over the world with it. The most eloquent among them would speak first; then all the rest would begin to sing the Praises of the Lord. Finally, their leader would say to the audience: 'Since we are God's *jongleurs* and deserve a reward for our songs, the one we ask is that you live from now on as good Christians.' "

Naturally, the Friars Minor had to preach too. We recall how their father had bidden them greet everyone they met with "God give you peace!" He soon permitted them to say more, and to recite a little exhortation to penance already mentioned, and which was less a sermon than an edifying refrain. Later on, those authorized by the Minister General could preach; and here again (let us insist), these were purely moral and practical exhortations, since Innocent III had forbidden the Franciscans to touch on dogmatic and biblical subjects; and the definitive Rule itself bade them to confine themselves to speaking "of vice and virtue, of punishment and glory, and not to preach long sermons, in imitation of our Lord who always spoke briefly when here on earth."

So Francis was not being inconsistent when he urged his friars to lay aside their books and to rely on the inspirations of grace to touch men's hearts. It was likewise the way Francis himself preached.

"Speaking from the heart," says Thomas of Celano, "avoiding all the apparatus of distinctions, of sounding words, and the subtleties of rhetoric, he expressed the inexpressible in a few words, and with flaming gestures rapt his audience to Heaven. If he ran out of words, he simply told his hearers that he could not recall what he had prepared. In this case, either the inspiration came back and he was more eloquent than ever; or else, not finding anything to add, he would dismiss the people with his blessing."

Laying aside the sermon "aids" and the dialectics so dear to pulpit orators of the period, his preaching was simple and clothed with mysterious power. We have contemporary accounts of two of his sermons. The first was given at Rome before Honorius and his court:

> After asking the Pope to bless him, the Little Poor Man began without the least timidity. He was so full of his subject that he began to gesticulate and to dance, if not like a tumbler, at the very least like a man intoxicated with divine love. No one thought of laughing; on the contrary, all were so moved that they could not restrain their tears—in admiration for the workings of divine grace in such a man. It was Cardinal Hugolin who had proposed that Francis should preach; and he was so fearful lest the thing should not go off well that he prayed all the time for God to help his friend.

The other sermon was the one the Poverello preached at Bologna on August 15, 1222:

"I was studying in that city," writes Thomas of Spalato, "when I had an opportunity of hearing Francis preach on the square of the Public Palace, where almost the whole population had assembled. He preached of angels, men, and demons with such eloquence and precision that the most learned were amazed that an untutored man could express himself so well. His discourse had nothing of the tone or mannerisms of the preacher. Rather it was like a conversation whose sole object was to extinguish hatred and restore peace. The orator was wretchedly garbed, his appearance frail, his face without beauty; but this did not hinder his words from reconciling the Bolognese nobles who had been slaughtering one another for generations. And so great was the enthusiasm that men and women rushed up to him to tear his garments to shreds and make off with the pieces."

Certainly, to find God and communicate him to others, Francis himself had no need to study. The current teaching of the Church, joined to meditation on the Gospels and liturgical texts, was sufficient for him. This inspired man found richer nourishment in the songs of birds and streams than in the laborious cogitations of the learned. And when God in addition communicated himself to his soul in prayer, what need had he of books?

To convert souls the way the Poverello did, no school was necessary. But on one condition—that of being as great a poet and as great a saint as he. Was it an illusion on his part to believe that his example could be followed by many?

How could one require of scholars sufficient heroism to close their books, forsake their beloved studies, and, in the words of Pascal, "consent to grow stupid"? This was no more to be expected than to see them continue to live in wattle huts.

And how could anyone make these eloquent men—once in the pulpit—"speak briefly of virtue and vice," foregoing all doctrinal instruction and the confounding of heretics? If a man needs to be instructed himself in order to teach others, where is he to find the true doctrine if not in the masters and in their works? Besides, was not the example of the Fathers of the Church and of St. Dominic there to show the possibility of allying theology and sanctity?

So thought a number of friars burning to widen the scope of their zeal and to follow in the footsteps of the Dominicans. Resistance was all the more vain, since the Roman Curia itself supported them, only too glad to have such valuable auxiliaries for its reform of ecclesiastical studies and in its battle against heresy.

It was Cardinal Hugolin who, with his customary skill, made Francis listen to reason. We do not know how he went about it and to what extent he really convinced his friend. The fact is that he did bring him to authorize the reopening of the great convent of Bologna and the resumption of the courses inaugurated there by Peter Staccia.

Now, since it was necessary for members of the Order to study, no one was better fitted to instruct them than Brother Anthony, who had just revealed his learning and sanctity in Lombardy. So it was he who was assigned to teach.

Born in Lisbon in 1195, Anthony of Padua was a canon regular at Santa Cruz in Coimbra, when in 1220 the remains of the first Franciscan martyrs were brought back from Morocco for burial in the church of the canons. Burning to follow in the footsteps of these heroes, he left his Order to enter that of the Friars Minor and set off for Morocco. However, almost immediately he fell ill. He re-embarked to return home, but was cast by a tempest off the coast of Sicily. He there joined some friars of Messina who were going to the General Chapter of 1221. At the Portiuncula nobody paid any attention to him; and the superiors would have even forgotten to give him an obedience, had it not been for Brother Gratian, Provincial of Lombardy, who agreed to take Anthony with him.

At the hermitage of Montepaolo, Anthony lived at first in a cave, which he left only to assist at the offices and to keep the house clean. His theological lore and his oratorical talents, however, were made manifest on an ordination day at Forli. When others refused to preach because unprepared, Anthony was bidden by his superior to preach extemporaneously. Thereafter, except for the time devoted to the lessons which he gave at Bologna, Toulouse, and Montpellier, he preached the rest of his life: in the Lombard region where he combated the Cathari with his great learning; in France, where he preached in Brive, Arles, Bourges, and Limoges; and, finally, in Padua, where he died at the height of his fame at the age of thirty-six. He was canonized less than a year after his death, and was named a Doctor of the Church in 1946.

This prodigious orator, who has become Christianity's most popular saint, is said to have spoken all languages. Even the fishes (the *Fioretti* assures us) heard him gladly. The fact is that immense crowds assembled to hear him, and merchants closed their shops when he preached. He confounded the most learned Patarini, and excoriated from the pulpit the immoral lives of prelates, a proof that the saints of the second Franciscan generation no longer had, as did their father, a horror of disputes and of attacks against individuals.

It is thought that it was in the winter of 1223 that St. Anthony inaugurated his lectures at the Bologna friary. At once, as at a given signal, schools were established in every province of the Order; and twenty years later, the Franciscans possessed chairs at Oxford, Paris, Cologne, and elsewhere, whose renown soon became universal. In them flourished those famous geniuses whose doctrines and works have been studied and republished for centuries: Alexander of Hales, the "irrefragable Doctor"; St. Bonaventure, the "Seraphic Doctor"; Roger Bacon, the "Admirable Doctor"; Ockham, the "Invincible Doctor"; and Blessed Duns Scotus, the celebrated rival of St. Thomas, who caused the doctrine of the Immaculate Conception to triumph in theology.

We may also be sure that Franciscan preaching was not long in liberating itself from every impediment; and in 1230, Hugolin, now pope, officially abolished the prohibition forbidding the friars to comment on dogma and the Scriptures from the pulpit.

Far from these famous universities, however, where Franciscans and Dominicans vied with each other in learning and eloquence, the humble "school" of Rivo Torto still endured, where Brother Leo and Brother Giles meant to preserve, with their disciples, the spirit of simplicity of the early days. It was this "school," as we know, that produced the *Speculum Perfectionis*, the *Sacrum Commercium*, and those incomparable *Fioretti*, so much appreciated by those who profit very little (alas) from the *Summas* and *Commentaries* of Oxford or Paris.

The simple brethren held that the friars did wrong in wanting to become scholars and have themselves talked about. "Ah, Paris, Paris!" exclaimed Brother Giles. "It is you who are ruining the Order of St. Francis!" Later on, the Franciscan poet Jacopone da Todi likewise accused Paris of having brought about the ruin of Assisi.

While venerating the theologians, Brother Giles sometimes found them tedious: "Of all your treatises, there are only two that I judge worthy of constant study—the first which teaches me to praise God for his benefits, and the second which teaches me to repent of my sins." He also counseled them to waste less time trying to explain the unexplainable, and said in regard to predestination: "Those who claim to know everything that the sea contains have only to jump into the water after it, if they so desire. For my part, I'll stay on shore where I can wash my hands and feet, or all of me if I like. Once I have learned how I ought to behave, why should I weary myself learning more?"

One day the ecstatic of Monte Ripido began to needle St.

Bonaventure. "When one thinks," said he, "of the light that great doctors like you receive from Heaven, how do you expect ignoramuses like us to be saved?"

"The all-important-thing for salvation," replied Brother Bonaventure, "is to love God."

"You're not trying to make me think that an illiterate man can love Him as much as a learned man?"

"Come now, Brother Giles! Not only as much, but sometimes more. Why, one sometimes sees old women surpassing the greatest theologians in this respect."

At that very moment an old beggar woman was coming down the road. Giles rushed to the garden and shouted to her over the hedge: "Rejoice, old lady! For I have just learned that if you will, you can love God even more than Brother Bonaventure does!"

Thereupon he fell into an ecstasy in which he remained for three hours.

CHAPTER SEVENTEEN

The Final Rule

WE HAVE SEEN that the Rule of 1221 was unable to restore harmony among the friars. Obviously, its greatest defect was its attempt to maintain the primitive characteristics of the Brotherhood and to conform to an outmoded state of things. But there was still another defect on which the party of Elias, upheld by Hugolin, could more honorably insist—the lack of definiteness and precision needed in a legislative document, a factor which consequently gave it no chance of securing Rome's approval.

Aided by the Cardinal-Protector, the Ministers persuaded Francis to elaborate a new text. Taking with him Brother Leo and Brother Bonizzo, a learned jurist, the saint climbed the wooded heights of Fonte Columbo near Rieti; and there in a cavern in the wilds above a narrow valley through which flowed a mountain stream, he set to work once more.

We know nothing of the Rule he then composed. Nevertheless, it is probable that it likewise was not pleasing to the opposition; for when the time came for discussion, Brother Elias, to whom it had been entrusted, declared that he had lost it.

If one way for a diplomat to achieve his ends is often to gain time, one may ask whether this loss was really involuntary. Was there some hope of exhausting the saint's patience? Or, knowing him to be ill, did the opposition count on his death before he had confirmed his intentions in writing?

Again accompanied by Brother Leo, Francis repaired once more to the hermitage of Fonte Colombo, where, fasting, praying, and lamenting before God, he attempted anew to draw up the Gospel code which he desired to bequeath to his sons. He passed through fearful hours of discouragement. The task to which the attitude of the dissenters condemned him seemed beyond his strength. How could their human views be harmonized with God's own demands? How was he to let his heart speak, and appeal from it to the hearts and loyalty of his friars, in a dry administrative ordinance in which he was no longer permitted to quote from the Gospel? Especially now when he had so much to say and insist on, when he sensed his authority reduced, his adversaries become more and more powerful, and his ideal less and less followed. And perhaps—poet that he was— he suffered additional pangs at the difficulty he had to be brief and to condense his thought.

Yet as the guide and father of an immense religious family, he could not abandon those loyal men whom he had induced to follow him.

One night he saw in a dream some famished friars who begged him for food. He attempted to gather up some crumbs he saw scattered on the ground; but like dust, they sifted through his fingers. "Francis," said a voice, "make a loaf from these crumbs, and in this way your friars can eat them."

Francis obeyed. Among the religious present, some eagerly ate of this mysterious bread; others, refusing, were immediately covered with leprosy. The saint understood that the crumbs were the words of the Gospel, that the loaf represented the Rule which he must continue to draft, and that the rebels were harming themselves and incurring God's punishment. This dream encouraged him to complete his task.

Meanwhile the ministers were anxiously wondering what the new text would be like. Some of them even went to Fonte Colombo to declare that they would never accept a rule that ran counter to their desires. Francis replied that he was writing under God's dictation and sent them away with his curse.

Not all the ministers were of this sort, for one wrote to Francis of the trials his office brought—so great that he longed to abandon his charge and take himself to a hermitage. To him Francis wrote:

> I do my best to reply to you on the state of your soul, to bid you not to be disturbed any more by the difficulties you are encountering, which (you say) keep you from loving the Lord God. Do not be afflicted by what it does not please God to grant you. Even if the brothers should beat you, you ought to look on all such treatment as a grace. Prefer, then, the duties of your charge to the life you might live in a hermitage. If one of your brothers should have committed all the sins in the world, so act, if he comes to you, that he shall not leave without having read forgiveness in your eyes and received from you some kind word. By this I shall know that you love the Lord and that you love me, His servant and yours. If the culprit does not come to you, then go to him yourself and ask him if he desires to be forgiven. And should he come to you a thousand times, you must love him more than you love me, to win him to God. Let the guardians know, when you are able, that you are fully resolved to act thus.

At Pentecost, with God's help and with the common consent of the brothers, we shall endeavor to bring together in one, all the chapters of the Rule relative to mortal sin. It will be worded something like this: 'If a brother fall into mortal sin, he must go to his guardian, and then to his custos, who will receive him mercifully, dealing with him as he would wish to be treated himself. And if the other friars learn of his fault, let them not shame or reproach the guilty one, but show great mercy toward him and carefully keep his secret.... And the confessor shall say to him, 'Go and sin no more,' and this shall be all the penance he shall impose.

In closing, Francis counseled the minister to think over the things still lacking in the Rule, and arranged to meet with him at the Chapter of Pentecost, where he hoped that everything could be peacefully settled.

Contrary to his expectations, the hoped-for agreement was arrived at only at the price of new and difficult negotiations. The documents are lacking which would permit us to describe them. Nevertheless, I surmise that they were long, drawn-out, often stormy, and fraught with immeasurable suffering for the Little Poor Man.

In May 1223, Francis attended the General Chapter of the Portiuncula. A few months later, he left for Rome, where his Rule, already so much worked over, received from Hugolin its definitive form. On November 29, Pope Honorius approved it by the Bull *Solet annuere*; and ever since it has constituted the official legislation of the Friars Minor.

This Rule differs entirely in its makeup from the previous plan. Three times as short as the Rule of 1221, quoting only ten verses from the Gospel, (whereas the other contained a hundred), it consists of twelve short chapters from which every prayer and effusion of the heart have almost disappeared. The words were chosen with great care, with the double intent of not wounding the susceptibilities of the intransigents nor of discouraging the demands of the moderates. But whereas the Rule of 1221 constituted—in a blending of lyrical prayer and touching supplication—a detailed description of Franciscan life as dreamed of by its founder, and was so worded that no learned commentaries could dilute it, that of 1223 on the contrary is a canonical text to be interpreted by jurists—a series of prescriptions and prohibitions for them to decide whether they oblige *sub gravi* or *sub levi*, and in which they would later find matter for twenty-seven mortal sins.

If, fundamentally, there is no glaring contradiction between the two documents, still we cannot affirm that the Rule of 1223 perfectly expresses the intentions of the founder. This is especially apparent in the suppressions and omissions to which he was obliged to consent.

For example, Francis desired to insert the following clause in his text: "If, in the course of their travels, the friars shall find the Blessed Sacrament reserved in unseemly vessels or places, they shall urge the priests to remedy matters; and if they refuse, they shall do so in their stead." This was an ordinance which would have been certain to engender conflicts with the clergy, and which the wise Hugolin ruled out.

It was doubtless the same hand that struck out the dangerous and anarchistic article authorizing the friars to judge the conduct of their superiors and to disobey any who would prevent them from observing the Gospel literally (chap. V).

Equally suppressed was the passing reference in the Rule of 1221 to the care of leprosy patients. An outstanding suppression was those words so characteristic of the first Franciscans: "And when they shall go through the world, they shall take nothing with them, neither wallet, nor bread, nor staff; and they shall not resist the evildoer, letting themselves be despoiled without resistance." In short, almost everything was done away with that commanded the Friars Minor to remain in the ranks of the truly poor.

From this time on, in fact, the friars were engaged in elevating themselves to the social rank of other clerics and religious. First, by means of study, of which, to be sure, the new Rule makes no mention. But it should be noted that it no longer forbids the friars to have books. Next, by means of favors gradually obtained from the Roman Curia and by the increasingly lenient interpretation of their vow of poverty.

It was Hugolin who discovered the legal formula permitting them to occupy suitable buildings from which it would no longer be possible to dislodge them. He already had this in mind when, in order to get Francis to let his friars go back to their convent at Bologna, he declared, as we have seen, that the building belonged to the Holy See. Extended to all conventual property, such an interpretation would do away with every type of difficulty and would render incalculable service in the future.

It was also thanks to the "governor, protector, and corrector of the brotherhood" that the friars obtained the Bulls that rapidly improved their status in the world and in the Church. For they soon had no further cause to envy the other mendicant orders on this score.

Already prior to 1221, pontifical letters recommend them to foreign prelates; in March, 1222, they obtained permission to officiate in their conventual churches in times of interdict; in 1225, they were authorized to celebrate Mass on portable altars without the bishops being able to object; in March 1226, friars going to Morocco received permission to use money; and Francis was hardly dead before Friars Minor were elevated to the episcopate. Finally, as soon as he became Pope Gregory IX, Hugolin granted two extremely important Bulls to the Franciscans: the one confers the privilege of exemption on them and withdraws them from that jurisdiction of and dependence on the bishops in which their father desired them to remain; and the other removes all force of law from the Testament of the saint.

These accommodations and mitigations, profoundly modifying the physiognomy of the Brotherhood, have been held by many against the authoritarian and powerful prelate. The Rule of 1223, privileges and exemptions, the abandonment of manual labor, the encourage-ment given to study, the prestige accorded clerics and the possibility of their being admitted to ecclesiastical dignities, the partial aban-donment of the original Gospel program—all this is in great part his work. Hence, some have accused him of "utterly disorienting the Franciscan movement in order to turn it completely to the profit of the Church."

Evidence is lacking, however, for so flat a condemnation. If we are to judge Hugolin fairly, it behooves us not to lay more responsibility at his door than is rightly his. Was it his fault if the ideal of the Little Poor Man could be entirely realized only by a few exceptional souls? The moment that this ideal became the common property of several thousand men, it had to be watered down, as it were, in order to remain accessible to all. Who could possibly make heroism and holi-ness the common law of this world?

The difficulties in which Hugolin soon found himself enmeshed stemmed from the fact that some, like Brother Giles and Brother Leo, looked on the primitive ideal as a thing realizable and not to be touched; while others, led by Brother Elias, held it to be slightly utopian and utterly impracticable.

These difficulties could only be aggravated by the growth of the fraternity, by the entry of learned men into the Order, and by the different ways in which the friars conceived of the apostolate: some wishing to exercise it only in strict fidelity to the spirit of Rivo Torto, and the rest thinking it should be revamped to adapt it to the requirements of study and to current conditions of apostolic effort.

Such was the conflict the Cardinal-Protector was called upon to resolve. This he did, to be sure, in accordance with his personal opinions and with an eye to furthering the reforms of Innocent III, but not without entering as fully as possible into the sentiments of St. Francis. His arbitration therefore was a meritorious compromise between the demands of the two parties involved.

As the official representative of the Church to which belongs the right to regulate the statutes of religious orders, it would have been easy for him—relying on Brother Elias and the papal authority—to crush the zealots of the primitive observance. Yet he always treated them with consideration. Later on, when he had become pope, far from seeking to destroy the writings from which their intransigence drew its support, he eulogized the Testament of St. Francis and assigned Thomas of Celano to relate the humble chronicles of Rivo Torto. And when Brother Elias had almost brought to triumph in the Order those tendencies capable of utterly destroying the Franciscan spirit, he removed him from office, covering him with ridicule in the eyes of Christendom.

Thus it was that in everything practicable the work of St. Francis was able to continue; the sons of the Poverello remained in possession of their father's heritage; and down through the centuries men have seen his sublime and inaccessible ideal, like a ferment of "holy discontent" laid in the hearts of his children, ceaselessly impel them onward to new and more holy reforms.

To be just toward Hugolin, we must remind ourselves that he always defended Francis against those prelates who desired to put a speedy end to the Franciscan adventure. And what would have become of the Poverello without the prudence of this great cardinal? When we realize that the saint's fate might otherwise have been settled like that of some Waldensian, that this extraordinary figure of history might thus have been lost in the crowd, and that nothing of him would have come down to us, we cannot do otherwise than honor the memory of his powerful friend.

Few men have suffered more than St. Francis. In addition to the infirmities due to his continuous state of poor health and the mysterious tortures of the stigmata, he constantly afflicted his body with fasting and vigils, with fatigue, penances, and mortifications of every sort. He habitually treated "brother ass" with such harshness that before leaving it, he felt the need of a reconciliation. "I bear it witness," he said, "that it has shown itself obedient in every circumstance, and has not pampered itself. I must acknowledge that it and I have always been of the same mind to serve our Lord."

Of all the Poverello's sufferings, the most dreadful was that which marked the period we have just studied. It was the one referred to by his biographers when, without being more specific, they speak of St. Francis's "great temptation." This was a unique trial, a torture particularly long and cruel, a distress of conscience so serious and so profound that divine intervention was necessary to deliver him from it.

It was a sort of intense anguish in which the Little Poor Man, almost abandoned by God, walked in darkness, a prey to indecision and doubt, almost, it would seem, to the point of despair.

Reduced to powerlessness ever since Elias and the other superiors of the Order loom between him and his friars, he sees the ministers and learned brethren resisting him, Hugolin enjoining him to make concessions—and so his work seems irreparably compromised. What is he to do? Was it not from the Lord that he received this form of life that he practiced and desired to transmit to his sons? Could he have been deceived? Under color of following the Gospel, had he been merely chasing shadows, deluded by self and the devil? Is it for the sins of his youth that God has forsaken him?

And so this heaven-inspired man, finding heaven now mute, is troubled in spirit. His assurance and optimism vanish. He is obsessed by fears of evil and devoured by scruples.

Many are the manifestations of this state of soul as reported by his biographers. For months, writes one of them, he refused to visit the Poor Ladies. It was Sister Clare, we know, who saved him from himself this time, succeeded in seeing him again and even in eating with him. "Do you believe," he observed afterward to his friars, "that I do not cherish with all my heart our Sisters of San Damiano? It would be cruel and sinful to abandon them."

Another time, he seems to reproach himself for defending his ideal against Hugolin; and the man who held obedience to be a joy and knightly service now goes to extremes and speaks of it in a macabre style: "The obedient man ought to be like a corpse which lets itself be placed anywhere and does not protest. If men clothe it in purple, it appears the more livid. If they seat it on a platform like a doctor, instead of raising its head, it will let it fall on its breast."

His moods shift like those of a soul that has lost its moorings. At times he is animated by holy wrath: "Let them be accursed by You, O Lord, those men whose evil example shame the good friars of the

Order and destroy by their conduct what it has pleased You to build up." Then, indignation giving way to discouragement, he confines himself to pitying those faithful religious whom the reformers may drive some day from the Brotherhood, reducing them to life in the woods.

This man who was so clear in his thinking and so assured in his progress had suddenly become unsure of his way, uncertain of his duty, troubled in spirit, entangled in the most contradictory resolutions. One day he dreams of authorizing the partisans of the primitive observance to leave the perjured community. Does he fear lest this will soon be his own fate? "Supposing," he says, "that the friars, ashamed of an unlettered superior like me, shamefully expel me from the Brotherhood. I tell you that I would not be a true Friar Minor if I did not rejoice to be treated that way."

But he soon reconsidered, recoiling before schism, and counseling submission. "Should a superior command something contrary to their spiritual good, though the friars should not obey him, let them never separate themselves from him, and let them love him in proportion of this persecution of them."

Finally Francis adopted for himself a middle course. Increasingly avoiding the society of the friars, he chose to withdraw with a few faithful friends to secluded hermitages. He would even have liked to go back to his first way of life and the care of lepers. From time to time he still wanted to fight. "If I go to the Chapter," he would shout, "I'll show them who I am!"

But these were only passing moods. Harshness was not his forte. "I am no executioner," he would say. The more often, he sadly resigned himself; and to those who reproached him for forsaking his friars, he replied that he loved the brothers "with all his heart." "But," he would add, "I would love them still more, and I would not be as a stranger among them, if they would follow in my footsteps and stop citing examples of what the other Orders do."

His distress at this period is evident—and what it cost him to witness the collapse of his dream. This martyrdom was prolonged up to Rome's approval of the Rule. God then made this obedient son of the Church realize that his role as founder was definitely over. "Poor little man," said our Lord to him, "Why are you so sad? Is not your Order My Order? Is it not I who am its Chief Shepherd? Cease to be afflicted then, and take care rather of your own salvation."

To this man stumbling in the night, distressed at no longer knowing God's will, these words brought back the light. And when, thereafter, the friars came to him to speak of books, of mitigations of the Rule, and of the practice of the older Orders, he would only say: "Do what you will. I am no longer obligated to do anything except pray for my friars and give them a good example."

The biographers relate the way in which this "great temptation" ended. One day at the Portiuncula when the saint was praying in tears, crushed by the weight of his responsibility and grief, a voice was heard saying: "Francis, if you had faith like a grain of mustard seed, you would say to this mountain, 'Be removed,' and it would obey you."

"What mountain, Lord?" asked Francis.

"The mountain of thy temptation," continued the voice.

"Lord," replied Francis, "let it be done to me according to Your word." And at once the temptation vanished.

Thereafter the conscience of the Little Poor Man was limpid and calm once more like a fair lake, and a great peace again filled his soul.

CHAPTER EIGHTEEN

Christmas at Greccio

THE STEPS PRELIMINARY to the approval of the Rule had compelled Francis to prolong his sojourn in Rome in November 1223. On this occasion he no doubt saw Brother Jacopa. Certain dignitaries of the curia also came to show him their veneration.

One day on returning to Cardinal Hugolin's palace at the luncheon hour, he drew from his sleeve the pieces of black bread he had just begged and offered them to the other guests. The prelate was very embarrassed, writes Thomas of Celano, for it was a state dinner, at which foreigners were being received by him for the first time. However, everyone was openly glad to share the Little Poor Man's quest and many kept their pieces as a souvenir.

When the meal was over, the cardinal drew his friend aside: "Brother," he asked, "why do you humiliate me by begging alms when you are my guest? Don't you know that my house and everything in it is yours?"

"My Lord," replied Francis, "since nothing is more pleasing to God than holy poverty, far from shaming you, is it not rather an honor for you to honor in your home our common Master, who deigned to live poor on earth for love of us? I must also think of my present and future friars, who would otherwise scorn to go out begging. I must act in such a way that there will be no excuse for them before God in this world or in the next at being ashamed to humble themselves."

Deeply moved, Hugolin embraced him, saying: "Son, do as you like, for it is plain that the Lord is with you and inspiring you."

At Rome, Francis had found Brother Angelo, one of the Three Companions, staying with Cardinal Brancaleone; for the first friars, as we have seen, often hired themselves out as domestic servants to earn their living. Giles himself lived for a while in Rieti in the house of Cardinal Niccolo di Chiaramonte. Evidently this custom was found to be edifying by the princes and prelates, since for a time it was quite the thing for them to have a Franciscan among their household servants. Some of the friars, however, began to grow overfond of living in palaces; and Thomas of Celano, in his *Vita secunda*, does not spare these degenerate penitents, who, "because of laziness, ambition, and a love of ease," preferred the dwellings of the great to their own wooden huts. One of these *Palatini*, as they were dubbed, who lived at the court of the King of England, came to a very bad end, according to Eccleston.

Brother Angelo, to be sure, did not deserve any such reproach. Having come to Rome no doubt on pilgrimage, if he was staying with a cardinal, it was only temporarily; and he was meanwhile living according to the Rule, by the work of his hands.

As nothing detained Francis there any longer, he decided to return to Umbria with Angelo. Cardinal Brancaleone, however, was most desirous to welcome Francis first at his palace. As it was winter and the weather was very bad, Francis surely could wait a little, it would seem, before starting home! "Besides," added the prelate, "you can live with me in as much seclusion as you like; and if you wish, you will be at liberty to take your meals with my poor." Joining his pleas to the cardinal's, Angelo offered to prepare for him a cell in a solitary tower at the foot of the garden where he could live as in a hermitage.

Francis accepted, on condition that he need not leave the tower or receive anyone there. But the first night he received a visit from the devil, who beat and harassed him in every way. Calling his companion, he said to him, "The demons are the constables and seneschals of the Most High, charged either with making those whom he loves expiate their former sins, or with compelling good religious who sin through ignorance to examine their consciences better. Since I do not recall any sin I have not confessed and done penance for, it must be that there is something else and that God does not want me here. And indeed, staying with a cardinal, they will surely say, 'Well there is a fellow who is taking his ease, while we are fasting and doing penance in our poor hermitages.' So I must leave here."

In the morning he climbed down from the tower and told the cardinal what had happened in the night, adding as he left: "My Lord, the man you took for a saint deserved to be driven from your house by fiends."

Leaving Rome, where he was never to return again, Francis set out for the Valley of Rieti. Freed from all responsibility, now that the Bull of November 29 had given definite status to the Order, a new era opened before him. He was nearing the final stage of his career, in which, while waiting for death, his one desire would be to live in peace, close to Christ. Apparently, he went back once more to the hermitage of Fonte Colombo which had recently witnessed his great trial; and as Christmas was approaching, he wanted—this year, at any rate—to celebrate it his own way.

Of all religious feasts, writes Thomas of Celano, Christmas was for Francis the most beautiful. For him it was the feast of feasts, the one that reminded him (he would say) of the day when God, become a little babe, was nourished by a woman's milk. The picture of Jesus in his Mother's arms made him stammer with emotion. Sometimes he would begin to weep at the thought of the destitution of the crib. One day at table, when a friar depicted the dire distress of the Virgin and her Son at Bethlehem, he got up at once from the table, shaking with sobs, and finished the rest of his meal on the bare ground in honor of their "royal poverty." "For," he explained, "is not this virtue of which Christ the King and the Virgin Queen wished to give us an example of royal virtue?"

Nevertheless, it was joy that predominated in him at the approach of the Savior's birth. One year, when the feast fell on a Friday, Brother Morico, the former Crosier, asked if the friars had to abstain from meat.

"Abstain!" exclaimed Francis. "Why, it's a sin to call that day Friday on which the Child was born to us! The very walls should have a right to eat meat today! And if that is impossible, we ought to rub them with fat, at least, so that they can eat meat their way." Asses and oxen, he said, ought to have a double ration of hay and oats in memory of the ox and ass that warmed Jesus in the crib with their breath. Another time he said: "If I saw the Emperor, I would ask him to scatter grain on the highways on Christmas for our brothers the birds, and especially for our dear sister larks."

So a fortnight before the Nativity of 1223, Francis sent for his friend, John Velita, the lord of Greccio, who had apparently forsworn the profession of arms to enter the Order of Penance. Opposite Greccio, which rises on a rocky shelf bordering a spacious valley, John possessed a steep hill, honeycombed with caves and surmounted by a small wood. The saint judged this site proper for the setting he had in mind. Since this was a novelty in the liturgy of the period, he had submitted the idea before quitting Rome to Pope Honorius, who had approved it.

"I should like," said he to his friend, "to celebrate the coming feast of the Savior with you. And I should like to commemorate His birth at Bethlehem in a way to bring before me as perfectly as possible the sufferings and discomforts He endured from infancy for our salvation. That is why I want you to set up a real manger on this mountain spot, with hay, and to bring in an ox and an ass like those that kept the Infant Jesus company."

John Velita was only too happy to lend a hand to this project; and Francis dismissed him, recommending him to hurry so that everything would be ready when he came.

It is from Thomas of Celano's *Vita Prima* that we shall paraphrase the account of the feast. It is almost contemporary, for he wrote it only four or five years afterward. The people of the country had joined with the friars of the surrounding hermitages, bearing torches and candles to lighten the darkness of this night that, like a star, has shone for centuries and will shine forever. Winding up the mountain, the procession wended its way toward the spot where—between a great ox and a little donkey—the crib was set up. Under the great trees it was as light as day, and from rock to rock the echo reverberated of the chanting of the friars, mingled with the pious refrains of the crowd. Standing before the crib, torn with compassion and filled with unspeakable joy, the Poverello, sighing deeply, awaited them.

The Mass commenced, at an altar placed in an overhanging niche. Never, the celebrant himself confessed, had he experienced such consolation while offering the Holy Sacrifice. Vested in the dalmatic, Francis assisted as deacon. At the proper moment, he intoned the

Gospel in a sonorous voice; then he preached a sermon to proclaim the joys of heaven to those men of good will who had flocked to his appeal. In words honey-sweet he spoke of the poor King who twelve centuries before, on such a night, was born in the little town of Bethlehem, calling him either "Jesus" or the "Babe of Bethlehem," and pronouncing the word "Bethlehem" like a bleating lamb. And whenever one of these divine names occurred in his sermon, he would pass his tongue over his lips that he might longer taste their sweetness.

Thus it was a night marvelous above all other nights; and we must not be surprised that God afterward wished to shower down his blessings upon his blessed spot. Many sick folk recovered their health here and even domestic animals who ate a few stalks of hay from the crib were cured. For it is true that on this hay the Savior of the world had miraculously rested.

John Velita in fact reported that he saw the little Jesus asleep on it, and that there was a moment when the Divine Infant awakened, opened his eyes, and smiled at St. Francis.

This stupendous vision, according to Thomas of Celano and St. Bonaventure, rewarded the zeal of the pious lord of Greccio; but it likewise symbolized the admirable work accomplished on earth by him who reawakened the faith slumbering in men's hearts—faith in Jesus Christ our Lord, who lives and reigns with the Father, in the unity of the Holy Spirit, world without end, amen. Alleluia! Alleluia!

CHAPTER NINETEEN

The Stigmata

FRANCIS PASSED THE rest of the winter and the following spring at the hermitage of Greccio. From time to time he preached in the surrounding villages, but on Easter Day it seemed to him that he owed a lesson to the friars themselves. On the occasion of their minister's visit, they had procured tablecloths, glasses, and other fine things to adorn their table. The meal was underway when a knock was heard at the door: "For the love of God," came a quavering voice, "an alms for a poor sick pilgrim!"

And they saw a little beggar come in, wearing an old hat and leaning on a staff. It was Francis who had disguised himself to remind the friars of their vocation. He held out his bowl, received a piece of bread, and sat on the ground before the hearth to eat it. "Since your table is too fancy for the poor who go begging at people's doors and who, more than other religious, are bound to imitate the Savior's humility," said he, "permit me to sit here like a real Friar Minor."

Thus, without seeking any more for opportunities, but taking them as they came, Francis continued to protest against the inroads made on his evangelical ideal.

Far from departing from it himself, he daily came closer to it. "Those who lived with him," wrote Thomas of Celano, "know that his mind dwelt constantly on Christ. Jesus filled his heart, was on his lips, and before his eyes; his bodily members, like the powers of his soul, were as though marked with the seal of Christ." His friars likewise admired his increasing resemblance to his divine Model. Everything in his life now recalled the life of the Savior. Under the garb of the pilgrim who had presented himself to them, wrote Friar Thomas, the religious of Greccio had immediately recognized the image of the Pilgrim of Emmaus. But what was this distant resemblance compared with that soon to be his?

Francis went from Greccio to the General Chapter of June 1224. It was the last one he attended.

A few weeks later, he left the Portiuncula for La Verna, a hundred miles north of Assisi. In his choice of this solitary summit for a residence, was there a presentiment of the sublime favor awaiting him there? We know only that he chose to take with him a few friars according to his heart: Leo, Angelo, Illuminato, Rufino, and Masseo, the faithful companions of so many other journeys.

They set out at the beginning of August, and Brother Masseo, who was good at meeting the public, was put in charge.

"You shall be our guardian," said Francis. "We will sleep wherever you say; at mealtime we shall beg our bread; and the rest of the time, faithful to our custom, we shall recite our hours, speak of God, or else walk along in silence."

The region of Casentino, toward which the little caravan was headed, forms a broad and imposing valley, filled with meadows, vineyards, and forests, with castles and charming villages perched on the hills. It is watered by the upper Arno, and hemmed in on all sides by the inaccessible summits of the Apennines. Among them, Mount La Verna rises, abrupt and isolated, about four thousand feet high, a lofty and solitary plateau.

Already it was visible, though doubtless still far away, when after one or two days of hiking, Francis became so exhausted that it was necessary to find a mount for him. A villager lent his donkey for the rest of the trip. He must have been an honest fellow, but with a dislike for being fooled, and he meant to have the saints repay any favor he did for them. As he followed his beast, he felt a desire to know God's servant better. Going up to him, he asked, "Tell me, are you really that Brother Francis of Assisi people talk about so much?"

"Yes," replied the saint.

"In that case, I want to give you some advice, and that is to be as good as people say you are, for you have a great reputation for holiness among us."

"Instead of taking offense at this lesson," writes the chronicler, "and saying (as some proud friars I know would have said), 'What a nitwit he must be, to preach to me like that!' Francis dismounted and knelt before the rustic, and, kissing his feet, thanked him for his charitable warning."

The heat became stifling. As they were climbing a very rugged slope, the peasant, who increasingly lagged behind, declared that he was dying of thirst. "Either you find me something to drink," said he, "or I'll die here!"

Again St. Francis dismounted, and raising his arms to heaven, prayed until a spring was discovered near a neighboring rock.

They arrived at the mountain that was to become the saint's Calvary and Tabor. After ascending the first escarpments, and before starting on the last incline, they paused a moment for breath. Francis sat down under a great oak, which lived, we are told, until 1602, and which a tiny chapel has since replaced. He was gazing at the beauty of the place and the countryside, when hundreds of birds flew down around him, fluttering and singing loudly. In a moment his head, shoulders, arms, and legs were covered with them. Francis thereupon said to his companions: "Dear brothers, I believe that our Lord Jesus Christ is pleased to have us settle here, since our brothers and sisters the birds are giving us such a joyous welcome."

In fact it was there that, by the impression of the stigmata, our Lord was about to complete his resemblance to him.

The summit of La Verna is an uneven plateau, supported by titanic rocks and covered with pines and beeches, where even today legions of familiar birds are loud in their song. A hermitage was built there for the saint by the Count of Chiusi, and also a little oratory which was dedicated in the late sixteenth century to St. Mary of the Angels. From this vantage point the eye takes in an immense panorama. On a clear day one may catch a glimpse of the Adriatic from La Penna, the summit of the mountain, nearly an hour's walk from the shrine.

As soon as Count Orlando learned of the arrival of Francis and his companions, he came from his castle to welcome them and bring them some provisions. Francis asked him to build him a hut "cell" under a large beech tree a stone's throw from the hermitage. When it was done, Orlando said to his guests: "Dear brothers, I do not mean to have you want for anything on this mountain wilderness, so that you may not be hindered in your spiritual exercises. So I say to you once and for all, feel perfectly free to come to me for anything you need. And if you do not come, I shall be very displeased."

Then he departed with his retinue.

The day was at its close. On Mount La Verna the late afternoons of summer are of surpassing beauty. Nature, which has lain prostrate under the burning sun, seems to take on new life. A thousand voices awaken in the branches of trees and in the clefts of the moss-covered rocks, forming a sweet and melancholy symphony; while for hours the sun still illumines the distant peaks of the Apennines with its iridescent afterglow, filling the heart of the laggard contemplative with what a Franciscan poet terms "the nostalgia of the everlasting hills."

Francis bade his companions to be seated and instructed them how friars living in hermitages should comport themselves, counseling them not to abuse the generosity of Count Orlando but to remain ever true to Lady Poverty. Speaking to them also of his end which he saw approaching, he said to them: "Because I see that I am drawing near to death, I wish to dwell here in solitude and bewail my sins before God. So if any laypeople come here, you are to receive them yourselves, for I do not want to see anyone except Brother Leo."

He then blessed them and retired into his hut of branches. From time to time, he would come out and sit down under the beautiful beech to admire the magnificent scenery.

One day when he was thus engaged, his eyes fixed on the gigantic cliffs huddled there before him, towering above the great chasms, he wondered what could have caused such an upheaval in the earth's surface. Then as he prayed, it was revealed to him that these huge crevices had been opened at that moment when the rocks on Mount Calvary, according to the Gospel, were rent. From that time onward, La Verna was for him a witness and constant reminder of Christ's Passion. His love for the crucified Savior increased, his prayer became continuous, and God now favored him with extraordinary mystical graces.

"With the best of intentions" (continues the chronicler), and with that biographer's indiscretion for which posterity will ever be grateful, "Brother Leo diligently spied on his spiritual father."

Sometimes he would hear him lamenting over his Order: "Lord," he would say, weeping, "what will become of this poor little family that You have entrusted to me, when I am gone?" But more often he surprised him in loving colloquy, or crying out for very love, or rapt in ecstasy. Thus it was, we are told, that he saw Francis lifted up several yards above the ground, sometimes even to the top of the great beech. Then he would silently draw near, and when the feet of the ecstatic were within reach, he would embrace them, saying, "Lord, be merciful to me a sinner. And by the merits of this blessed Father, may I find grace in Your sight!"

Meanwhile the Assumption drew near in which Francis had decided to begin a Lent which would last until the feast of St. Michael the Archangel. Resolved to keep his too curious observer away, he enjoined Brother Leo to station himself at the door of the hermitage, saying, "When I call you, you are to come."

Then going some distance away, he called to him in a loud voice. Brother Leo came running. "Son," said Francis, "I am still not far enough away. We must find a place where you cannot hear me."

Finally they found the right spot. On the mountainside, hollowed out in the stone, there was a sort of ledge overhanging a chasm some hundred and twenty feet deep. The friars had to place a log as a bridge over the chasm to reach this ledge and erect on it a little hut of reeds. When this was done, their father dismissed them, saying:

"Return to the hermitage; for with God's grace, I desire to live here in absolute silence and not be disturbed by anyone. You, Brother Leo, may come only twice a day, the first time to bring me bread and water, then about midnight to recite Matins with me. But before crossing the bridge, you are to take care to announce yourself by saying: *Domine, labia mea aperies.* And if I answer, *Et os meum annuntiabit laudem tuam*, you are to pass over. But if I do not, you are to go back at once."

When the Feast of the Assumption came, Francis commenced his great fast.

We are approaching the truly seraphic period in the life of the Poverello, days when, as if lost in God, his soul consummated its final alliance with and conformity to the very soul of Christ.

As the history of mystical phenomena offers nothing similar, and no one has ever been able to claim that he has drawn aside the veil from such mysteries, it is here especially that the historian must limit himself to reproducing the statements of authoritative witnesses. For us these are principally Brother Leo, the saint's confessor; St. Bonaventure, the Seraphic Doctor; and the author of the *Considerations on the Most Holy Stigmata*—himself dependent in part on the *Actus beati Francisci* and Thomas of Celano, and in part of the tradition of the friars residing at La Verna.

They report that at this time the Poverello's fervor and austerities were redoubled, that he suffered dreadful pain, and was horribly tormented by the Evil One. "Oh," he would sometimes say to Brother Leo, "if the Brothers only knew what I have to endure from the devil, there is not one of them who would not have compassion and pity for me."

Nevertheless, in the midst of this painful purification, God still sometimes sensibly visited his heart. Thus it was to console him and give him a foretaste of heaven—that he sent him an angelic musician. Once and only once, the celestial spirit passed the bow over his viol, but "the melody that came forth was so beautiful," declared the saint later, "that I almost swooned: and if the angel had drawn his bow a second time, I know that my soul would have left my body, so boundless and unbearable was my joy."

Francis also enjoyed the friendship of a falcon that nested near his cell. Every night before Matins, this affectionate creature would beat its wings against the walls of the hut. But if the saint was too ill or too tired, the compassionate bird would let him rest and not waken him until later.

Likewise Brother Leo, no less charitable, did not insist when the saint did not reply to his *Domine, labia mea aperies*. Once, though, he crossed the bridge anyway.

Not finding Francis in the hut, he started out in the moonlight to look for him in the woods. He found him in ecstasy, conversing with someone invisible. "Who are You?" the saint was saying, "and who am I, Your miserable and useless servant?" Leo also saw a ball of fire descend from heaven and return almost immediately.

Seized with awe at this supernatural spectacle, and fearing lest his curiosity might lead St. Francis to dispense with his services, the indiscreet friar attempted to flee, but the rustling of the leaves betrayed him.

"Who is there?" cried Francis.

"It is I, Father: Brother Leo."

"Didn't I forbid you, dear little Sheep, to spy on me this way? Tell me under obedience, did you see or hear anything?"

Brother Leo confessed what he had seen and heard and asked for some explanation. The saint admitted to his friend that our Lord had just appeared to him and he told Leo that something wonderful was going to happen soon on the mountain.

What was this wonderful thing? As was his habit, Francis wanted to consult the Gospels about it. In the hermitage chapel where Brother Leo said Mass, he asked his friend to open the missal three times at random, and each time it opened at the story of the Passion. "By this sign," writes St. Bonaventure, "the Saint understood that, having imitated Christ in his life, he was also to imitate Him in the sufferings that preceded His death. So, filled with courage, despite his ruined health and physical exhaustion, he made ready for martyrdom."

The feast of the Exaltation of the Cross had come. It commemorated the victory which had permitted Heraclius to regain the Savior's cross from the Muslims; and no feast was more popular at that time among Christians, who were continually being called on to take the cross in the Crusades. It was probably on this day, September 14, 1224, that the miracle of the stigmata took place.

In that hour which precedes sunrise, kneeling before his hut, Francis prayed, his face turned toward the east. "O Lord," he pleaded, "I beg of You two graces before I die—to experience in myself in all possible fullness the pains of Your cruel Passion, and to feel for You the same love that made You sacrifice Yourself for us."

For a long time he prayed, his heart aflame with love and pity. Then "suddenly," writes St. Bonaventure, "from the heights of Heaven a seraphim with six wings of flame flew swiftly down." He bore the likeness of a man nailed to a cross. Two of his wings covered his face, with two others he flew, and the last two covered his body. "It was Christ Himself, who had assumed this form to manifest Himself to the Saint. He fixed his gaze upon Francis, then left him, after imprinting the miraculous Stigmata" of the Crucifixion on his flesh.

"From that moment," continues the Seraphic Doctor, "Francis was marked with the wounds of the Divine Redeemer. His hands and feet appeared as though pierced with nails, with round black heads on the palm of the hands and on the feet, and with bent points extruding from the back of the hands and the soles of the feet. In addition, there was a wound in the right side, as if made by a lance, from which blood frequently flowed, moistening his drawers and tunic."

There had been no witnesses to the prodigy, and although it had left visible marks, the saint's first thought was to keep it secret; then, after much hesitation, he decided to ask the counsel of his companions. "So he asked them in veiled words if they thought that certain extraordinary graces ought to be kept secret or revealed."

Brother Illuminato, who well deserved his name, remarks St. Bonaventure, divining that something out of the common order had occurred, spoke up:

"Brother Francis, it might be wrong for you to keep for yourself that which God has given you to edify your neighbor."

Timidly, then, the saint told what had happened; but without showing his wounds, which he always took care afterward to cover up with bandages. He even formed the habit of keeping his bandaged hands in the sleeves of his habit.

However, as the stigmata never disappeared, a number of persons were able to see them. Among them were Brother Leo, whom Francis took as his nurse and who regularly bathed the oozing wound in the side; Brother Rufino and several others who gave sworn testimony about them; and all those present at the death of the saint or who were able to venerate him in his coffin, especially Brother Jacopa and her sons, and Sister Clare and her daughters. In addition, Pope Alexander IV, who in a sermon heard by St. Bonaventure, averred that while Francis was still alive he had seen the miraculous marks with his own eyes.

Some rationalist scholars have indeed attempted to impugn their existence, although the presence of "nails embedded in the flesh," proved most vexing to them. But their opinion bears no weight; and while waiting for them to furnish proof, we may refer to the judgment of the Holy See which, by a favor not granted to any other saint and by the advice of St. Robert Bellarmine, extended to the whole Church the annual observance of the Feast of the Stigmata of St. Francis at the time of Pope Paul V (1605–1621); and although the changes made in 1960 reduced this feast to a commemoration, the feast is still observed by the Franciscan Order, to which it was granted by Pope Benedict XI (1303–1304).

In addition to his habitual maladies and infirmities, the Little Poor Man now experienced an increase of mysterious inner torment. No doubt he also continued to suffer from the betrayal of some of his own sons, but his soul was overflowing nonetheless with happiness and serenity. What other saint had ever received such proof of God's love and assurance of salvation? The litany that he wrote soon after the great miracle expresses the fullness of his joy. It is the Magnificat of the stigmatized Poverello:

> You are the Holy one, the Lord.
> You alone are God. You alone do wonders.
> You are mighty and great.
> You are the Most High.
> You are King omnipotent, O Holy Father, King of Heaven
>   and earth.
> You are three and one, the Lord God, every good.
> You are good, every good, the highest good,
> The Lord God, living and true. You are charity and love.
> You are wisdom, humility, patience, tranquility, happiness
>   and joy.
> You are justice, temperance and all-sufficient riches.
> You are beauty and mildness.
> You are our protector, defender, and guardian.
> You are our strength and our refreshment.

You are our faith, hope, charity, and our infinite sweetness.
You are our life eternal, Lord wonderful and great;
God omnipotent, Savior most merciful!

Now while Francis thus sang of his happiness, Brother Leo had become depressed. He was a victim, as he himself tells us, "of the most painful of spiritual trials." Perhaps he had begun to despair of his salvation. Be that as it may, so great was his distress that nothing would have induced him to speak of it to anyone. "Oh, if only," he thought, "my blessed Father would write me a few words of encouragement in his own hand, it would comfort me, or perhaps even cure me!"

Francis divined the spiritual anguish of his beloved companion and condescended to his desire. He took the sheet of paper with his *Laudes* on it and wrote on the back these three Scripture verses: "May the Lord bless you and keep you! May the Lord show His face to you and be merciful to you! May the Lord lift up His countenance upon you and give you peace!" adding in his large handwriting, "God bless you, Brother Leo!" Sketching a crude head which some suppose to be that of Brother Leo, he drew the letter TAU over this portrait, then handed the parchment to his friend, saying: "Take this, Leo, and keep it as long as you live."

We can imagine the surprise and joy of Brother Leo, and the happiness he felt at seeing himself marked on the forehead with the sign of the elect. On the instant, he was freed from his obsession, which never troubled him again. And for the forty remaining years of his life, he always carried the beloved talisman on his person.

That is why the priceless autograph, preserved at the Sacro Convento of Assisi, is so worn and dim today. The paleographers, however, have deciphered it perfectly. In addition to the phrase mentioned, it contains fifteen handwritten lines by which Leo himself takes pains to authenticate it. We read, among others, these words under the blessing: *Beatus Franciscus scripsit manu sua istam benedictionem mihi frati Leoni*; and under the man's head traversed by the TAU: *simili modo fecit istud signum tau cum capite manu sua* ("This blessing was given to me, Brother Leo, by Blessed Francis who wrote it in his own hand, and it is also his hand that drew the head and the T").

The feast of St. Michael had arrived, and the saint's fast came to an end. Already the snow was beginning to fall on the mountaintops, and soon the hills that Francis must cross to get back to the Portiuncula would be impassible.

An apocryphal document attributed to Brother Masseo relates how the Little Poor Man took leave of La Verna:

> The morning of September 30, 1224, Francis assembled us in the chapel where, following his custom, he had heard Mass. After commanding us always to love one another, to apply ourselves to prayer, and to take great care of the oratory, he commended the holy mountain to us, and ordered that friars present and future were to hold it in veneration. "Brother Masseo," said he, "my desire is for the superiors to send only God-fearing religious here, chosen among the best in the Order."
>
> He then said, "Farewell, farewell, Brother Masseo! Farewell, farewell, Brother Angelo" And in the same way he took leave of Brother adding, "Live in peace, my dear children. Farewell! For I return to the Portiuncula with Brother God's Little Sheep, never to return again. My body goes away, but I leave you my heart. Farewell, farewell to you all! Farewell, Mount La Verna! Farewell, Mount of the angels,

beloved mountain! Farewell, Brother Falcon: once more I thank you for your kindness to me. Farewell, great rock, I shall see you no more. Farewell, St. Mary of the Angels! Mother of the Eternal Word, to you I entrust these children of mine."

We all broke into sobs. He went away, weeping, bearing our hearts with him.

Accompanied only by Brother Leo, Francis took the path over the nearby Monte Casella and then down to Montauto and Borgo San Sepolcro. When they reached the last peak from which Mount La Verna is still visible, the saint dismounted, knelt down, and blessed it for the last time: "Farewell, mountain of God, holy mountain, *mons pinguis, mons in quo beneplacitum est Deo habitare*. May the Father, Son, and Holy Spirit bless you, Mount La Verna! Peace to you, beloved mountain, which I shall never see again."

CHAPTER TWENTY

The Canticle of Brother Sun

THE RETURN TO the Portiuncula was by way of Borgo San Sepolcro, Monte Casale, and Citta di Castello. Francis was obliged to ride on a donkey, so painful had walking become for him. And it was this way that he traveled in future, although St. Clare had made special shoes for him to ease his wounded feet.

Apparently, Brother Leo had not denied himself the pleasure of telling about the miracle that had just occurred, for their way was marked by popular demonstrations and by miraculous cures. Everyone wanted to see and touch the stigmatic of La Verna, who had become as a living relic, endowed with supernatural virtue. Even his donkey's bridle was believed to help mothers in difficult child-birth obtain a happy delivery.

Francis, meanwhile, humble and absorbed in God, did not hear the murmurs of veneration by which he was accompanied. Pulling the sleeves of his habit over his bandaged hands, he extended only his fingertips to be kissed by his admirers, not even looking around him.

"Shall we reach Borgo San Sepolcro soon?" he inquired, long after they had passed the town.

They made a short halt at the hermitage of Monte Casale, where he restored an epileptic friar to health. Stopping also at Citta di

Castello, he delivered a possessed woman who "barked like a dog," and cured a young boy "whose wound healed over in the form of a red rose."

Already the first snows had made their appearance on the mountains. One night when our travelers, prevented by a storm from reaching shelter, had been forced to take refuge under an overhanging rock for the night, they were unable to light a fire—a thing which put the muleteer in a bad humor. "It is all Francis's fault," he grumbled, "that we are in this fix and liable to freeze to death."

The saint touched the grumbler on the back, and (writes St. Bonaventure) the mere touch of his stigmatized hand made the shivering man warm again. A few minutes later he dozed off, and as he himself related later on, he never slept better in his life.

No sooner had Francis arrived at the Portiuncula than, as though filled with new zeal, he wanted to resume his apostolic tours. But the aggravation of his gastric disorders and the pain caused by the stigmata and his weakness from the loss of blood, troubled the friars. They begged him to seek medical treatment, but he gaily calmed their fears. Did not his honor as Christ's knight require him to die in harness? And throughout that winter and the following spring, mounted on a donkey, Francis continued to go about Umbria, preaching in as many as three or four villages in a day.

At Foligno, Brother Elias told him of a dream he had had about him: an old priest all in white appeared to him, warning him that Francis would die in two years. This announcement filled the Poverello with joy, but his infirmities soon increased to the point that the friars feared lest he should succumb before that date. He became almost blind and suffered from excruciating headaches.

As Honorius III and the Curia, driven from Rome by a popular uprising, were lodged in Rieti, Cardinal Hugolin urged Francis to consult Teobaldo Saraceni, the pope's physician. Now the saint had a horror of doctors, and in order to get him to agree to treatment, Elias had to appeal to his spirit of obedience and quote this Scripture verse: "The Most High hath created medicines out of the earth, and a wise man will not abhor them" (see Sirach 38:4).

It was in the summer of 1225 that Francis consented to go to Rieti. Taking with him those who remained his nurses to the end—Brother Masseo and the Three Companions—he decided first to take leave of St. Clare, whom he feared never to see again. Upon his arrival, his condition became so grave that he had to give up going any farther. He stayed about seven weeks at San Damiano, where St. Clare had the consolation of caring for her spiritual father. She had a hut of reeds built for him between the chaplain's house and the convent, like the one he occupied at the Portiuncula; but before getting any rest there, he spent some dreadful hours.

One would have thought that, "summoned by the devil, all the mice in the country had met there to torment him." The wattles of his cabin were full of them, and the ground was covered with them. They climbed up on the table where he ate and into the bed in which he was attempting to sleep, and scurried squeaking over his face. One night, his patience exhausted, and tempted to despair, the Poverello cried out to God who seemed to have forsaken him. It was then that a familiar voice was heard:

> "Francis, if in exchange for all these evils, you were to receive a treasure so great that the whole earth—even if it were changed into gold—would be nothing beside it, would you not have reason to be satisfied?"
>
> "Certainly, Lord!"

"Then, be happy, for I guarantee that one day you shall enjoy the Kingdom of Heaven, and this is as certain as if you possessed it already."

What did they matter now—after such an assurance—the mice, the suffering, and the other inventions of the Evil One? The divine words filled Francis with heavenly joy; the cabin of torments became a place of delight; and this malefic night inspired the invalid, overwhelmed by every ill, with the most optimistic song ever to spring from a human heart.

We like to think that it was at San Damiano that the Poverello composed it. For did not everything in this place which had seen the birth of his vocation, recall God's mercies toward him? The cave in which he had hidden to escape his father's "prison." The stone bench where the old priest had sat and talked to him. The miraculous crucifix that had shown him his way. And this chapel rebuilt by him, whence in the silent night he could hear the chant of the Poor Ladies. No doubt, the thought of Sister Clare—the perfect incarnation of his ideal—the nearness of the four good brothers who cared for him with such tender devotion, and the thought of so many more of his sons who followed the Gospel so well in their poor hermitages, were added consolations.

So Francis blessed his fruitful and beautiful existence. He blessed all nature and life, victorious over death and evil; he blessed the sun that illumines man's joys and sorrows, his struggles and triumphs; he blessed the earth, where man may merit heaven; and he thanked God for having created him. When the sun had risen, he called his companions and said to them: "The Lord has deigned to assure me that I shall one day enter His Kingdom. So to show Him my gratitude, I desired to compose this new song which you are about to hear." And the blind saint, for whom the least ray of light was a torture, sang to them what he called "The Canticle of Brother Sun":

Most High Almighty Good Lord,
Yours are praise, glory, honor and all blessing.

To You alone, Most High, do they belong,
And no man is worthy to mention You.

Be praised, my Lord, with all Your creatures,
Especially Sir Brother Sun,
Who is daylight, and by him You shed light on us.
And he is beautiful and radiant with great splendor.
Of You, Most High, he is a symbol.

Be praised, my Lord for Sister Moon and the Stars.
In heaven You have formed them clear and bright and fair.

Be praised, my Lord, for Brother Wind
And for air and cloud and clear and all weather,
By which You give Your creatures nourishment.

Be praised, my Lord, for Sister Water,
For she is very useful, humble, precious and pure.

Be praised, my Lord, for Brother Fire,
By whom You light up the night,
For he is fair and merry and mighty and strong.

Be praised, my Lord, for our Sister Mother Earth,
Who sustains and rules us
And produces varied fruits with many-colored flowers and
    plants.

Praise and bless my Lord
And give Him thanks and serve Him with great humility.

Such is the hymn that won for the Poverello the title of the "Orpheus of the Middle Ages," the incomparable psalm which Renan considered the "most beautiful piece of religious poetry since the Gospels." Sister Clare probably was the first to hear it, she who loved poetry and music and who also showed herself so grateful to God for the gift of life. Francis dictated it in Italian, such as we still have it; then had it sung by his companions to a melody he had adapted for it. And he himself was so pleased with it that for a moment he thought of sending Brother Pacifico through Europe to sing it to everyone.

An occasion did come soon to call on the talents of the former troubadour.

A violent quarrel had once more set the civil and religious authorities of Assisi at loggerheads. Bishop Guido had excommunicated the podesta Oportulo who had countered by forbidding all relations between the bishop and the officials. Nothing could be more painful to the saint than to see his fellow citizens at odds. Immediately adding a new stanza to his poem, he called Brother Pacifico and said: "Go find the podesta for me, and invite him with his worthies to come to the bishop's palace to hear my song."

There was a great crowd in the bishop's courtyard when the King of Verse appeared with his musicians: "You are about to hear," he announced, "the 'Canticle of Brother Sun' which Francis has just composed to the glory of God, and for the edification of his neighbor. And he himself asks you through me to hear it with great devotion." Brother Pacifico then intoned:

Most High Almighty Good Lord,
Yours are praise, glory, honor and all blessing.

To You alone, Most High, do they belong,
And no man is worthy to mention You.

Be praised, my Lord, with all Your creatures,
Especially Sir Brother Sun,
Who is daylight, and by him You shed light on us.
And he is beautiful and radiant with great splendor.
Of You, Most High, he is a symbol.

Alternating with their leader, the friars repeated the stanza in unison. Meanwhile the podesta, writes the author of the *Speculum*, "had risen, and, with hands joined and tears in his eyes, was listening with reverent attention." The entire audience imitated him, moved by these accents of a beloved voice and at hearing their dear saint singing the beauties of a world he could no longer see.

Be praised, my Lord for our Sister Mother Earth,
Who sustains and rules us
And produces varied fruits with many-colored flowers and
plants.

It was at this point that Francis had introduced his plea for pardon and peace, his true heart's message to his fellow citizens:

Be praised, my Lord, for those who grant pardon for love of
You,
And bear sickness and tribulation.
Blessed are they who shall bear them in peace,
For by You, Most High, they shall be crowned.

At these words, the emotion of the assemblage was at its height, and sobs choked them as the podesta turned toward the bishop. Falling on his knees before him, he said: "Even if he had killed my own son, there is not a man in the world that I would not want to forgive now, for love of God and His servant Francis. With much greater reason, my Lord, I am ready to make whatever satisfaction you may desire."

Bishop Guido was no less prompt to admit his own errors. Raising the podesta to his feet and warmly embracing him, he said: "I likewise ask your forgiveness. Pardon me for not fulfilling my charge with proper humility and for having yielded once more to anger."

They separated completely reconciled; and, thanks to Francis, charity and peace won out once more among the people of Assisi.

As soon as he was able to be moved, the saint left Sister Clare, whom he was never to see again, and with his companions, headed for Rieti, fifty miles away. They passed near Terni, then along the winding course of the Velino, coming at last into a lovely plain at the end of which was to be seen—etched against the somber mass of Monte Terminillo—the smiling city where the papal Curia was staying.

Rieti was preparing a triumphal welcome for the stigmatized saint of La Verna. To avoid it, or because of his exhausted state, three miles before reaching his destination Francis asked hospitality of the parish priest of San Fabiano. He was a poor priest whose income was derived from a vineyard. He gave Francis and his escort a warm welcome, but was soon to repent having a saint in his home. For his house was invaded by crowds of pilgrims. The horses of the prelates of the Curia trampled down his garden, and the thirsty throngs picked his choicest grapes and ravaged his vineyard. As he was blustering against the people who had ruined him, Francis observed: "Father, there's no use in crying over spilled milk. But tell me, how much does your vineyard bring you in the best years?"

"Fourteen measures."

"Well, then! If you will agree not to call people names any more, I'll guarantee you twenty from this vintage. And if you fall short, I promise to make up the difference."

But the saint did not have to make up anything, for when the grapes were harvested, the priest had his twenty measures. And this was a real miracle, for his vineyard had never yielded more than fourteen before.

The arrival of Francis at Rieti gave full scope to the popular devotion. The bishop's palace, where Hugolin installed him, was the scene of sometimes stormy demonstrations. People fought over his garments, his combings, and even his nail parings. A farmer who had collected the water in which Francis had washed his hands, sprinkled his sick flock of sheep with it and they were immediately healed. The case is also told of a canon named Gideon, who was also sick, but as a result of his debaucheries, and who came up to Francis weeping and asking him to bless him.

"How can I make the sign of the cross over you," Francis asked him, "a man who lives only for the flesh? I will bless you, though, in Christ's name; but know that evil will befall you again, if you ever return to your vomit."

And the prediction came true; for when the cured canon went back to his sinful life, he alone was killed when the roof fell in at the house of a fellow canon where he was passing the night.

Meanwhile, the saint's condition grew steadily worse. His stomach, liver, and spleen were seriously affected, while he continued to suffer horribly in his head and eyes. At that time, wishing to hear some music, he summoned a friar who had been a troubadour in the world, and begged him to borrow a viol and give him a little concert. "It would do Brother Body so much good," he remarked, "to be a little distracted from his sufferings."

But the former troubadour, who believed that a saint ought to stay in character, observed that some people might be scandalized.

"Then let's not say any more about it," replied Francis, "for we do have to make concessions to public opinion."

But the next night, a mysterious visitor came and played the viol under his windows. In the morning, Francis sent for the scrupulous friar. "God consoles the afflicted," he observed. "Last night, to make up for the concert you refused me, He permitted me to hear one infinitely more beautiful than all the music of earth."

Not wanting, however, to tarry longer in the palace of the Bishop of Rieti, he asked to be taken to the hermitage of Fonte Colombo. It was there that he underwent treatment by a doctor.

The treatment consisted of cauterizing with a red hot iron the flesh around the more affected eye, from ear to eyebrow.

The sick man shuddered at the sight of the preparations, then addressed the glowing iron: "Brother Fire, the Most High has made you strong and beautiful and useful. Be courteous to me now in this hour, for I have always loved you, and temper your heat so that I can endure it."

"We fled," confessed his companions, "so as not to witness his sufferings. But our Father said to us: 'Men of little faith, why did you run away, when I did not feel anything at all?' Then turning to the doctor, he said: 'If it wasn't done right, you may do it again!' "

And this the doctor did, for he opened the veins over Francis's temple, after which another physician thought it his duty to pierce both ears with a red-hot iron.

With all this, Francis enjoyed great spiritual happiness. Sometimes the brothers heard him singing new hymns, whose words and music he had composed. Some of them he sent to St. Clare, who was also ill and much worried about him. His heart was more eager than ever, and his head teemed with impossible projects. "Brothers," he would say, "let us start serving our Lord, for so far we have done nothing."

For Francis would have liked to live his life over again, seeking new apostolic and knightly adventures. Since this was impossible, he began to dictate letters, two of which, at least, have come down to us.

In one, addressed to the "rulers, consuls, judges, and governors of all countries," Francis urged these highly placed personages to "think of death which waits for no man, not to transgress God's Commandments, and to receive frequently our Lord's sacred body and blood." Then perhaps recalling what he had seen in Muslim lands, he begged them to "appoint a public crier or other means to invite the people every night to praise and thank the Lord."

In the other letter, addressed to all the guardians of his Order, he asked them to urge clerics and bishops to venerate the Body and Blood of Jesus Christ above everything else, and to use only proper chalices, corporals, and linens at the altar. And so it was that the Little Poor Man spent his last winter on earth.

When spring came again, Elias and Hugolin had Francis taken to Siena, where it seems there were also some very celebrated physicians. It was during this journey in the plain extending south of San Quirico d'Orcia, that a meeting occurred that has become legendary.

Francis saw three old women coming toward him, so perfectly alike in age, height, and features, that one would have thought them triplets. As they passed him, they bowed reverently and greeted him: "Welcome, Lady Poverty!" "Never," writes Thomas of Celano, "did a greeting give so much pleasure to St. Francis." Believing them to be beggar women, he requested the doctor who accompanied him to give them something. Dismounting, the latter gave each of them some money. Thereupon the three sisters disappeared so suddenly that our travelers, who had turned around almost at once, were unable to see what had become of them. "It was doubtless a celestial vision," writes St. Bonaventure, "symbolic of the virtues of poverty, chastity, and obedience, to which Francis had always been so faithful. But as poverty," he adds, "was incontestably his chief title to glory, it was natural that it was this virtue these mysterious virgins wished especially to honor in him."

The reception Francis received at Siena was no less enthusiastic than that of Rieti. Clergy and laity vied with one another in their display of both curiosity and veneration. The biographers tell us that a knight made Francis the gift of a pheasant that did not want to leave him and that refused to eat whenever it was separated from him. They also speak of a learned Dominican who came to propose to him a theological difficulty from which he extricated himself with honor. They further declare that it was there, with the connivance of Brother Pacifico, that a friar of Brescia succeeded in seeing the sacred stigmata. "I forgive you," said the saint later to the King of Verse, "but you have caused me much pain."

As for the doctors of Siena, their efforts were as ineffectual as those of the pope's physician. One night the saint vomited such a quantity of blood that the friars believed his last hour had come. Gathered round his pallet, they were inconsolable: "What is to become of us," they mourned, "poor orphans that we are, abandoned by him who was father, mother, and good shepherd to us?"

They besought him to leave them a written testimony of his last wishes, to guide them in the future. Francis had Brother Benedict of Pioraco, who had celebrated Mass several times at his bedside, summoned. "Write," he said, "that I bless all my friars present and to come. And as I am not able to speak longer, here, in a few words, is what I want them to know: In memory of me who have blessed them, let them always love and honor one another. They must ever love and honor our Lady holy Poverty, and they must ever humbly and faithfully obey the prelates and clergy of our holy Mother the Church."

Meanwhile, Brother Elias, who had been alerted, hastened to the invalid to take him "home" to die. Francis himself desired to breathe his last at the Portiuncula; while his fellow citizens, who had just been despoiled by the people of Bettona of the body of St. Crispolto, did not intend to be dispossessed this time.

Assuredly, it is rather painful to observe the preoccupation of Elias and the Assisians during the last months of the Poverello's life. But we must remember that the people of the Middle Ages were a little less hypocritical than we; and we should likewise recall the development that the cult of relics had taken on at this period. Nothing outweighed for a city the advantage of possessing the body of a servant of God to place on its altars. Piety, patriotism, and self-interest were here in accord; and men were as willing to shed their blood then for holy relics as they have since been for assuredly more futile motives.

Led by the Minister General, the cortege wended its way toward Cortona; and the invalid stopped for a few days at the hermitage of Le Celle, a league from the city. There, a poverty-stricken man who had just lost his wife and had several children to care for, came to Francis to ask for alms. Francis gave him his cloak, saying, "It is very fine, as you see. That is why, if you dispose of it, be sure to make whoever wants it pay you well."

It was a new cloak, for it replaced the one the saint had taken off on the same trip to give another poor man. The brothers lost no time trying to get it back; but the beggar held on to it so stubbornly that they had to hand him a good sum to make him give it up.

Some time after returning to the Portiuncula, with the onslaught of the summer heat, they decided to take Francis up to the healthier air of the hermitage of Bagnara, in the mountains east of Nocera. Later, while there, the saint seemed at death's door. The swelling of his legs had gone up to his abdomen, and he could not take any nourishment. Fearing the worst, the municipality of Assisi dispatched its men at arms to meet the cortege. Thus escorted, the group reached the village of Satriano in the mountains. There, driven by hunger and thirst, the knights and their retinue attempted in vain to procure some provisions. "It's up to you, then," they said laughingly to the friars, "to feed us, since the people here refuse to sell us anything whatever."

"You should have gone about it differently," replied Francis, "and put your trust in God and not in flies." By flies he meant their money. "Ever since man sinned, all earthly goods are alms that God gives with equal kindness to good and evil men. So go to them and ask them for what you need for the love of God." They obeyed and this time obtained all they desired.

The arrival at Assisi was in the nature of a triumph. "Everybody exulted," writes Celano; "for they hoped that the Saint would soon die, and they blessed God for bringing him back to their city." However, as the Portiuncula was in the open, exposed to an enemy raid, Brother Elias—for greater surety—had Francis carried inside the ramparts. He installed him in the bishop's palace, and the municipality posted armed men about it to forestall a kidnapping.

CHAPTER TWENTY-ONE

The Testament and Death

NOTHING WAS TO be lacking in the life of the Poverello to make it a perfect masterpiece, and his death was the harmonious culmination of his life. His last weeks on earth are like the close of a beautiful day, wherein the setting sun seems to shed on the world all its remaining splendor. Thus, before leaving his friars, Francis expressed to them once more his most intimate thoughts, poured out upon them all his tenderness, and then, serene and filled with gratitude, went home to God.

Regardless of what one thinks of Brother Elias, we do well to recognize the loving care with which he surrounded St. Francis till the end, imposing no restrictions on his liberty or choice of companions. Assuredly, he is not without merit, for he could not help reflecting that what was said and written at the invalid's bedside might tend to be unfavorable to him.

It was apparently to his faithful attendants that Francis drew the portrait of the ideal head of the Brotherhood. Uneasy over what was to become of it, and themselves too, once Elias had a free hand, one of them urged Francis to designate someone to fulfill the post of Minister General after he was gone.

"I do not see anyone capable of being the shepherd of so great a flock," he replied, "but I shall enumerate, nonetheless, the qualities he ought to have.

The head of the Order ought to be a very austere and pious man, sympathetic and discerning, loving all his friars without acceptation of persons, a man of prayer. I should like to have him rise early in the morning, placing Holy Mass at the beginning of his day and praying at length for himself and his flock. Then let him put himself at the disposal of all, answering all requests pleasantly and kindly, receiving both the learned and the unlearned, and letting himself be despoiled, if I may so speak, by all those needing him.

If he is a scholar himself, far from priding himself on his learning, let him be diligent above all to be humble and simple, endeavoring to preach by example rather than by word. And let him not be a collector of books, lest study make him neglect the duties of his office. As the head of a family of poor men whose model he is to be, let him hate money, convinced that there is no greater corrupter for us, no deadlier foe. Thus he will never wrongly use money-boxes. Let him limit himself to having for his own use one habit and a little copy of the Rule, with writing materials and a seal for the service of the brethren.

He will also be the one to console the afflicted, restore hope to the despairing, humble himself to bend the incorrigibles, and sometimes forego his own rights to gain souls for Jesus Christ. He will show mercy to deserters of the Order, reminding himself how terrible must have been the temptations capable of bringing about such falls and that he himself would surely have succumbed to them if God's grace had not preserved him. Finally, he will close the mouths of tattlers and beware of talebearers, deeming himself under obligation to find out the truth for himself. However, let this leniency not go so far as to favor laxity; for it devolves on him to make himself feared as well as loved. Let him not be a man whom a selfish desire to remain in office would keep from a manly enforcement of justice; instead, he must be one to whom such a high office is rather an onus than an honor.

The brothers, for their part, are to honor him as Christ's vicar; charitably providing for his needs, and procuring for him such supplements of nourishment as may be required by his weakness and fatigue. In such case, the minister shall not eat secretly, but in public, for the encouragement of those who are ill, that they may not be ashamed of letting themselves be cared for. Let him take no pleasure in his prerogatives, and let him take as much pleasure in receiving insults as praise. Finally, I desire his helpers and companions likewise to give an example of every virtue, and to receive gladly all those who resort to them.

Understandably, Francis was unable to attend the Chapter of Pentecost in 1226. To make up for his absence, he dictated the *Letter to the General Chapter and to all the Brothers*. In this long epistle, the saint reverts to the reverence due to God's Word and to the Holy Eucharist. Addressing himself especially to the priests of the Order, he says:

Listen, my Brothers. If the Blessed Virgin Mary is justly honored for having carried the Lord in her most chaste womb, if St. John trembled at baptizing Him, not daring, as it were, to place his hand on God's Chosen One; if the tomb wherein Jesus reposed for a few hours is the object of such veneration; then how worthy, virtuous, and holy ought he to be who touches with his fingers, receives in his mouth and in his heart, and administers to others, Christ, no longer mortal, but eternally triumphant and glorious! Let every man tremble, let the whole world shake and the heavens rejoice, when upon the altar the Son of the living God is in the hands of the priest!

Fearful lest familiarity should dull reverence and holy poverty be endangered, Francis urged the friars to celebrate only one Mass a day in their friaries.

He next begged forgiveness of God and of the brethren for having sometimes "through negligence or infirmity or simplicity, sinned against the Rule," commending to them the exact observance of its prescriptions, saying: "Those who do not recite the office as prescribed by the Rule, or who go about as they please and care nothing about observing the Rule, I do not consider Catholics. For this reason, until such time as they mend their ways, I refuse to see or speak to them."

The *Testament* which the Poverello dictated at the approach of death is too important a document not to be reproduced in its entirety. The saint begins by telling the origin of his vocation:

> This is how the Lord gave me, Brother Francis, the grace to begin a life of penance: when I was yet in my sins, it seemed to me unbearably bitter to look at victims of leprosy. And the Lord Himself led me among them, and I showed kindness towards them. And when I went away from them, that which had at first seemed bitter to me was now changed for

me into sweetness of soul and body. And then I tarried but a little while, and left the world.

Here Francis's thought turns toward him whom he loved, served, and did his best to imitate: toward our Lord living among us in the Eucharist and still manifesting himself in the Scriptures:

And the Lord gave me such a faith in the churches, that in simplicity I would thus pray and say: "We adore Thee, O Lord Jesus Christ, here and in all Thy churches which are in the whole world, and we bless Thee, because by Thy holy Cross Thou hast redeemed the world." Then the Lord gave me, and gives me now, towards priests who live according to the law of the Holy Roman Church, so great a confidence, by reason of their priesthood, and even if they sought to persecute me, I would nonetheless return to them. And if I were to have as great a wisdom as Solomon possessed, and were to meet with poor priests of this world, I do not wish to preach without their consent in the parishes in which they dwell. And these and all others I desire to reverence, love and honor as my lords. And I do not wish to discover if they are sinners, because I behold in them the Son of God, and they are my lords. And for this reason I do this: because in this world I see nothing with my bodily eyes of Him who is the most high Son of God except His most holy Body and His most Blood, which they receive and which they alone minister to others.

And these most holy mysteries above all else I desire to be honored and adored and kept in precious places. Whenever I shall find writings with His most holy names and words in unbecoming places, I wish to gather them up and I ask that they be gathered up and laid in a more worthy place. And all theologians and those who impart the most holy words of God, we must honor and reverence as those who minister to us spirit and life.

Going back to the past, the Poverello then tells of his life with his first companions:

And after the Lord had given me brethren, no one showed me what I was to do, but the most High Himself revealed to me that I should live according to the pattern of the Holy Gospel. And I caused it to be written in few words and simple manner, and the Lord Pope confirmed it to me. And those who came to us to accept this way of life gave to the poor whatever they might have had. And they were content with one habit, quilted inside and out if they wished, with a cord and breeches. And we had no desire for aught else. The clerics among us prayed the office like other clerics, while the laics said the Our Father. And quite willingly we would live in poor and abandoned churches. And we were simple and without learning, and subject to all.

And I was wont to work with my hands, and I still wish to so do. And I earnestly wish that all the friars be occupied with some kind of work, as long as it becomes our calling. Those who do not know how should learn, not indeed out of any desire to receive the pay which the work may bring, but to give a good example and to avoid idleness. And if there are times when no pay is given for our work, then let us have recourse to the table of the Lord, and beg alms from door to door. As for our greeting, the Lord revealed to me that we were to say: "The Lord give you peace!"

After these reminiscences of the life led by the first Franciscans, the saint speaks out for the last time against the changes some would force on his work. A paragraph forbids the friars "to receive churches, houses and all else built for their use, unless these are truly in keeping with holy poverty," and bids them "consider themselves simply as guests therein," since they are but strangers and pilgrims on earth. Another reminds them of their duty of nonresistance and of not seeking papal favors: "I firmly command all the friars by obedience that, wherever they may be, they do not dare to ask for any letter of privilege at the Roman Curia, either directly or through intermediaries, whether concerning a church or any other place, or under the pretext of preaching, or even as protection against persecution. Rather, if they have not been welcomed in one place, let them depart to another and there do penance with the blessing of God."

Then comes a personal protestation of obedience and orthodoxy, with the sanctions to be enforced against friars suspected of insubordination to the Church:

And it is my firm desire to obey the Minister General of his brotherhood, as likewise the guardian whom it has pleased him to give me. And I wish to be as a prisoner in his hands, that I can neither move nor act apart from obedience to him and without his consent, because he is my master. And though I am simple and ailing, I wish always to have a cleric who may recite the office with me, as it is prescribed in the Rule. And all the other friars are to be bound in like manner to obey their guardians and to say the office in the manner prescribed by the Rule. And should some be found who are not saying the office according to the prescript of the Rule but are trying to introduce some other form of it, or who are not Catholics, all the friars, wherever they are, are to be bound in obedience to present any such, wherever they may find him, to the custos nearest to the place where they have found him. And the custos is to be firmly bound by obedience to guard him day and night as a prisoner, so that he cannot escape his hands, until he shall in his own person deliver him into the hands of his minister. And the minister is to be firmly bound by obedience to send him by such friars who will day and night guard him as prisoner until they bring him before the Lord of Ostia, who is the master of this whole brotherhood and has it under his protection and correction.

The *Testament* closes with these lines:

And the friars should not say "This is another Rule," because this is a reminder of our past, an admonition and exhortation, and my testament, which I, the little Brother Francis, am making for you, my blessed brothers, to this end, that we may observe in a more Catholic manner the Rule we have promised the Lord. And the Minister General and all other ministers and custodes shall be bound by obedience not to add to these words or take away from them. And let them always have this writing with them together with the Rule. And in all the Chapters they hold, when they read the Rule, let them read these words also. And all my brothers, both clerics and laics, I firmly charge by obedience not to make any explanations on the Rule or of these words and say: "Thus they are to be understood." Rather, as the Lord has granted me simply and plainly to speak and write the Rule and these words, so simply and without gloss you are to understand them, and by holy deeds carry them out until the very end.

Next comes the blessing:

And everyone that shall observe these things, may he be filled in Heaven with the blessing of the most high Father; and may he be filled on earth with the blessing of His beloved Son in fellowship with the most Holy Spirit the Comforter and all the powers of Heaven and all the Saints. And I, Brother Francis, your little servant, as much as I can, confirm to you within and without this most holy blessing. Amen.

Such was the Last Will and Testament of St. Francis, and the way he interpreted the Rule of 1223. But, as we have seen, the Order had evolved too far for it to be still possible to take his intentions into consideration. Thus in 1230, Hugolin, having become pope, gave to that Rule the interpretation for which many of the friars had been waiting, at the same time declaring that the Testament was not legally binding. This intervention was not immediately decisive. The struggle between the intransigents and the moderates continued and grew; and it took a century, as we know, to eliminate the "Spirituals" from the Brotherhood.

As for Francis, now that, following the example of the knights and martyrs, he had once more testified to his faith and said his *Credo* before dying, there remained nothing more for him than to await the hour of death.

A doctor friend from Arezzo came to pay him a visit. His name was Buongiovanni or "Good John"; but in obedience to the Gospel, wherein Jesus says that "God alone is good," Francis always called him "Finiatus" or "Bembegnate." He asked him, "What do you think of my dropsy, Bembegnate?" "Brother," replied the physician guardedly, "I think that with God's grace, all will be well."

"Please tell me the truth! For whether I live or die makes no difference to me. My great desire is to do God's will."

"In that case," replied the doctor, "I shall tell you that according to medical science, your disease is incurable; and my opinion is that you will die either at the end of September or the beginning of October."

Raising his arms to heaven the happy invalid exclaimed; "Welcome, Sister Death!" Then addressing a brother, he said, "Call Brother Angelo and Brother Leo so that they can come and sing by my bed."

Despite their sobs, the pair intoned the "Canticle of Brother Sun"; but this time, before the final doxology, the invalid stopped them and added the following verses:

> Be praised my Lord, for our Sister Bodily Death,
> From whom no living man can escape.
> Woe to those who die in mortal sin.
> Blessed are they whom she shall find in Your most holy will,
> For the second death shall not harm them.

And it was this new stanza that his companions sang him the "Canticle of the Creatures" from that time onward. "They sang it several times a day to comfort him, and even in the night to edify and entertain the armed guard in front of the palace."

But was it seemly for one of God's servants whose relics they would soon be venerating, to behave thus in the face of death? Some people, and among them Brother Elias (who doubtless already was thinking about his basilica), did not think so.

"Dear Father," said he to the saint, "I am glad to see you so merry. But in this city, where people look on you as a saint, I fear lest they be scandalized at seeing you prepare for death this way."

"Leave me be, Brother," replied Francis. "For in spite of all that I endure, I feel so close to God that I cannot help singing."

The ravages of the disease now spread all through him. The dropsy had been followed by extreme emaciation; and the doctors were astonished that this "skeleton" still lived. His sufferings were atrocious. To a brother who asked him if he would rather be executed than suffer such dreadful pain, he replied: "My choice is whatever God sends me. But I must admit that the cruelest martyrdom would be easier to bear than three days of pain like this."

There was an alarming moment, when believing he was about to die, the friars knelt round his bed to receive his final blessing. Unable to see, Francis asked if it was on Elias's head that his right hand was placed. Being assured that it was, he then said, "My blessing on you, my son. I bless in you, as much as I am able, all my friars and my dear sons. My children, always live in the fear of God, for great temptations threaten you and the time of tribulation is near. But I am hastening to the Lord, and I go full of trust to Him whom I have desired to serve with all my heart."

It was a false alarm—the Poverello was not to die in a palace.

In accordance with Francis's wishes, Brother Elias decided to move him to the Portiuncula. To this the magistrates of Assisi gave their consent, provided that he was accompanied by an armed escort. The procession went through nearby Porto Moiano and wended its way to the plain along a path lined with olive trees. When they reached

San Salvatore delle Pareti near the Crosiers' leprosarium, Francis asked them to set down his litter and turn his face toward Assisi.

At that spot the whole city is to be seen, with its ramparts and towers, its winding streets and storied houses, and a little to the right, the tiny convent of San Damiano. Higher up, rises the bare Rocca with the ruins of its demolished castle at the summit; while afar off in the rear the heights of Mount Subasio appear, marked by the ravine in which the hermitage of the Carceri lies hidden.

Francis had himself raised to a sitting position, and for a long time he seemed to gaze upon the familiar landscape that his blinded eyes could no longer see. Then, painfully raising his hand, he made the sign of the cross: "God bless you, dear city," he murmured. "You that were once a den of robbers, have been chosen by God to become the dwelling place of those who know Him and who will pour out upon the people the fragrance of their pure lives. Lord Jesus, Father of mercy, remember, I entreat You, the abundance of good things that You have shown it, and may it ever be a dwelling place of those who will glorify Your blessed name forever and ever. Amen."

The procession, now midway to its destination, resumed its course and soon reached St. Mary of the Angels.

The invalid was settled in a hut a few feet from the chapel. This wooded solitude, so often visited by the Spirit of God, assuredly supplied an appropriate setting for his death—a death of radiant beauty. Francis took leave of the world with the same simplicity and courtesy that had marked every act of his life. He forgot nothing. His sons and daughters, the places he loved, the lady of his thoughts, all living creatures, his brothers who had been so close to him, all shared in his farewells and blessings.

He commended his beloved Portiuncula to his disciples. "This place," he said to them, "is holy. Always hold it in veneration and never forsake it. If men drive you out one door, come back in by the other; for it is here that the Lord has increased our numbers, illumined us with His light, and set our hearts on fire with His love."

In honor of his lady, Poverty, he had himself placed naked on the ground, and covering his wounded side with his hand, he said to his friars: "My work is done. May Christ teach you to do yours!"

He waited until—like a final alms—a few garments were given him for the little time that remained to him. His guardian brought them to him, and, in a voice choked with sobs, said: "I lend you these breeches, this tunic and hood. And to keep you from thinking that you are the owner, I forbid you, under obedience, to give them away to anyone at all."

At these words, the poor blind man with his fleshless body and head marked with fearful wounds, trembled with joy. Then they put him back in his bed.

Those present then asked his forgiveness for the pain they had caused him, and implored anew his blessing. Laying his hand on the head of each in turn, he declared that he forgave them their faults and offenses; and, addressing himself to Bernard of Quintavalle, he added: "I also absolve and bless, as much as I am able, and even more than I am able, all my absent brothers. Tell them what I have said and bless them in my name."

Rightly fearing lest his oldest comrade, the veteran of his knightly band, might soon undergo persecution, he continued: "I ordain that in the Order special affection shall be shown to my dear brother Bernard, who was the first to give his goods to the poor and to enter with me upon the Gospel way."

Francis took care not to forget Sister Clare, whom they had just learned was in tears at the thought of the coming loss of her father and supporter. He had the following message brought to his dear "little spiritual plant":

"I, little brother Francis, desire to follow to the end the life and poverty of our Lord Jesus Christ and of His most holy Mother. And I entreat you, my Ladies, whatever advice you may receive in future, never to depart from it. And you are to tell the Lady Clare," he added, addressing the messenger, "that I forbid her to give way to grief, for I promise her that she and her Sisters shall see me again."

He likewise thought of his friend Jacopa in Rome. "It would sadden her too much," he observed, "to learn that I have left this world without telling her beforehand." And he began to dictate for her the following letter:

"To the Lady Jacopa, servant of God, Brother Francis, Christ's little poor man, greetings and fellowship of the Holy Spirit in our Lord. Dearest friend, you must be told that the end of my life is at hand, as our Blessed Lord has shown me. Come at once, if you want to see me alive. Bring haircloth with you to wrap my body in, and whatever is necessary for my burial. And please bring with you some of the good things you gave me to eat when I was ill in Rome."

The dictation had reached this point and the messenger was waiting for it, ready to set off on horseback, when the sound of a cavalcade was heard. It was the Lady Jacopa arriving from Rome with her two sons and her retinue. God himself, as she declared later on, had inspired her at prayer with the resolve to start at once for Assisi. A brother rushed up to the invalid's bedside. "I bring you good news," he whispered, without saying what.

"God be praised!" murmured Francis. "Open the door for her, for the ban on women entering here is not for Brother Jacopa."

Jacopa had brought everything necessary for the Poverello's burial—a veil to cover his face, the cushion in which his head would rest in his bier, the haircloth shroud, and all the candles required for the wake and the funeral. She also brought some of the almond pastry he loved; but he could only taste a morsel, and so he asked Brother Bernard to eat it. As Francis's condition suddenly improved, the Lady Jacopa thought of returning to Rome; but Francis begged her to stay until Sunday, assuring her that he would not last longer than that.

"When I am dying," he said, addressing himself to those around him, "lay me on the ground the way you did three days ago; and when I am dead, leave me there for the space of time it takes to walk a mile."

More and more frequently now, the strains of the "Canticle of Brother Sun" rose from the hut, with the stanza of praise to Sister Death. On Friday, October 2, Francis had bread brought, blessed it, and like Christ in the Upper Room, distributed it to the brothers present.

The following day, which was to be his last, the Passion According to St. John was read to him at his request. "The guest to whom no man willingly opens his door," did not come until twilight. As soon as the Little Poor Man saw her enter, he greeted her courteously, "Welcome, Sister Death!" And he asked the doctor to announce, like a herald-at-arms, the solemn arrival of the expected visitor, "for," he added, "it is she who is going to introduce me to eternal life."

The friars laid him on the ground on a coarse cloth; and to honor his dread guest, he had them sprinkle him with dust and ashes. Then in a barely perceptible voice, he intoned the one hundred and forty-first psalm, which those present continued with him:

"*Voce mea ad Dominum clamavi*. I cried to the Lord with my voice: with my voice I made supplication to the Lord.... In this way wherein I walked, they have hidden a snare for me.... There is no one that hath regard to my soul. I cried to Thee, O Lord: I said: Thou art my hope, my portion in the land of the living.... Deliver me from my pursuers.... *Educ de custodia animam meam*. Bring my soul out of prison, that I may praise Thy name: the just wait for me, until Thou reward me."

Then in the darkling cell there was a great silence. Francis lay motionless, and the brothers who bent over him saw that he had ceased to breathe. He died singing, in the forty-sixth year of his age, and the twentieth of his conversion.

At this very instant, a great flock of larks alighted on the roof of the hut, their twitterings a mixture of sadness and great jubilee. In the same hour, a holy friar saw a flaming star borne on a white cloud over the waters, ascending straight to heaven. It was the Poverello's soul winging its flight to the regions of eternal bliss.

As for Francis's body, it was as though transformed. His limbs, which had been long contracted by suffering, became supple like those of a child; his face was as beautiful as an angel's; the wound in his side appeared a rosy red hue; and on his once swarthy flesh—now white as milk—the stigmata of his hands and feet stood out like black stones on white marble. One might have thought, as Brother Leo said later, that it was the Divine Crucified taken down from his cross who lay there.

All night long the great forest resounded with the chanting of psalms by the friars, mingled with the murmur of the voices of the throngs who had flocked there. At dawn on Sunday, October 4, a procession formed to conduct the mortal remains of the saint of

Assisi. The Friars Minor, singing hymns, were joined by the neighboring populations, bearing palm branches and candles. They were in haste to cross the ramparts, for a surprise attack by the Perugians was always to be feared.

At a given point, however, the procession turned, and, to fulfill the dead saint's wish, went on to San Damiano. The open bier was brought inside the cloistered nuns' chapel; and so it was that Clare could see the face of her beloved father once more. She bathed the holy corpse with her tears and covered the sacred stigmata with kisses.

Then the cortege resumed its march toward the Church of San Giorgio, where the first interment of the Poverello took place. About four years later, May 25, 1230, the body was transferred to the crypt of the basilica being erected by Brother Elias. And it is in this grandiose monument—so unlike Francis—that men continue to come to venerate his dust.

INDEX